PRACTICAL THEOLOGY

PRACTICAL THEOLOGY

An Introduction

Richard R. Osmer

WILLIAM B. EERDMANS PUBLISHING COMPANY
GRAND RAPIDS, MICHIGAN / CAMBRIDGE, U.K.

Published 2008 by

Wm. B. Eerdmans Publishing Co.

2140 Oak Industrial Drive N.E., Grand Rapids, Michigan 49505 /

P.O. Box 163, Cambridge CB3 9PU U.K.

www.eerdmans.com

Printed in the United States of America

23 22 21 20   15 14 13 12

Library of Congress Cataloging-in-Publication Data

Osmer, Richard Robert, 1950-

Practical theology: an introduction / Richard Robert Osmer.

p.   cm.

Includes bibliographical references and indexes.

ISBN 978-0-8028-1765-5 (pbk.: alk. paper)

1. Theology, Practical.   I. Title.

BV.086   2008

253 — dc22

2007048488

Unless otherwise noted, the Scripture quotations in this publication are from the New Revised Standard Version of the Bible, copyright © 1989 by the Division of Christian Education of the National Council of Churches of Christ in the U.S.A., and used by permission.

With thanks,
to

Don S. Browning
Charles V. Gerkin
Johannes A. van der Ven

Pigmaei gigantum humeris impositi plusquam ipsi gigantes vident.

Contents

—ᴥᴥ—

Preface

———⤬—

This book is dedicated to three giants in the field of practical theology: Don Browning, Chuck Gerkin, and Hans van der Ven. As a young scholar, I had the good fortune of their colleagueship and, later, their friendship. This book reflects the influence of their work on my thinking. The widely quoted metaphor of dwarfs standing on the shoulders of giants was attributed to Bernard of Chartres in the twelfth century by John of Salisbury. In his *Metalogicon,* John wrote: "Bernard of Chartres used to say that we are like dwarfs on the shoulders of giants, so that we can see more than they, and things at a greater distance, not by virtue of any sharpness of sight on our part, or any physical distinction, but because we are carried high and raised up by their giant size." This captures nicely the way my understanding of practical theology builds on the groundbreaking contributions of these three practical theologians.

Special thanks also are due four colleagues and friends: Jack Stewart, Friedrich Schweitzer, Wentzel van Huyssteen, and Rodney Hunter. They too have contributed in countless ways to my understanding of practical theology. Jack has guided me through the literature on congregational studies and leadership. He knows more about these subjects in his little finger than I will ever hope to know. Friedrich introduced me to the European discussion of practical theology and is a brilliant practical theologian in his own right. As we collaborated in writing *Religious Education between Modernization and Globalization,* I learned an enormous amount from him.

Wentzel has influenced enormously my thinking about cross-disciplinary issues and introduced me to the recent philosophical discussion of rationality. Rod, one of my professors as a doctoral student at Emory, has remained an important dialogue partner over the years. Whenever we meet, our conversation always involves an intense discussion of practical theology from which I learn a great deal. It also was in one of Rod's classes many years ago that I first began to explore the Wisdom literature as a resource for thinking about practical theology, an idea that has finally germinated in this book.

I also am surrounded by outstanding colleagues in the department of practical theology at Princeton Theological Seminary. We learn from and support one another in many ways. I am especially blessed with two exceptionally bright and creative colleagues in Christian education, Kenda Creasy Dean and Gordon Mikoski. We work together, teach together, and even pray together. What more could one hope for? Through our many conversations, Kenda and Gordon have contributed to this book in ways that I can no longer even recognize. Special thanks to the two of you!

Special thanks to my editor at Eerdmans, Tom Raabe, who did wonderful work on this manuscript. Thanks also to Sam Eerdmans, with whom I initially talked about this project, and Linda Bieze, who provided editorial oversight of the publication process.

Finally, I want to express my deepest gratitude to my partners in love and life, my wife, Sally, and children, Richard and Sarah. Sally and I journeyed together through many of the incidents described in this book. Her thoughtful comments about these events and the book generally have strengthened my writing in countless ways. Thanks to all of you for your loving support.

In recent decades practical theology as a field has passed through a period of creative ferment. This began in the 1960s with the so-called "new discussion" of practical theology. This discussion gained momentum in subsequent decades with the publication of a number of exceptional texts in practical theology and the creation of the International Academy of Practical Theology. Today the discussion of practical theology is truly international in scope and is a conversation to which many outstanding scholars contribute.

During this period a decisive break was made with older models of practical theology. Today it is no longer accurate to view this field as solely concerned with application, with helpful techniques and skills applied to the life of the church. Practical theologians carry out diverse research programs and make their own constructive, scholarly contribution to the theological enterprise as a whole. Nor is it accurate to view this field as concerned solely with the tasks of clergy or the life of congregations. The scope of the field includes matters of public importance beyond the church, and often is directed toward shaping public policy and social transformation. In recent years, for example, van der Ven has led a research project on the attitudes of young people toward human rights, giving special attention to the impact of religion on these attitudes. Likewise, Browning recently led a research team that studied the American family and contributed to the highly charged political debate over family values in the United States. These are two of many examples in which practical theologians focus on matters important to the common good and not simply to the church. Indeed, I will argue in this book that the scope of practical theology comprehends the web of life.

It is important to point to the broad scope of contemporary practical theology at the outset, for it allows me to locate this book within the new discussion. The subject matter of this book is practical theological interpretation by the leaders of congregations. It is written for students in master of divinity and doctor of ministry programs, as well as for leaders currently serving congregations. This may appear to be a return to the older clerical paradigm of practical theology. This is not how I understand the matter, however.

Rather, the method of practical theology explored in this book, which includes descriptive-empirical, interpretive, normative, and pragmatic tasks, may be brought to bear on *any* issue worthy of consideration. This is apparent in the projects of van der Ven and Browning, noted above. Within the broad scope of contemporary practical theology, focusing on leadership in congregations is only one of many possible topics this field may take up. Yet teaching students and church leaders how to engage in practical theological interpretation is an important goal of theological education. The quality of leadership in congregations has much to do with their long-term prospects and their contribution to public life. This is the specific concern of the chapters that follow. While not the only topic worthy of consideration by contemporary practical theologians, it is an important one.

Finally, three matters of writing practice must be mentioned. First, the cases, events, and interviews appearing in this book are altered to protect the identity of the persons and communities involved. Second, instead of using the cumbersome practice of writing "he or she," I alternate gender-specific pronouns, using "she/her" sometimes and "he/his" at other times. I have attempted to balance this equally over the course of the book. Finally, I have left all quotations from other writers in their original form, even when their lack of gender-inclusive language may grate on us today.

Four Tasks of Practical Theology

—◦◦◦—

When my wife, Sally, and I graduated from divinity school, we were copastors of two yoked congregations in the mountains of eastern Tennessee. Our first child was born during our final semester, and since parenting was something we both thought important, we decided to share ministry. Eager but inexperienced, we somehow muddled through the messiness of blending marriage and ministry while living in a parsonage not far from one of our churches. It was a shock at first to hear someone call to you while walking into the Food Lion, "Hey, Preacher . . ." As I recall, I was called this more than Sally — they didn't quite know what to call a "lady preacher," as they sometimes put it — until they discovered what a wonderful preacher and leader she was and is.

We learned a lot during these years about ourselves, our congregations, and mountain culture. We learned that many decisions in our churches were not made when the church council met but occurred down the road at the gas station restaurant where the farmers gathered for a cup of coffee after their morning chores. We learned the perils of navigating around the "hollers" to visit shut-ins, guided by landmarks like a big oak stump and a couple of rusted-out cars. One of us even had a very nice conversation with an elderly woman just out of the hospital, only to discover as we were leaving that she was Sylvia Leatherwood and we had set out to visit Edra Leatherwood. We learned there are Free Will Baptists, Primitive Baptists, and Premillennial Baptists, as well as Southern Baptists. We learned that ministerial colleagues, with whom we sometimes conducted funeral services, would point to the casket and tell those gathered: "Right there, that's why it's time to get right with God. Not tomorrow, but this very minute. Don't put it off, for there we all shall someday be."

It was during these first years of ministry that I fell in love with Christian education. The summer lab schools at Lake Junaluska, an assembly ground of the United Methodist Church, had a lot to do with this. But what I learned about the importance of Christian education to the overall health and mission of a congregation also had something to do with it. One of our churches had been without a Sunday school for over twenty years. There were no families with children in the church, though a lot of young families lived in the area. So I set out to start a Sunday school, beginning with Nancy Boyd, the daughter-in-law of a long-term member. It took a while and all the creativity and energy Nancy and I could muster. But after two years we had a nursery, three age-level classes, and a youth group of young people from four churches. We gradually were becoming known as a church with a future and not just a past, a place with something to offer young families. We even put a swing set next to the covered picnic area where the children could play while the parents shared conversation and coffee after worship. In the past, the church used the picnic area only once a year for a barbecue during homecoming, a gathering of church friends and family.

Two weeks after the swing set was put in, I pulled into the church parking lot and noticed that something was not quite right. It was the sort of feeling you get when you walk into a familiar room and the pictures or TV has been moved. It took me a minute, but then I realized that the swing set was gone. I hurried out of my car and walked over to the picnic area. Sure enough, four freshly filled dirt holes were all that remained. I walked around to the back of the church building, and there was the swing set — now solidly cemented into its new home. It took a few days to find out what had happened, but this was a small town and nobody had secrets.

Mary Jo James, the longtime church treasurer, had hired some men to move the swing set in the dead of night. One of the men later told me, "She said to dig the holes deep and fill them with concrete. That's what we did." The parents were pretty mad. As one of them put it at the next church council meeting, "What kind of church is this? Don't you want us here? Sneaking around in the middle of the night to do something like this!" The other church members were as puzzled and outraged as he was. They voted to put the swing set back in place, and suspended the meeting on the spot, jumping in their trucks to go home for sledgehammers and shovels. Some of the men stayed long into the night taking turns breaking up the cement and digging up the swing set, returning it to its rightful place. The next day, it was solidly set in concrete.

The young people were appeased. I was told to visit Mary Jo James. This excited me about as much as a visit to the dentist for a root canal. But visit her I did. I had always liked Mary Jo and appreciated her work as treasurer of the church, a job she had carried out for fifteen years. I admit it did irritate me when she sometimes turned around to shush the children during worship. But more than once she had shared appreciation for the new members and their contribution to the finances of the church. I had no idea what was going on.

As I drove up to Mary Jo's home, I noticed that she peeked out of the closed curtains to see who had pulled into her driveway. One knock and she was at the door, holding the ledgers in which she had carefully recorded the financial matters of the church over the years. "I quit," she said, handing me the large stack of ledgers. "I'm quitting the church too. No sense in coming in. No way you're going to change my mind." She shut the door, leaving me standing on her porch weighed down with a pile of records lovingly kept for so many years.

I wish at that time I had known something about practical theology. I wish that at least one class of my theological education had given me the knowledge and skills to make sense of what I was experiencing. I realize, in ministry, experience is one of our most important teachers. But experiences like this one in which lives and years of work are at stake can leave us bewildered. Ministry, like life, can be stranger than fiction.

My goal in this book is to teach you a way of approaching situations like this one with at least some knowledge and skills in hand. I cannot promise that you will make the right decisions or take the right actions. Good ministry is never merely a matter of solving problems; it is a mystery to be ventured and explored. But we can journey into this mystery with knowledge and skills that help us find our way as we move along. Or we can stand where I did, on a porch with only my gut to tell me whether I should knock again or leave.

The Core Tasks of Practical Theological Interpretation

Chances are good, if you are the leader of a congregation, that you will someday run into a situation like this one. Over the course of this book we explore four questions that can guide our interpretation and response to situations of this sort:

What is going on?
Why is this going on?
What ought to be going on?
How might we respond?

Answering each of these questions is the focus of one of the four core tasks of practical theological interpretation:

- *The descriptive-empirical task.* Gathering information that helps us discern patterns and dynamics in particular episodes, situations, or contexts.
- *The interpretive task.* Drawing on theories of the arts and sciences to better understand and explain why these patterns and dynamics are occurring.
- *The normative task.* Using theological concepts to interpret particular episodes, situations, or contexts, constructing ethical norms to guide our responses, and learning from "good practice."
- *The pragmatic task.* Determining strategies of action that will influence situations in ways that are desirable and entering into a reflective conversation with the "talk back" emerging when they are enacted.

Together, these four tasks constitute the basic structure of practical theological interpretation. I make no claim to originality in my description of these tasks. While the terms may differ, something like each of them is taught in clinical pastoral education, doctor of ministry courses, and courses on preaching, pastoral care, administration, Christian education, and evangelism in schools of theology. Moreover, pastors and church leaders carry out these tasks in ministry.

To see more clearly what each task involves, let us return to the case of the moved swing set. What is going on in this situation? This is the key question of the descriptive-empirical task of practical theological interpretation. Over the course of several weeks I was able to piece together Mary Jo James's story. She married late in life after many years as a single woman who worked as an accountant for a local business. When Jimmy James's first wife was killed in an automobile accident, Mary Jo was one of many church members who offered him support. A year later they were married. Mary Jo was too old at that point for children, but, by all accounts, they had ten happy years before James died of cancer. Not long after his death, Mary Jo gave money to the church for a covered picnic area in honor of her husband. Her church friends recall her saying at the time, "Jimmy never liked it much when they put those plaques in the church saying so-and-so had given the money for the 'Leatherwood' room. So I don't want any kind of plaque on the picnic area. We'll know in our hearts who we're remembering. Jimmy always did like a good barbecue." The problem was, as the years passed and new members joined, many people did not remember. They had no idea when the swing set was placed next to the picnic area that it would bother Mary Jo so deeply. Even her closest friends didn't know how she felt — until she paid to have the swing set moved and the church was in an uproar.

Gathering information that helps us discern patterns and dynamics is the descriptive-empirical task of practical theological interpretation. Often, in ministry this takes place informally. In this case I sought out Mary Jo's closest friends in the church and asked them to help me learn more of her story and what they thought might be going on. This information was helpful in placing her actions in a longer narrative framework. When Mary Jo allowed me to visit her several weeks later, I tried to gain more information about her perspective. By that time I knew she had given the money for the picnic area in honor of her husband, but I wanted to discern what this meant to her in her own words. How did she interpret the decision to put a swing set right next to the picnic area? While I was drawing her out, I also was listening with a "third ear," as it is sometimes put in counseling. I attended to her feelings and body language. I looked for signs of depression or other psychological disorders. Beyond Mary Jo, I also began to attend more closely to what was going on in the church as a whole, paying particular attention to any signs of tension between the new, younger members and the long-term, older members.

Much of the time, congregational leaders carry out the descriptive-empirical task of practical theological interpretation along these lines, through informal information-gathering, careful listening, and looking more closely at patterns and relationships that are taken for granted. Yet, many times leaders may desire to gather information in ways that are more systematic. They might like to build up a demographic profile of new families moving into their area. They might want to develop a clearer picture of what the young people are getting out of confirmation or to evaluate the entire adult education program. A new pastor may decide that she needs to work hard during the first year at understanding her congregation's "culture," using the research activities of congregational studies. A pastor long in a church may believe that his preaching is growing stale and desire ways of discovering life issues his members really care about. There are many reasons for congregational leaders to learn how to carry out the descriptive-empirical task of practical theological interpretation in a more systematic and disciplined fashion. The first chapter will explore further some of these reasons and offer an introduction to research projects and approaches.

Once I had discerned some of the important patterns and dynamics surrounding the swing set episode, I needed to step back and make sense of what I had found. Why did this incident take place? What sorts of theories might help me better understand and explain the patterns and dynamics I had begun to discover? These are the key questions of the interpretive task of practical theological interpretation. At least three lines of interpretation come to mind, two of which I saw at the time and one I detected in hindsight.

While I grew up in North Carolina, my family lived in a midsized city. I attended a state university and a divinity school in the Northeast. My ministry in these congregations, thus, was my first exposure to the mountain culture of eastern Tennessee. Of the many things I learned about this culture that may be relevant to the interpretation of this situation, one thing particularly comes to mind: the honoring of the patriarchs and matriarchs in families, churches, and local communities. This takes place through storytelling, homecomings, memorials, statues, and other rituals and symbolic markers. Such activities and monuments are important ways of building corporate identity and maintaining ties with the past.[1] It is likely that Mary Jo invested the picnic area with this kind of symbolic importance. Treating it casually and altering it without consulting her was, in her

---

1. John Westerhoff and Gwen Kennedy Neville, *Learning through Liturgy* (New York: Seabury Press, 1978); Westerhoff and Neville, *Generation to Generation: Conversations on Religious Education and Culture* (New York: Pilgrim Press, 1979).

mind, quite literally the desecration of holy ground. The cultural context in which this event took place, thus, is an important line of interpretation.

It also is possible to interpret this incident in terms of family systems theory, which has been extended to congregations in the writings of Edwin Friedman and others.[2] In family systems theory, individuals sometimes are portrayed as playing the role of the "identified patient," expressing the pain of the family system as a whole.[3] It is quite possible that Mary Jo's "acting out" was expressing tensions within the system of the church family. Changes were taking place in the church, largely driven by the younger and newer members. These included changes in programming, worship, outreach, and administration. It may be that Mary Jo was not alone in feeling left out and unappreciated. The congregational context, thus, is a second line of interpretation worth considering.

Finally, what of Mary Jo herself, in terms of her stage in life and individual biography? Until midlife she lived as a single woman, which in this setting carried something of a stigma. Her marriage to a patriarch of the church and a man of land and wealth issued, not only in an altered social status, but also, in her words, in "the happiest years of my life." When Jimmy died, her most important social network was her friends in the church. Her work as treasurer made her an insider whom key leaders consulted regularly. The fact that no one recognized the significance of the picnic area to Mary Jo may have felt like a blow to the most important relationships in which she was invested. As a widow facing the early stages of old age, these relationships were more important than ever. A psychological line of interpretation, thus, also is worth considering.

Other fruitful lines of interpretation also might be explored. But enough has been said to illustrate the importance of different kinds of theories that bring into focus different dimensions of this situation. The interpretative task of practical theological interpretation draws on theories of this sort to better understand and explain why certain events are occurring. In chapter 2 we examine this task in greater depth, and will offer a

2. Edwin Friedman, *Generation to Generation: Family Process in Church and Synagogue* (New York: Guilford Press, 1985); George Parsons and Speed Leas, *Understanding Your Congregation as a System: The Manual* (Bethesda, Md.: Alban Institute, 1993); Peter Steinke, *Healthy Congregations: A Systems Approach* (Washington, D.C.: Alban Institute, 1996).

3. See, for example, Virginia Satir, *Conjoint Family Therapy: A Guide to Theory and Technique* (Palo Alto, Calif.: Science and Behavior Books, 1967); William Lederer and Don Jackson, *The Mirages of Marriage* (New York: Norton, 1968).

model that will help you analyze and assess theories that may be helpful in your interpretation of particular episodes, situations, and contexts.

The use of theories from other fields like anthropology and psychology is an important part of practical theological interpretation. Such theories, however, can take congregational leaders only so far. As members of the Christian community, they face further questions: What ought to be going on? What are we to do and be as members of the Christian community in response to the events of our shared life and world? These questions lie at the heart of the normative task of practical theological interpretation. In chapter 3 this task will be portrayed as threefold. First, it involves a style of theological reflection in which theological concepts are used to interpret particular episodes, situations, and contexts. In light of what we know of God, how might God be acting? What are the fitting patterns of human response? Second, it involves the task of finding ethical principles, guidelines, and rules that are relevant to the situation and can guide strategies of action. Third, it involves exploring past and present practices of the Christian tradition that provide normative guidance in shaping the patterns of the Christian life.

At the time of the swing set incident, I probably reflected less on this task than on the others. My theology classes in divinity school had focused primarily on church doctrine, giving me little practice in using theology to interpret particular incidents or contexts. Looking back, I can discern a number of theological concepts I might have used to help the congregation interpret these events but will offer only one here. I also can discern an ethical stance that implicitly informed the actions I undertook.

If I was correct in interpreting Mary Jo's "acting out" as indicative of broader tensions in the church family as it began to change, then this might have been interpreted theologically with the concept of the people of God. More than the organic concept, body of Christ, it implies movement through time, the journey of God's people into new circumstances and God's faithfulness in the midst of change.[4] Throughout Scripture we find God's people recalling stories of God's action in the past, which allow them to discern ways God may act in the present and future.[5] A key dy-

4. See Hans Küng's discussion of the differences between the concepts of people of God and body of Christ in *The Church* (New York: Sheed and Ward, 1967), pp. 107-50.

5. For an especially nice example of this in Deutero-Isaiah, see Richard Bauckham, *God Crucified: Monotheism and Christology in the New Testament* (Carlisle, U.K.: Paternoster Press, 1998), pp. 71-72.

namic is at work here. The recitals of God's actions in events like the exodus and wilderness wanderings provide identity descriptions of God. Yet these very descriptions of God's identity are reinterpreted to articulate the new thing God is doing and will do as the people of God continue on their journey.

Normatively, thus, one of my tasks in this situation might have been to encourage this congregation to see itself as God's people who can trust that God will travel with them as they begin to change and journey toward the future. This opens up certain strategic lines of thinking: preaching and teaching the stories of Scripture in which God's people recall God's actions in the past to guide them in time of change and crisis. I also would have done well to discover stories of the congregation's history when it faced changes or crises and the understandings of God that sustained it in such times. I might have drawn on and reinterpreted these understandings to portray the new stage of its journey as God's people.

It is worth noting in passing that gathering stories of the congregation's past leads me back to the descriptive-empirical task. Moreover, I was directed to the concept of the people of God on a journey by my interpretation of the swing set incident as indicative of tension in the church family. This sort of interaction between the tasks of practical theological interpretation is common. They interpenetrate in the living practice of ministry. It also is worth noting that making sense of this episode impacts many forms of ministry. It influences the pastoral care offered Mary Jo, my preaching and teaching, and the administrative approaches I might have used.

I did not in fact engage in this sort of theological interpretation at the time. But in retrospect, I wish I had. Rather, my actions were guided by an implicit theological ethic, an ethic of reconciliation. Even here, however, I worked more intuitively than with the guidance of a clear ethical principle. My thinking at the time went something like this: it is wrong for this long-time church member, who has given so much over the years and is now a widow, to be estranged from the community; this is not the kind of church God wants us to be. I wish I had thought about this incident in terms of an explicit ethic of reconciliation, which has important implications for the congregation's attitude toward Mary Jo. It cannot simply write her off as a stubborn old-timer standing in the way of progress. It must strive for some sort of reconciliation. This is what God has called the church to do and be.

Without the clear guidance of theological interpretation or ethical principles, I coped with this incident as best I could. I strategized with

Mary Jo's friends about how to best reach out to her. I also began to realize that I needed to do a much better job of honoring the contributions of the older, long-term members of the congregation in public events and inter- personal communication. Moreover, I began to realize that this congrega- tion offered its members very few resources with which to deal with con- flict. It had long bothered me that two members of the congregation whose farms adjoined, with mailboxes only ten feet apart, were caught up in a feud that had begun more than ten years earlier. They literally would not speak to one another! When Mary Jo quit the church, I worried that she might respond in the same way. Bad blood could last a long time in this community. Why had the congregation never taught its members how to resolve its differences in the spirit of Christian love? Or, as I might put it today, why were there no practices of reconciliation present in the church? Exploring models of "good practice" might have provided normative guid- ance in my leadership of the church.

These kinds of issues open out to the pragmatic task of practical theolog- ical interpretation. How might we respond in ways that are faithful and ef- fective? The pragmatic task focuses on strategies and actions that are under- taken to shape events toward desired goals. In chapter 4 we give special attention to the sort of leadership required in situations like the one we have been following. Such leadership requires competence in ministerial tasks like preaching, teaching, administration, and pastoral care. But it involves more. It takes leaders who can see things "whole," leaders who think in terms of the entire congregational system and the church's relationship to its context.

We now have before us an outline of the central argument of this book. Practical theological interpretation involves four key tasks: the descriptive- empirical, the interpretive, the normative, and the pragmatic. It is helpful to conceptualize these four tasks with the image of a hermeneutical circle, which portrays interpretation as composed of distinct but interrelated mo- ments.[6] As we have begun to see, the four tasks of practical theological in- terpretation interpenetrate. Problems emerging in the pragmatic task may open up issues that need to be explored empirically. Theories used to inter- pret particular events may bring to the fore issues calling for normative re- flection. The interaction and mutual influence of all four tasks distinguish practical theology from other fields. The social sciences, for example, do

6. Richard Palmer, *Hermeneutics* (Evanston, Ill.: Northwestern University Press, 1969), pp. 25-26, 87-88, 118-21.

not develop normative *theological* perspectives to interpret research and, often, do not attempt to shape the field they are investigating.[7] Yet the normative and pragmatic tasks are central to practical theology as an academic discipline.

The Four Tasks of Practical Theological Interpretation

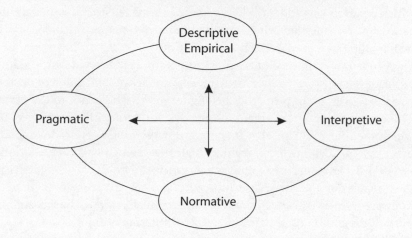

Often, thus, it is helpful to think of practical theological interpretation as more like a *spiral* than a circle. It constantly circles back to tasks that have already been explored. Interpreting the congregation's relationship to Mary Jo with an ethic of reconciliation might have led me to look again at how the congregation handles conflict, the descriptive-empirical task. Practical theological interpretation often circles back like a spiral as insights emerge.

Before proceeding, it may be helpful to clarify three categories used repeatedly in this introduction: episodes, situations, and contexts. I use these categories throughout to distinguish different focal points of practical theological interpretation. They are a convenient way of differentiating units of time and space that are increasingly comprehensive.

7. While some social scientists *do* conduct and interpret research in ways that are value-laden, this almost never is based on a theological perspective. Moreover, some view their research as contributing to the common good and offer proposals to this end. My point is that theological, ethical, and pragmatic dimensions are central to practical theological interpretation, distinguishing it from the social sciences. When social scientists include ethical and pragmatic dimensions in their work, practical theology may overlap these features, intersecting them in some ways while diverging in others.

An *episode* is an incident or event that emerges from the flow of everyday life and evokes explicit attention and reflection. It occurs in a single setting over a short period of time. An episode describes what took place on Mary Jo's front porch when I called on her. A *situation* is the broader and longer pattern of events, relationships, and circumstances in which an episode occurs. It often is best understood in the form of a narrative in which a particular incident is located within a longer story. As the ramifications of moving the swing set unfolded over time and included more people, they are best described as a situation.

A *context* is composed of the social and natural systems in which a situation unfolds. A system is a network of interacting and interconnected parts that give rise to properties belonging to the whole, not to the parts. The congregation as an organizational system is one of the contexts in which the swing set situation unfolded. But this system is nestled within other systems that are local, regional, national, and global. Context, thus, serves a flexible purpose, calling attention to micro- and macrosystems that are relevant to a given case. Moreover, systems are open and dynamic. They are influenced by other systems. Contextual analysis, thus, is an important dimension of practical theological interpretation.

Practical Theological Interpretation: A Bridge Concept

It may also be helpful at the outset to clarify my use of the term "practical theological interpretation." I use this term to indicate three corollaries of my central argument about the fourfold nature of practical theology: (1) practical theological interpretation takes place in all the specialized subdisciplines of practical theology; (2) the same structure of practical theological interpretation in academic practical theology characterizes the interpretive tasks of congregational leaders as well; (3) acknowledging the common structure of practical theological interpretation in both the academy and ministry can help congregational leaders recognize the interconnectedness of ministry.

Bridging the Subdisciplines of Academic Practical Theology

The first corollary makes the claim that the basic structure of practical theological interpretation is common to *all* the specialized subdisciplines of practical theology. Attention to the four tasks outlined above takes place in preaching, pastoral care, evangelism, spirituality, Christian education, and other ministerial practices.

Preaching, for example, gives special attention to the interpretation of biblical texts and to proclamation on the basis of this interpretation in the context of worship. As such, it carries out a task that is inherently normative. Yet preaching does not take place in a vacuum. Sermons are crafted with an eye to a particular group of people on a specific occasion in a particular congregational context. Today, many prominent voices in preaching are attending to the cultural and congregational context in which preaching takes place — what I have called the descriptive-empirical and interpretive tasks.[8] Moreover, sermons are performed through bodily gestures and patterns of speech; they use certain forms that offer listeners something to feel, think about, and do during the preaching event. They strive to evoke the imaginations of hearers. The artistry of preaching warrants precisely the sort of strategic thinking and acting brought into focus by the pragmatic task.

The basic structure of practical theological interpretation is found in the other subdisciplines of practical theology as well. This is not to say that preaching, Christian education, pastoral care, and other forms of ministry are identical. Each focuses on a particular task of ministry, which involves specific practices, skills, and concepts. But it *is* to say that they overlap in significant ways and share a common structure of practical theological interpretation.

Bridging the Academy and Ministry

The second corollary of my central argument makes the claim that the same structure of practical theological interpretation informing academic practical theology characterizes the interpretive tasks of congregational

---

8. Thomas Long, *The Witness of Preaching* (Louisville: Westminster John Knox, 1989); Leonora Tubbs Tisdale, *Preaching as Local Theology and Folk Art* (Minneapolis: Fortress, 1997); John McClure et al., *Listening to Listeners: Homiletical Case Studies* (St. Louis: Chalice, 2005); Ronald J. Allen, *Hearing the Sermon: Relationship, Content, Feeling* (St. Louis: Chalice, 2004); Mary Alice Mulligan et al., *Believing in Preaching: What Listeners Hear in Sermons* (St. Louis: Chalice, 2005); McClure, *The Four Codes of Preaching: Rhetorical Strategies* (Minneapolis: Fortress, 1991).

leaders as well. As we saw in the discussion of the case study, pastors and other leaders face the focal questions of the four tasks of practical theological interpretation: What is going on? Why is this going on? What ought to be going on? How might we respond? A key pedagogical task of practical theology courses is to educate students in ways that prepare them to carry out practical theological interpretation in their future ministries.

The importance of this sort of preparation is something I learned first-hand when my mother was in a car accident. The accident occurred only a few blocks from my parents' home. My father was driving them on some errands when a car in front of them suddenly braked and my father could not stop in time. My mother's head snapped forward and hit the dashboard. She was taken to the hospital and appeared to be fine, so my parents returned home. But later that night she lost consciousness and was rushed to the hospital where she was placed on life support. When my father called, he was so upset that I could barely make out what had happened. I flew home early the next morning and suddenly confronted a life-or-death situation. The accident had precipitated a subdural hematoma in which blood was trapped between the brain and the skull. This is particularly dangerous for older adults on blood thinners like my mother.

My father was emotionally distraught. I was very fortunate that the pastor of my parents' church, in which I was raised, arrived at the hospital only minutes after I did. He was present when the doctor later told us that my mother had suffered massive damage to all parts of her brain and that her prospects were not good. The doctor recommended keeping her on life support for a few days to see if she showed any signs of recovery. I heard the doctor's words, but I needed to have our pastor interpret them for me later in the waiting room. When it became clear that my mother would not recover and that the life-support systems were taking over basic functions like breathing, I needed this pastor to help me let go of my mother, re-minding me of the certainty of God's love in life and death. He noticed that it really bothered me that I had not been able to tell her good-bye. So together, we entered her room and confronted her body, suspended pre-cariously over the precipice of life and death on the slender threads of so many tubes and machines. Lifted up by this pastor's strength, I talked to my mother and we prayed over her. When the life support was removed later that week and my mother died, I was sustained by what we had done; I was also sustained by the beautiful funeral sermon this pastor later preached.

It is only with the passing of many years that I can look back at this experience and see how this pastor carried out the tasks of practical theological interpretation. I was very fortunate to have a minister educated in pastoral care along these lines, seasoned by years of experience. Not only did he draw out the story of what had happened, but he also was there to interpret for me the doctor's diagnosis and prognosis. He helped me realize that in the midst of this crisis my father was too distraught to face the decisions before us and that I needed to take over more of this role than I ordinarily might have. He interpreted these terrible circumstances biblically and theologically without any jargon. He gently reminded us of the promises of God and asked us to stand on these promises. He recognized my need to say good-bye and led me to actions that allowed me to do so.

I offer this very personal story to underscore the importance of ministry adept in practical theological interpretation. Theological education that equips leaders to carry this out is engaged in far more than an academic exercise. It is preparing people to provide leadership in the face of life-or-death decisions.

The Web of Life: The Interconnectedness of Ministry

The third corollary of my argument makes the claim that acknowledging the common structure of practical theological interpretation in both academic practical theology and ministry can prepare congregational leaders to recognize the interconnectedness of ministry. In the personal example just described, it was no accident that the pastor who offered such helpful pastoral care also preached just the right sermon for our situation. Ministry in its various forms is interconnected.

Unfortunately, many contemporary schools of theology do not prepare leaders to grasp these interconnections. This is a by-product of specialization in the academy, which has resulted in sharp divisions between scholarly fields and subject areas in the curriculum. In practical theology this often results in courses that focus exclusively on one form of ministry like preaching, pastoral care, or Christian education. What gets lost in this educational pattern is the interconnectedness of ministry in the congregational system and the congregation's interaction with its context.

A helpful perspective on this issue is offered by pastoral theologian Bonnie Miller-McLemore. She describes the focus of practical theological interpretation as the "living human web," drawing attention to various forms of interconnection.[9] Just as the strands of a spider's web are interconnected, so too are the bonds that link individuals, families, congregations, communities, and larger social systems. This image also reminds us of the World Wide Web, which creates information flows connecting individuals, communities, and systems around the world.

Miller-McLemore develops this image, in part, to correct the individualistic, therapeutic focus of pastoral care in the past century. This is too narrow, she argues, for it does not attend to the interconnections between individual crises and broader patterns in families and communities, which often create such crises in the first place.[10] Pastoral care, thus, does more than offer healing, sustaining, and guiding to individuals in need, the widely influential definition of Seward Hiltner.[11] Rather, it attends to the web of relationships and systems creating suffering through ministries of compassionate resistance, empowerment, nurturance, and liberation.[12]

I want to extend Miller-McLemore's helpful image with the work of Fritjof Capra.[13] Capra reminds us that social systems are located in an interconnected web of natural systems. It is important, thus, to think in terms of the *web of life*, not just the living *human* web. Capra offers a "new synthesis" of the life sciences in which living systems share three characteristics: a pattern of organization, structures that embody this pattern, and

9. Bonnie J. Miller-McLemore, "The Living Human Web: Pastoral Theology at the Turn of the Century," in *Through the Eyes of Women*, ed. Jeanne Stevenson Moessner (Minneapolis: Augsburg Fortress, 1996), chapter 1. See also Miller-McLemore, "The Human Web: Reflections on the State of Pastoral Theology," *Christian Century*, April 7, 1993, pp. 366-69. In both articles Miller-McLemore not only corrects the individualistic, therapeutic approach but also expands Anton Boison's widely influential description of the starting point of pastoral theology as the study of "living human documents."

10. For an excellent example of pastoral care that takes account of this living human web, see Pamela Couture, *Blessed Are the Poor? Women's Poverty, Family Policy, and Practical Theology* (Nashville: Abingdon, 1991).

11. Seward Hiltner, *Preface to Pastoral Theology: The Ministry and Theory of Shepherding* (Nashville: Abingdon, 1958). This definition of pastoral care was augmented with the task of reconciling by W. A. Clebsch and C. R. Jaekle in *Pastoral Care in Historical Perspective* (Englewood Cliffs, N.J.: Prentice-Hall, 1983).

12. Bonnie Miller-McLemore, "Feminist Theory in Pastoral Theology," in *Feminist and Womanist Pastoral Theology*, ed. Bonnie J. Miller-McLemore and Brita L. Gill-Austern (Nashville: Abingdon, 1999), p. 80.

13. Fritjof Capra, *The Web of Life: A New Scientific Understanding of Living Systems* (New York: Anchor Books, 1996).

processes by which a living system takes in, transforms, and creates output in its interactions with other systems, renewing its own pattern and structures as it does so.[14] These characteristics are found in *all* living systems — from cells to organisms to social systems to the entire planetary system. Moreover, living systems are nestled in other systems, which together make up the web of life.

The concept of the web of life extends Miller-McLemore's initial insight and proves helpful to our understanding of practical theological interpretation in three ways. First, it reminds us that focusing exclusively on individuals is too limited. We must think in terms of interconnections, relationships, and systems. Miller-McLemore's critique of the individualistic focus of recent pastoral care is applicable to other forms of ministry as well. Second, this image draws attention to the interconnection of various forms of ministry. Experienced pastors are the first to recognize that their preaching is deeply connected to the level of biblical literacy they can presuppose in the pulpit, fostered by the teaching ministry. This, in turn, is connected to the quality of Christian education offered in the home, which, in turn, is related to parents' spirituality, and so forth. Ministerial tasks are part of an interdependent whole. Third, this image reminds us that congregations are embedded in a web of natural and social systems beyond the church. When health-care systems force the elderly to choose between buying medicine or food, this impacts the congregation's care of older adults and its mission as an advocate of justice. When a small town's zoning commission is controlled by real estate developers, resulting in numerous strip malls and housing developments that reduce the wetlands, pollute the air, and overload the sewage system, local churches are caught up in these changes, whether they like them or not. Taking account of the web of natural and social systems in which congregations are situated is an important part of practical theological interpretation. Systems are nestled within systems. Practical theological interpretation, thus, is deeply contextual. It thinks in terms of interconnections, relationships, and systems.

To summarize, practical theological interpretation is an important bridge concept in this book. It creates a bridge between the subdisciplines of academic practical theology and between the academy and the church. It draws attention to the web of life in which ministry takes place. This perspective potentially opens up a new way of thinking about congregational

---

14. Capra, *The Web of Life*, chapter 7.

leadership that integrates the various tasks of that leadership. This is found in the model of the congregational leader as interpretive guide.

Congregational Leaders as Interpretive Guides

While a doctoral student at Emory University, I had the good fortune of studying with the pastoral theologian Charles Gerkin. I was his research assistant while he was writing *The Living Human Document,* and he later was a member of my dissertation committee.[15] One of Gerkin's most important contributions in the final part of his career was to develop a new model of pastoral leadership: the pastor as *interpretive guide.*[16]

In part, this model reflects the movement away from a hierarchical view of pastoral authority in many churches and denominations during the modern period. The social trends that brought this about include the following:

1. The rise of public education during the nineteenth century and the expansion of high school and college education during the twentieth century. Pastors are no longer the most highly educated persons in their communities. Indeed, they often have far less social status than other professionals like doctors, psychiatrists, and lawyers.
2. The spread of democratic values and governments over the past two centuries, which encourage people to think for themselves and hold authorities accountable, including pastoral leaders.
3. Greater cultural pluralism in many Western nations, including religious, lifestyle, and ethnic diversity. People have freedom to choose whether or not they will affiliate with a religious community and how

15. Charles Gerkin, *The Living Human Document: Re-Visioning Pastoral Counseling in a Hermeneutical Mode* (Nashville: Abingdon, 1984).

16. Charles Gerkin, *An Introduction to Pastoral Care* (Nashville: Abingdon, 1997), pp. 113-14. This image first emerges, I believe, in *The Living Human Document,* p. 54. It is developed further in *Widening the Horizons: Pastoral Responses to a Fragmented Society* (Philadelphia: Westminster, 1986), in which Gerkin offers a narrative hermeneutical theory of practical theology portraying the entire task of practical theological thinking as interpretive guidance. See especially chapter 5. He continues to develop this image in *Prophetic Pastoral Practice: A Christian Vision of Life Together* (Nashville: Abingdon, 1991), pp. 68-70.

much or how little they will participate. Pastors no longer automatically have special authority because everyone goes to church. Rather, they must "earn" their authority.

4. The secularization of modern institutions, which pressures religion to remain in the private sphere of personal meaning and family life. This compartmentalization of religion to a very narrow sphere of life results in the perception that pastors have neither the right nor the competence to address issues in other areas of life, like work, politics, public education, and so forth.

Gerkin argues that these trends created a new social context in which "the pastor's right to be heard and taken seriously is defined more in terms of the parishioner's perception of both the reasonable wisdom . . . of what is said and the quality of relationship communicated."[17] As he notes, this is not altogether a negative development. What pastors lost in hierarchical authority, they gained in access to the everyday experiences and problems of ordinary people. Too often in the past, people hid their personal issues and questions from the pastor and put on their "best Christian face." In our present social context, Gerkin believes, "a relationship of mutual exploration and reflective consideration of options may be possible" between pastor and people, facilitating greater freedom and honesty on both sides.[18] It is this new understanding of pastoral authority that Gerkin seeks to capture in his model of the pastor as interpretive guide, a kind of "master model" that runs across and, potentially, integrates the various tasks ministers carry out. Both sides of this model are important: the leader as guide and as interpreter.

We often think of a guide as someone who plays a key role in an outdoor vacation, like rafting down the Colorado River in the Grand Canyon. The guide has traveled the route many times and knows where the most dangerous rapids and the best places to stop for the night are located. She also must be a good judge of the people on a particular trip — their physical capabilities, stamina, and prior rafting experience. All this is implied in Gerkin's model of interpretive guide, with one important difference. The pastoral guide does not take people on the same old trip but travels with them into *new* territory. Together, they must learn the lay of the land and

17. Gerkin, *Widening the Horizons,* p. 99.
18. Gerkin, *Widening the Horizons,* p. 99.

the paths available to them. This is a collaborative activity. The guide must attend carefully to the resources of the travelers and the particular journey they hope to take, as well as contributing her own expertise.[19]

The central task carried out by the pastoral guide is *interpretation*. This is pivotal to Gerkin's portrait of pastoral leadership and, by implication, to congregational leadership generally. Moreover, the "turn" to interpretation, or hermeneutics, informs virtually every theory examined in this book. Thus, it is worthwhile to pause here and explain what this means. We will then return to Gerkin's description of the interpretive activity offered by pastoral guides.

Hermeneutics: The Art and Science of Interpretation

Throughout the modern period scholarly reflection on interpretation was associated with the field of *hermeneutics*. Initially, hermeneutics focused on the art and science of the interpretation of ancient texts. The classics of literature and the sacred scriptures of religious communities often are difficult for people to understand because they were written in historical eras and cultural contexts quite different from the present.

This was particularly true as people began to live in a scientific, industrialized world and became more and more aware of the differences between the past and the present. Hermeneutics arose initially to cope with this problem, providing guidelines for the interpretation of ancient texts. It helped people find meaning in texts that were an important part of their cultural and religious heritage.

In the twentieth century hermeneutics as a "regional" field, focusing on the interpretation of ancient texts, was expanded by hermeneutic philosophy in two important ways: (1) hermeneutics was broadened to include the interpretive activity of ordinary people in everyday life; (2) it was recog-

19. Like Miller-McLemore, Gerkin is attempting to move pastoral care beyond the individualistic, therapeutic paradigm, a paradigm informing his work until the last part of his life. But he values careful attention to individuals in all their particularity, which was championed by pastoral care in the past century. He does not want to throw the baby out with the bathwater. For a nice summary of this element of the pastoral care and counseling movement in the twentieth century, see Rodney Hunter and John Patton's historical perspective in *Pastoral Care and Social Conflict*, ed. Pamela Couture and Rodney Hunter (Nashville: Abingdon, 1995), pp. 24, 35-36.

nized as a dimension of all forms of scholarship, the hermeneutical, or interpretive, dimension of the sciences and humanities.[20]

Humans as Interpretive Beings

The first point indicates the way that interpretation came to be viewed as an activity that lies at the heart of human existence, what the philosopher Martin Heidegger called an *existentiale* of human existence in *Being in Time*.[21] Humans are inherently "hermeneutical" beings, engaged in the activity of interpreting and making sense of their experience. Heidegger portrayed this interpretive activity as grounded in the already-interpreted world into which human beings are born and socialized.

In everyday life, much of this interpretive activity is practical in nature. Objects and people are interpreted in ways that allow individuals to get on with their ordinary routines. In the morning we are awakened by an alarm clock; we shuffle into the bathroom and use the toilet; we walk to the kitchen and open several cabinets to get cereal and a bowl; we take a carton of milk out of the refrigerator. At no point do we stop and think: this is an alarm clock, toilet, cereal, bowl, or milk. We simply interpret and relate to these objects as part of an already-interpreted world that is largely oriented around practical use.

Usually, only the experience of being brought up short causes us to become aware of the interpretive activity we are taking for granted. The alarm clock fails to sound because the electricity has gone off briefly in the middle of the night. As we lean over to pull out a new gallon of milk from the refrigerator, we wrench our back. These sorts of events puncture our taken-for-granted world and make us aware of the interpretive activity in which we are already engaged. When such events are serious, they may even call into question key elements of our interpretation of the world. The unexpected loss of a job may undermine our sense of financial security or our self-image as a rising star in a company. The death of a child may puncture our belief that God watches over "good people" and does not let bad things happen to them.

20. This account of hermeneutics builds on Paul Ricoeur, *The Conflict of Interpretations: Essays in Hermeneutics,* ed. Don Ihde (Evanston, Ill.: Northwestern University Press, 1974), especially chapter 1. A helpful overview of this process is found in Palmer, *Hermeneutics,* cited above, and A. C. Thiselton, *New Horizons in Hermeneutics* (London: HarperCollins, 1992).

21. Martin Heidegger, *Being in Time* (New York: Harper and Row, 1962), pp. 182-95.

When events call into question the taken-for-granted assumptions of our world, it makes us aware that our interpretive activity is very human and built on a fragile foundation. This may evoke anxiety, and even dread. In their profounder forms such experiences represent the threat of nonbeing to our way of being in the world. Heidegger said our response to these threats takes two basic forms. We can shrink back and deny the challenges these experiences present, attempting to buttress and repair our already-established patterns of interpretation. Or we can embrace the challenges they represent to our way of being in the world, learning from them and accepting responsibility for creating new interpretive patterns. These represent inauthentic and authentic responses, respectively.

The Hermeneutical Dimension of Scholarship

One of Heidegger's students, Hans-Georg Gadamer, was important to the second expansion of hermeneutics noted above: the recognition of the interpretive dimension of scholarship. Like Heidegger, Gadamer argued that all interpretation begins in an already-interpreted world. In his book *Truth and Method,* he pointed out that this is true of scholarship as well.[22] He was particularly critical of the way modern science since the Enlightenment tried to eliminate the interpretive starting point of inquiry, bracketing out all "prejudices," or preunderstandings, that would compromise a scientist's objectivity. In contrast, Gadamer argued that all interpretation begins with preunderstandings that come to us from the past.

In science (and scholarship generally), this takes the form of research traditions that provide the scientist with a language, conceptual framework, and research practices with which to begin his inquiry. Rather than pretending to bracket out all preunderstandings in the futile attempt to hold a neutral, objective point of view, scholars do better to acknowledge their interpretive starting point, the particular research tradition that guides their work. It was only the Enlightenment's "prejudice against prejudice" that led modern science and scholarship to deny the positive role of preunderstanding.

But Gadamer went further. The preunderstanding with which we begin interpretation, he argued, does not necessarily determine the end point of interpretation. He developed the important concept of a *hermeneutical*

22. Hans-Georg Gadamer, *Truth and Method* (New York: Continuum, 1975).

experience to describe the sort of interpretive activity that is open to encountering and learning something genuinely new.[23] Gadamer portrayed this sort of experience along the lines of a hermeneutical circle, composed of five moments:

- *Preunderstanding.* This comprises the interpretive judgments and understandings with which we begin interpretation; they come to us from the past.
- *The experience of being brought up short.* This is the experience of running up against something in our investigation that calls into question some facet of our preunderstanding.
- *Dialogical interplay.* To allow the text, person, or object to reveal itself to us anew, we listen for its "voice" and open ourselves to the "horizon" it projects. The concept of horizon is based on a visual metaphor. It indicates the farthest point that can be seen from a particular vantage point. In Gadamer, it indicates both the scope and limitations of a particular point of view. Interpretation, thus, is like a dialogue in which there is a back-and-forth interplay between the horizon of the interpreter and the horizon of the text, person, or object being interpreted.
- *Fusion of horizons.* Like a conversation, interpretation yields new insights when the horizons of the interpreter and the interpreted join together. Both contribute something.
- *Application.* New insights give rise to new ways of thinking and acting in the world.

Scholarship at its best partakes of this hermeneutical circle. New understanding emerges when scholars are open to hermeneutical experiences in which they become aware of the preunderstandings with which they begin their interpretative activity and are willing to put them at risk in a dialogical encounter with the objects, people, or texts they are interpreting. The hermeneutical, or interpretive, dimension of scholarship is widely acknowledged today. It would be difficult to overstate the influence of Gadamer's critique of the Enlightenment's "prejudice against prejudice."[24]

---

23. Gadamer, *Truth and Method*, pp. 310-25.

24. For an excellent introduction to the "interpretive" turn in the social sciences, see the appendix ("Hermeneutic Social Science and Practical Theology") in Don Browning et al., *From Culture Wars to Common Ground: Religion and the American Family Debate*, 2nd ed. (Louisville: Westminster John Knox, 1997), pp. 335-41.

Guiding Interpretation:
The Integrative Task of Congregational Leaders

Gerkin's portrait of pastors (and congregational leaders) as interpretive guides builds on these developments in contemporary hermeneutic philosophy. Three tasks of interpretation emerge in his writings, which are portrayed along the lines of a dialogue.

1. *Guiding the congregation as a community of interpretation.* Gerkin portrays humans as interpretive beings, who are socialized into an already-interpreted world. Within the web of relationships and communities in which Christians participate, their congregations play a formative role. When individuals join or grow up in a congregation, they become part of a community of interpretation, a community that embodies a particular understanding of the Christian tradition in its ritual actions, practices, and beliefs.

One of the tasks of congregational leadership is guiding the congregation as a community of interpretation. This is a matter of facilitating a dialogue between interpretive activity already taking place and interpretations generated by Scripture, tradition, and other sources of Christian faith. The dialogical interplay and fusion of horizons found in genuine hermeneutical experiences mean that this dialogue must be two-way conversation. The interpretive guide must attend carefully to the interpretative activity in which people are already engaged. This takes careful listening and empathy, as well as analysis and critique of the social systems shaping their interpretive patterns. This attentiveness is crucial to the interpretive guide's ability to relate the normative sources of the Christian tradition to the issues people actually face in their everyday lives.

2. *Guiding interpretation evoked by the experience of being brought up short.* Congregations and their members encounter experiences that bring them up short, which has the potential of evoking new interpretive activity. Losing a job at midlife, going through a divorce, discovering that our government is practicing torture, or changes in the congregation's neighborhood can puncture taken-for-granted interpretations of God, morality, and what it means to live as a faithful Christian. They can call into question personal and corporate identities.

A second task of congregational leadership, thus, is entering into a dialogue with people when life brings them up short, helping them rework their interpretations of self, marriage, church, work, or political commitment. It is not uncommon for people to draw back from experiences that call into question cherished notions of self, church, or nation and to settle for inauthentic forms of faith. Leaders, thus, face the task of providing the appropriate measures of support, encouragement, and confrontation. Their goal is to facilitate a dialogue between people whose interpretation of life has unraveled and the resources of the Christian community.

3. *Guiding the dialogue between theology and other fields of knowledge.* To a certain extent, this third task of the interpretive guide is the special responsibility of leaders who have received a theological education, which has taught them how to bring theology into conversation with other fields. In this book we describe this general task as cross-disciplinary dialogue and give it special attention in chapter 3. Facilitating dialogue between theology and other fields is important in the congregation's interpretation of events unfolding inside and outside the church. It is common for congregations to include people with expertise in medicine, business, law, recovery, education, and therapy. Such expertise can be a great resource in the congregation's reflection on its life and mission, contributing to the practical wisdom of the entire community. The task of the guide is to draw out this expertise while making sure that the perspectives of theology and ethics also are taken seriously.

The Spirituality of Congregational Leaders

One final introductory matter remains. Throughout the book I use the term "congregational leaders" instead of "pastors" or "ministers" to refer to interpretive guides. This is intentional and takes us beyond Gerkin's focus on *pastoral* guides. Clergy are not the only people who provide guidance in congregations. Indeed, a strong theological case can be made that mutual guidance belongs primarily to the whole people of God and only secondarily to people set aside by this community in ordination.[25]

---

25. For an insightful treatment of the relation between clergy and congregation, see Long, *The Witness of Preaching*, chapter 1. For discussion of edification as belonging to the entire congregation, see Richard Osmer, *The Teaching Ministry of Congregations* (Louisville: Westminster John Knox, 2005), pp. 17-25.

A Communication Model of Leadership

We need a perspective, thus, that portrays leadership as broader than the official leaders of a community or organization. One such perspective is the communication theory of leadership developed by Michael Hackman and Craig Johnson.[26] They define leadership as "human (symbolic) communication, which modifies the attitudes and behavior of others in order to meet shared group goals and needs." There are three key components of leadership in this definition.

First, leadership is the exercise of *influence.* While it includes the influence of designated leaders like preachers, teachers, and caregivers, it also involves the influence of people who are not official leaders. In a small-group Bible study, for example, it often is not the teacher who provides the most important insights about the Bible passage and moves the discussion in fruitful directions. This is common throughout congregations. Influence flows in many directions, from official, designated leaders and informal leaders as well.

Second, leadership is the exercise of influence through many *different forms of communication.* Communication is meant broadly here. It includes words, nonverbal communication, and actions, which help a group achieve shared goals and meet the needs of its members. Research indicates, for example, that young people are most likely to be involved in a congregation when it offers relationships they trust and in which they feel valued and accepted. Leadership that is responsive to these needs encompasses all forms of communication that build these kinds of relationships, including actions as well as words. Indeed, leaders' actions often communicate more than their words.

Third, leadership is *collaborative.* Leaders work with others to achieve shared goals. This is particularly important in voluntary organizations in which motivation and participation go hand in hand. Leaders, thus, must empower — give power to — others. Yet the failure to collaborate often is the point where congregational leadership breaks down. A leader may have a vision of where he would like the church to go, but if he does not empower others to participate in the process of shaping this vision, then he is unlikely to achieve lasting change.

26. Michael Hackman and Craig Johnson, *Leadership: A Communication Perspective* (Prospect Heights, Ill.: Waveland Press, 1996), p. 12.

The Spirituality of Congregational Leaders

Leadership in the Christian community is inherently a spiritual matter. Using influence to modify the attitudes and behaviors of others is not to be taken lightly, even when this is carried out in a collaborative fashion. Accordingly, I develop a theology of congregational leadership over the course of this book, giving special attention to the spirituality of leaders. By spirituality I mean leaders' openness to the guidance of the Holy Spirit as she forms and transforms them toward the image of Christ in his body and in the service of the church's mission. Some Christian traditions have used the term "piety" instead of "spirituality," for reasons that were relevant in the sixteenth century. Today, however, "piety" and "pietism" have connotations that make it difficult to use these terms. In recent decades, moreover, fresh theological thinking about the Holy Spirit has led many Protestant communions, originally hostile to spirituality, to become more open to its role in the Christian life.

In offering a theology of the spirituality of congregational leaders, I move away from a general description of the tasks of practical theological interpretation that are found in the writings of many contemporary practical theologians. I offer a *theological* perspective that is my own. It is not necessary to agree with it to accept my description of the tasks of practical theological interpretation, however. Many practical theologians frame these tasks with very different theologies. This is one of the sources of pluralism in practical theology. In articulating my own perspective, I draw on the tradition of the threefold office of Christ, which has received much attention in Reformed theology. It is one way this tradition has portrayed the interrelatedness of the Old and New Testaments, providing a starting point for theological reflection on leadership in congregations.

In this theological tradition God's election of Israel is viewed as an act of divine grace. It does not confer special privilege on Israel but is God's way of forming a community that will serve as a sign and witness to the divine purposes for creation. This election takes the form of a covenant between God and Israel and brings into being a covenant community, whose way of life is to embody a relationship of trust in God and right-relatedness among human beings. Over the course of this unfolding covenant relationship, God provides Israel with leaders, anointed with the Spirit of God, to help it live with covenant fidelity. Priests play a special role in Israel's worship of God, overseeing the cult and offering sacrifices to God on the people's behalf. Judges, sages, and kings provide leadership in the organization of the covenant community, offering wise teachings, settling disputes, guiding its political affairs, and protecting it against external threats. Prophets speak God's Word to Israel, announcing divine judgment when it strays from covenant fidelity, calling it to repent, and offering hope if it turns back to God.

The New Testament draws on biblical traditions related to each of these offices within Israel to describe Christ in order to make two basic points. First, the God who entered into a covenant with Israel and promised to remain faithful to this covenant community has "in the fullness of time" fulfilled these promises. Christ is the true priest, king, and prophet. The one for whom Israel longed has now arrived. Second, Christ transforms these offices, even as he fulfills them. Christ does more than offer sacrifices to God; his very life and death is a sacrifice pleasing to God. Christ does more than rule wisely as God's viceroy; he is God's Wisdom in person and establishes God's royal rule in the form of a servant. Christ does more than utter words from God; he is God's Word. God's covenant promises are transformed in Christ Jesus, even as they are fulfilled. A new possibility is opened up in the salvation Christ brings, resulting in the election of a new covenant people.

As theologians in the Reformed tradition reflected on the many ways the New Testament portrays the themes of promise and fulfillment and God's new covenant in Christ, they brought them together in the concept of the threefold office of Christ. Technically speaking, this is one office in three forms. The unity of Christ's work in salvation is that of a mediator, who stands between God and humanity in order that the broken relationship between God and creation might be set right. 1 Timothy 2:5 puts it like this: "For there is only one God, and there is only one mediator between God and humanity, himself a human being, Christ Jesus" (NJB). This one office is described from three perspectives — Christ as priest, king, and prophet — to bring into focus different dimensions of mediation.

Building on the tradition of the threefold office, I develop a practical theology of leadership in which the four tasks of practical theological interpretation are portrayed as facilitating the congregation's participation in Christ's priestly, royal, and prophetic mediation of salvation. To anticipate what follows, the descriptive-empirical task is a form of priestly listening, grounded in a spirituality of presence: attending to others in their particularity within the presence of God. The interpretive task is a form of wise judgment, grounded in a spirituality of sagely wisdom: guiding others in how to live within God's royal rule. The normative task is a form of prophetic discernment, grounded in a spirituality of discernment: helping others hear and heed God's Word in the particular circumstances of their lives and world. The pragmatic task is a form of transforming leadership, grounded in a spirituality of servant leadership: taking risks on behalf of the congregation to help it better embody its mission as a sign and witness of God's self-giving love.

In short, the leaders of congregations carry out the tasks of practical theological interpretation to guide their community in participating in the priestly, royal, and prophetic office of Christ. For leaders to carry out these tasks well, they need to acquire a rich array of knowledge and skills. But they need more than professional competence alone. They must learn to rely on the guidance of the Holy Spirit, rooted in their spirituality. Their being and becoming in the Spirit are integrally related to their doing and leading in Christ's body and this body's service of the world.

CHAPTER 1

The Descriptive-Empirical Task: Priestly Listening

—◦◦◦—

O livia Potter twisted the handkerchief again and again as she stood in the airport baggage area waiting for her parents. She had been looking forward to this visit for weeks, but now that it had finally arrived she grew more and more anxious. She knew that her mother would immediately notice how much weight she had lost and the big circles under her eyes. She would tell them what was going on in her life in good time, but not at the airport. So she put on her best smile and began to scan the faces of the people coming down the escalator.

Later that evening Olivia decided it was time to "fess up," as she put it. After clearing the dishes from the table and pouring coffee for her father, she asked her parents to join her in the small living room of the condominium. "Well, I guess you must be wondering why John isn't here," she said. "We've decided to separate. I've told you that he was drinking a lot, but I didn't tell you everything. He never, ever comes home at night. After work he jumps in the truck and is off to meet his drinking buddies. I think the earliest he's gotten home this week is two in the morning. He's too hung over to say much at breakfast, although he's promised me more than once that he will be home in time for supper. I let him make that promise one last time this Monday, and when he didn't show up, I went through the house and got all the money I could find and went to stay with Patty. You met her last time you were down here. I'm only back in the condo for your visit. Then I'm packing up and moving out. I've already got something lined up."

Olivia reached over and took her father's mug. As she went into the kitchen, she tried unsuccessfully to hold back the tears. Her parents quickly joined her in the kitchen, and they placed their arms around her as she wept. Through her sobs Olivia went on: "That's not all. With all this stuff going on with John, I've started to drink a lot myself. When he doesn't show up at night, it makes me so angry I start drinking, and the more I drink, the angrier I get. Things have been terrible at work too. I never knew real estate agents and developers were such con artists. And they're not just doing it to the clients, they've been conning me too. Remember how excited I was when I told you that I'd been promised a car and a big raise? Well, I've been working my butt off for two months now, and it's pretty obvious that they're not going to give me any of that. I hate going to work. I hate coming home. I've even been thinking pretty often about driving my car off the road and ending it all."

As Olivia began to sob again, she whispered, "Daddy, I want to do God's will. I really do. I'm trying to figure that out. But I feel so tired right now. I'm ready to give up."

After a moment her father responded, "Olivia, one thing I'm pretty sure of. God's will isn't for you to be working these kinds of hours and to be living in such a rotten marriage and to be so unhappy. Please, please, go see a pastor. Get some help."

Two weeks later, after she had moved, Olivia called up Pastor Dorothy Gains, the associate pastor of a local church. She had found out about Rev. Gains from the wife of one of her coworkers. So here she was, sitting in Rev. Gains's office. "So what brings you here?" Rev. Gains began.

"I guess I'm more unhappy than I've ever been in my life," Olivia responded. "I've even had thoughts about driving my car off the road and ending it all."

What if you were Rev. Gains? You know nothing about Olivia Potter other than what you have just heard. Where do you go from here?

The purpose of this chapter is to teach the leaders of congregations how to carry out the descriptive-empirical task of practical theological interpretation. In seminary, students learn how to interpret many different kinds of texts. They learn the skills of exegesis and interpretation of biblical texts. They study classic texts and ancient liturgies of the Christian tradition and explore their meaning for today. Practical theology invites such

~~students to interpret the texts of contemporary lives and prac~~tices, what Anton Boison once called "l~~iving human documents~~."[1]

If you were Rev. Gains, the chances are good that you would try to draw Olivia Potter out and get more information. You might ask her how frequently she had suicidal thoughts and how serious she was about acting on those thoughts. You might pay close attention to her physical appearance. Does she look thin and tired? How is her hygiene? You might attend to the way she communicates. Does she tear up as she talks? Is her speech faltering and subdued? Are the feelings accompanying her words flat or sad? Since Olivia shared suicidal thoughts, you would feel obligated to assess how serious they were. You would spend time drawing out more of her story to decide if a referral to a mental health professional might be in order. At the end of this chapter I describe Olivia's life story more fully.

Congregational leaders experience episodes like this all the time as people share their problems, seek help, are hospitalized, lose loved ones, and pass through the stages of life. When they make observations and gather information in the face of such incidents, they are attempting to answer the question, "~~What is going on?" This question lies at the very~~ heart ~~of the descriptive-empirical task of practical theological interpreta~~tion. Yet it is important to view this task as broader than gathering information in the face of problematic or crisis situations like the example given above. It has to do with the quality of attentiveness congregational leaders give to people and events in their everyday lives. This is helpfully explored in terms of a spirituality of presence.

A Spirituality of Presence

In recent decades discussion of the spirituality of presence has been widespread and has moved in a number of directions.[2] Here it describes a spiri-

1. See Charles Gerkin's account of Boison's use of this phrase in *The Living Human Document: Re-Visioning Pastoral Counseling in a Hermeneutical Mode* (Nashville: Abingdon, 1984), p. 200 n. 1. As we saw in the introduction, Bonnie Miller-McLemore broadened this to the living human web, which I have extended to the web of life.

2. See, for example, Jean Stairs, *Listening for the Soul: Pastoral Care and Spiritual Direction* (Minneapolis: Fortress, 2000); Margaret Guenther, *Holy Listening: The Art of Spiritual Direction* (Cambridge, Mass.: Cowley, 1992); Tilden Edwards, *Living in the Presence: Spiritual Exercises to Open Our Lives to the Awareness of God* (San Francisco: HarperSanFrancisco, 1987).

tual orientation of attending to others in their particularity and otherness within the presence of God. The key term here is "attending," relating to others with openness, attentiveness, and prayerfulness. Such attending opens up the possibility of an I-Thou relationship in which others are known and encountered in all their uniqueness and otherness, a quality of relationship that ultimately depends on the communion-creating presence of the Holy Spirit.

Developing a spirituality of presence is a great challenge to congregational leaders. Most of us who have led congregations have experienced some of the following at different times in our ministries. We are so busy that we become completely task-oriented, relating to people solely in terms of the job we need to accomplish. Even when talking to another person, our minds race ahead to the next thing on our schedule; we are preoccupied, listening with only half of our minds. Often this leads us to make snap decisions without pausing to find out what is going on and at stake. Or we rush to judgment, making quick value judgments about others without even bothering to find out who they are and what they face.

Even worse, we may begin to act like the religious leaders who walked by the traveler in distress in the parable of the Good Samaritan. We fail to even notice — much less stop and help — those individuals and groups who are suffering and in need. Our society is good at keeping such people hidden. But all of us encounter at some point those trapped in poverty or on drugs, ravaged by mental illness and disease, or excluded because they are different. Too often we walk on by because attending to their plight is inconvenient or too threatening to our own way of life.

Ultimately, the descriptive-empirical task of practical theological interpretation is grounded in a spirituality of presence. It is a matter of attending to what is going on in the lives of individuals, families, and communities. This poses certain challenges that congregational leaders must face up to. How can we lead if we fail to attend to others in their particularity and otherness? What sort of influence do we have to offer if we have not struggled to overcome our own tendency to not listen, to rush to judgment, and to ignore suffering others in our midst? Struggling with these kinds of issues lies at the heart of a spirituality of presence. It is a matter of opening ourselves to the forming and transforming Spirit of God who remakes us in the image of Christ within his body. Unless we first learn to attend, we cannot really lead.

Priestly Listening

In *The Bible in the Pulpit,* Leander Keck offers a helpful theological starting point for thinking about attending in the descriptive-empirical task of practical theological interpretation. Intercessory prayer, he notes, is a priestly act only when the leader does not merely pray *about* the people but also offers prayer to God *from* the people on their behalf. As Keck puts it: "The pastor is truly a priest when the prayer articulates the situation of the congregation through his or her prayer. For this to happen, one must listen to the people and establish a critical identity with them. . . . To pray on their behalf, one must enter into their lives to the point that one begins to feel what they feel, yet without losing one's identity."[3]

Keck captures nicely the twofold movement of intercessory prayer. It requires entering into the situation of others through personal contact, listening, and empathetic imagination. It then moves upward to God, placing their needs and concerns before God in prayer on their behalf. This twofold movement reflects the pattern of the priestly office of Jesus Christ. In his incarnation Christ entered fully into the suffering and beauty of finite existence; in his life of obedience and sacrificial death he made an offering to God on humanity's behalf.

In the New Testament the entire Christian community is portrayed as a holy and royal *priesthood* (1 Pet. 2:5, 9; Rev. 1:6; 5:10), which is joined to Christ, the one true high priest and sacrifice (Heb. 2:17). All in the community are to act in a priestly way, praying for one another (Eph. 6:18), confessing their sins to one another (James 5:16), and bearing one another's burdens (Gal. 6:2). Drawing on the imagery of the priestly cult, Paul portrays the Christian moral life as a "living sacrifice" that should be pleasing and acceptable to God and as a form of "spiritual worship" (Rom. 12:1). Here, too, all in the community are to build up and encourage one another in living holy lives (1 Thess. 5:11).

It is important to begin with this understanding of the priestly ministry of the entire congregation. Priestly listening is, first and foremost, an activity of the entire Christian community, not just its leaders. It reflects the nature of the congregation as a fellowship in which people listen to one another as a form of mutual support, care, and edification. Within the

---

3. Leander Keck, *The Bible in the Pulpit: The Renewal of Biblical Preaching* (Nashville: Abingdon, 1978), p. 62.

priesthood of all believers, congregational leaders are set apart by the congregation to carry out ministries that will enable it to participate more fully in the priestly office of Christ. When leaders engage in priestly listening, they therefore do so on behalf of the congregation as a whole. Two contemporary practical theologians, Thomas Long and Leonora Tubbs Tisdale, provide much help in considering what this entails.[4]

Building on Keck's description of intercessory prayer, Long and Tisdale emphasize the importance of priestly listening in the preaching ministry. As Long puts it in *The Witness of Preaching*, when preachers turn to the Bible to prepare their sermons, they must bring with them an awareness of the life situations of the hearers, for preaching "speaks to particular people in the concrete circumstances of their lives."[5] Otherwise, they will not be capable of articulating the concrete claim of a biblical text on the members of their congregation. Long continues: "Going to the Bible on behalf of the people is a priestly act. As an exercise of the priestly office, the preacher represents the people before the text as a way of representing them before God." Like intercessory prayer, "the preacher goes to the biblical text as a priest, carrying the questions, needs, and concerns of congregation and world, not as an agenda to be met but as an offering to be made."[6] Priestly listening — attending to the people addressed by the sermon in all their particularity and otherness — is crucial to every step of sermon preparation.

In *Preaching as Local Theology and Folk Art*, Tisdale further develops Long's depiction of priestly listening as important to the preaching ministry.[7] She argues that it is important for preachers to do more than enter intuitively and imaginatively into the circumstances of listeners. Just as preachers explore the meaning of scriptural texts with the methods of biblical exegesis, so too they must learn to use "methods for 'exegeting' the congregation in all its sociocultural particularity." As Tisdale puts it: "Congregational interpretation is a necessary 'first step' (as well as an ongoing process) through which the pastor can listen attentively in order to deepen his/her understanding of the congregation *on its own terms*."[8]

---

4. Thomas Long, *The Witness of Preaching* (Louisville: Westminster John Knox, 1989); Leonora Tubbs Tisdale, *Preaching as Local Theology and Folk Art* (Minneapolis: Fortress, 1997).

5. Long, *The Witness of Preaching*, p. 55.

6. Long, *The Witness of Preaching*, p. 57.

7. Tisdale, *Preaching*, pp. 11, 24-25.

8. Tisdale, *Preaching*, p. 25.

Why is this important? As Tisdale notes, unless preachers attend to the culture of their congregations, as well as the diverse groups in these communities, they are likely to preach abstract sermons to a generic humanity that do not address the real-life situations of their hearers.[9] Too often, for example, sermons fail to connect with the youth of the congregation. The preacher does not understand youth culture and almost never has in-depth conversations with young people or participates in their activities. It is little wonder that the examples, issues, and language of sermons fail to connect with young people. Accordingly, Tisdale offers a very helpful introduction to the perspectives and methods of congregational studies to guide the priestly listening of preachers in a systematic way.

Just as priestly listening is needed in intercessory prayer and preaching, it also is needed in teaching, pastoral care, and other forms of ministry. *Attending* is important in every facet of congregational leadership. Moreover, Tisdale's depiction of priestly listening as deepened by the methods of congregational studies brings into focus a very important dimension of my understanding of a spirituality of presence. While it involves attending to others in personal relationships, it also includes investigating the circumstances and cultural contexts of others in more formal and systematic ways.

A Continuum of Attending

It is helpful to conceptualize the relationship between a spirituality of presence and the descriptive-empirical task of practical theological interpretation along the lines of a continuum.

The Descriptive-Empirical Task in a Spirituality of Presence

Informal attending ————————————————— Formal attending

Semiformal attending

At one end of the continuum is *informal* attending. This has to do with the quality of attending in everyday life. It includes active listening and attentiveness in interpersonal communication. It also includes our openness to the beauty and tragedy we encounter day by day. It is pausing to notice

---

9. Tisdale, *Preaching*, p. 23.

the beauty of nature as it gives witness to the glory of God. It is attending to a young Latino man riding by on a bicycle and pausing to wonder about the long journey that has brought him to this place and his quiet heroism in working so hard to send money back home. It is opening ourselves to the pain of those we encounter in a back story of the newspaper or sitting across from us in our office. Attending in these kinds of informal ways does not come naturally or easily. An orientation of openness, attentiveness, and prayerfulness is nurtured by our participation in spiritual disciplines that help us attend to others within the presence of God.

Semiformal attending involves the use of specific methods and activities that provide structure and regularity to our attending. They help us pay attention to our experience as we bring it to expression in words and reflect or meditate on it. Many people find journaling to be helpful for this purpose. Likewise, participation in a small group can help us pay closer attention to our experience. Some ministers form pastoral groups that meet regularly to reflect on the ongoing events of their ministries.[10]

Semiformal attending may be woven into activities that are part of a leader's work. Fred Craddock, for example, encourages preachers to set aside time every week to engage in a structured practice of empathetic imagination as part of their sermon preparation.[11] Bringing to mind people they have recently encountered, they try to enter vicariously into their experience, jotting down a response to questions like these: What is it like to be . . . facing surgery, fourteen years old, falsely accused by your company of embezzling money, taking a day off to hike the Appalachian Trail, and so forth. Likewise, church committees and youth groups can include times for people to "check in" with one another, sharing what has been going on in their lives since they last met.[12] Staff meetings, also, can support semiformal attending, allowing pastoral leaders to reflect together on events taking place in the congregation, community, and world. In these and other ways congregational leaders attend to others in semiformal ways.

Formal attending is investigating particular episodes, situations, and contexts through empirical research. This is what Tisdale has in mind when she encourages preachers to deepen their "priestly listening" with

10. An excellent guide to this sort of group is John Patton's *From Ministry to Theology: Pastoral Action and Reflection* (Nashville: Abingdon, 1990).

11. Fred B. Craddock, *Preaching* (Nashville: Abingdon, 1985), p. 97.

12. Charles Olsen, *Transforming Church Boards into Communities of Spiritual Leaders* (Washington, D.C.: Alban Institute, 1995).

the methods of congregational studies. Such methods allow congregational leaders to attend to others in a systematic and intentional fashion. On the surface, empirical research by congregational leaders might seem like the very opposite of a spirituality of presence. Does not such research turn people into "objects" that are prodded and probed to produce data for the researcher? Does not this sort of objectification of others represent the antithesis of attending as described above?

While research sometimes does objectify others, this is not always the case. Especially when the methods of qualitative research are used, empirical research is a disciplined way of attending to others in their particularity. It allows leaders to deepen their understanding of what is going on in particular episodes, situations, and contexts and is a genuine expression of a spirituality of presence. A chance encounter at Starbucks with the mother of a confirmand is one source of feedback about the confirmation program. But it is no substitute for an evaluation based on firsthand observation of the program's activities and interviews of a carefully selected sample of recent participants in confirmation. Such observing and listening is a way of taking the young people in the program seriously, of attending to what they are getting out of confirmation and what they might like to see changed.

Attending and Guiding

There is a deep connection between attending and guiding in congregational leadership. We began this chapter with part of the story of Olivia Potter, leading up to her decision to seek the help of Rev. Dorothy Gains. Rev. Gains could have responded to Olivia in a variety of ways. Suppose she had felt too busy and harried to listen carefully to Olivia's problems? After all, Olivia was not a member of her congregation at that point. Why not refer her to Alcoholics Anonymous and send her on her way as quickly as possible? She then could move on to the "real work" of her ministry. But this is not how Rev. Gains responded. She attended carefully to Olivia's story and invited her back for another meeting. As she formed a deeper understanding of what was going on in Olivia's life, she was able to guide her in ways that helped Olivia turn her life around.

When I look back at the swing set episode of Mary Jo James, described in the introduction, I view it, in part, as a failure to attend on my part. This was my first church, and I was eager to get the congregation moving. Perhaps my achievement orientation and ambition clouded my ability to notice the signs that the longtime, older members of the congregation were uneasy with the changes taking place. Our ability to attend is always caught up in mixed motives of this sort, and we must struggle with our spiritual blindness through God's grace and the Spirit's guidance. Perhaps if I had done a better job of attending to what was going on in the congregation, the swing set episode would never have taken place and Mary Jo would have been spared a great deal of pain. But once these events were set in motion, I could at least come to terms with what I had missed and attend more fully to what was going on in the future.

There are no quick and simple techniques to remove the many obstacles that may cloud our ability to attend, especially to attend to others within the presence of God. Yet our ability to offer guidance as leaders depends on our willingness to engage the limitations of our attending as a spiritual challenge. While we will never completely eliminate these limitations, we *can* do certain things that will discipline and develop our attending in informal, semiformal, and formal ways.

It is helpful to think of the relationship between attending and guiding in terms of Charles Gerkin's depiction of congregational leaders as *interpretive guides,* discussed in the introduction. When a guide is leading people through new territory, it is very important for her to gain an accurate picture of the lay of the land. She needs the best picture possible of the pathways and obstacles ahead to help the travelers negotiate the terrain. It would be discouraging and perhaps even fatal to lead them over a dangerous mountain pass only to discover upon reaching the other side that the way forward is blocked by a wide and rapid river. So too, interpretive guides need to form the best picture possible of the lay of the land as they lead the people of God on their journeys of faith, especially when entering new territory. This requires attending on their part, paying close attention to others in their particular life circumstances.

In the remainder of this chapter we focus on formal ways of attending, the use of empirical research in the descriptive-empirical task of practical theological interpretation. While this is only one form of attending in the work of congregational leaders, it is an important one. We proceed in two steps. We begin by exploring examples of empirical research by scholars that might assist interpretive guides in forming a picture of the congregational landscape. These are organized around questions congregational leaders sometimes face when guiding a conversation between their congregation or people brought up short and the resources of the Christian faith. As we saw in our reflection on Gerkin's work in the introduction, facilitating this sort of conversation is central to the work of interpretive guides. We then examine a framework that congregational leaders might use to design research projects that may deepen the quality of attending in their own ministries.

Drawing on the Empirical Research of Scholars

Guiding the Congregation as a Community of Interpretation

Much of the ongoing work of congregational leaders focuses on facilitating a dialogue between the congregation's shared life and mission and the normative sources of the Christian faith. Empirical research proves especially helpful in allowing interpretive guides to better understand the people who participate in this dialogue. It also helps them recognize social trends that are impacting people's lives and shaping the context of ministry. Here I offer two questions commonly faced by congregational leaders and some of the ways the empirical research of others might guide their response.

1. *How can we do a better job of communicating the faith to our youth, who often are less involved in church after confirmation and drop out after leaving home?*

In *Soul Searching*, Christian Smith offers findings from the most comprehensive and sophisticated research on adolescent faith in decades. This project dispels many widely held myths about adolescence perpetuated by the media. Adolescence, for example, is *not* a time of rebellion against parental faith. Rather, young people generally reflect their parents' patterns of participation in religion, and parents continue to play an important role in shaping their adolescents' faith.[13] Even without parental support, moreover, youth are likely to become active in a congregation if it invests significant resources in ministry with youth, especially supporting a full-time youth minister and quality programs for young people.[14]

13. Christian Smith, *Soul Searching: The Religious and Spiritual Lives of American Teenagers* (Oxford: Oxford University Press, 2005), p. 68, chapter 3.
14. Smith, *Soul Searching*, pp. 112-14.

Quite alarming, however, is Smith's finding that adolescents have an extremely limited grasp of the beliefs and values of their faith traditions. Most hold what Smith calls "moralistic therapeutic deism": God created and orders the world; God wants people to be good, nice, and fair, but is not particularly involved in the world except when a problem arises; the central goal of life is to be happy and feel good about oneself; good people go to heaven when they die.[15]

Smith's research offers the interpretive guide a vantage point from which to interpret what is going on in her congregation's ministry with youth. It particularly shines the spotlight on the role of parents and quality youth programs in facilitating a dialogue between young people and the normative resources of the faith. It challenges leaders to guide their congregations in doing a much better job of teaching their youth the basic beliefs and values of the Christian tradition.

2. *Why aren't older programs like the Sunday school, women's circles, and midweek Bible studies working so well anymore?*

Wade Clark Roof in *Spiritual Marketplace* and Robert Wuthnow in *After Heaven* investigate the changes taking place in religion in the United States since the middle of the past century and identify the emergence of new patterns of spirituality and church affiliation.[16] Roof describes this as the emergence of a quest spirituality, and Wuthnow, of a seeker spirituality. Both scholars describe the far-reaching implications of this shift for institutional religion. Individuals now affiliate with religious communities, not out of denominational loyalty, but because they believe a congregation has something to contribute to their personal spiritual quest. Individual seekers, moreover, tend to piece together their beliefs and practices from many sources beyond the congregation, including self-help literature, talk shows, recovery groups, and parachurch organizations.

Congregations, thus, are now competing in a spiritual marketplace for individuals who define their relationship to the church in terms of their own issues and needs. This may help us understand why older, traditional practices like the Sunday school and women's circles do not appeal to many new members. Seekers, often, are resistant to long-term commit-

15. Smith, *Soul Searching,* pp. 162-63.
16. Wade Clark Roof, *Spiritual Marketplace: Baby Boomers and the Remaking of American Religion* (Princeton: Princeton University Press, 1999); Robert Wuthnow, *After Heaven: Spirituality in America Since the 1950s* (Berkeley: University of California Press, 1998).

ments, traditional norms and authority, and practices of spiritual growth that are demanding. These patterns of spirituality have real implications for the ways leaders interpret the normative sources of the faith. They face the challenge of helping congregations develop new programs and practices that appeal to seekers, while also developing pathways into more demanding and costlier forms of Christian discipleship.

Guiding Interpretation Evoked by the Experience of Being Brought Up Short

When Olivia Potter showed up in Rev. Gains's office, it is possible that Rev. Gains knew very little about depression or alcoholism. Quite often congregational leaders must deepen their understanding of issues coming to the fore when ministering to people who have been brought up short, consulting professionals or reading books about the issues before them. The following are two examples of empirical research that might prove useful in the face of scenarios that bring many congregational leaders up short.

Scenario One: How can I make sense of conflicts in my congregation?

A fight erupted in the congregation's largest adult Sunday school class last week between new and long-term members. It had to do with the congregation's new after-school program for neighborhood children, which uses the fellowship hall and several classrooms. The program is designed to reach out to the many single-parent families in new apartments near the church. In two years the program has attracted over fifty children, and several of their families have joined the church. A passing comment by one of the long-term members about "the brats who are trashing our church" elicited an angry response from one of the leaders of the program, a relatively new member. The fight escalated from there.

In *Congregations in Conflict*, Penny Becker studied church conflicts in twenty-three congregations in the greater Chicago area.[17] She discovered that the types of conflicts and the ways they were handled were influenced by the "church model" shared by the members. These models are deeply

---

17. Penny Edgell Becker, *Congregations in Conflict: Cultural Models of Local Religious Life* (New York: Cambridge University Press, 1999).

held understandings of ~~the "core tasks" of the chur~~ch — what it means to be a church and the "bundle" of practices and activities it is supposed to carry out. She identified four church models:

Houses of Worship. This model views the core tasks of the church as worship, promoting the spiritual development of individuals, and Christian education of children. Little emphasis is placed on cultivating a sense of community among members, and the staff and a few key laypeople handle all leadership responsibilities. Conflicts tend to focus on administrative matters like budget, remodeling, or changes in worship, music, etc.

Family Congregations. The model emphasizes strong, family-like feelings of belonging among a relatively small membership. Knowledge of how the church family does things is shared among all members. Conflicts tend to focus on "outsiders" (the pastor or new members) who want to introduce new ways of conducting the church family's business.

Community Congregations. This model places great emphasis on building a strong sense of community among a diverse membership and on promoting an understanding of the faith that is meaningful to the members of this community, even if this means revising church tradition significantly. Emphasis on participation and "ownership" of congregational programs and practices means that congregations with this model tend to have the most conflict, which is not viewed negatively. Conflict tends to focus on how the congregation might make its practices more meaningful and relevant, as well as on debate about contemporary social issues.

Leader Congregations. The model strives to have a highly visible public presence in the local community and to influence its affairs. Its pastor is often a "player" in local politics, school boards, and other public forums. The congregation is seen as the bearer of an authoritative tradition with distinctive beliefs and values, which guide its public presence. The desire to impact the local community outweighs the desire to build up a strong sense of community within the congregation. Conflicts tend to focus on determining the "right" position on public issues and the strategies that might best influence the local community.

Becker's research found that one of these church models was dominant in nineteen of the twenty-three congregations she studied.[18] Congregational leaders who are faced with a conflict like the above scenario might begin by trying to determine the church model held most widely by the members of their congregation. This may offer insight into what is going on. Perhaps the family model of church is dominant, and the long-term members are expressing dissatisfaction with the "outsiders" (pastor, new members, program participants) who are disrupting the ways the church family has always done things. Or perhaps it is the sort of disagreement that regularly occurs in a congregation where the community model is dominant; the members disagree as part of the process of owning new programs. These call for very different intervention strategies by the leader.

But Becker also discovered that the most intense church fights were "between frame" conflicts.[19] One group holds one church model and another group holds a different one. The groups have very different ideas about what it means to be a church. If this is what has surfaced in the conflict described above, then congregational leaders face the difficult task of helping different groups begin to grasp one another's perspectives and to build trust and respect across their differences.

Scenario Two: How can we better support families in our congregation that appear to be under much pressure?

In a recent church staff meeting the conversation quickly turned to Mary and Paul Barnwell's recent separation. Both are influential leaders of the congregation, and they have two elementary-age children. Rev. Starbuck, the senior pastor, commented: "I think we all are pretty shocked. I sure didn't see this coming. And it's the fourth divorce in our church in the past two years. I'm at a loss at what to do." Elaine Brown, the church educator, added: "I'm hearing all kinds of problems in the Baby Group (for mothers of newborns). A lot of them are really struggling with being home all day after so many years of working. They're not too happy with their husbands' lack of help around the home either. It seems like the dads think that's their job now."

18. Becker, *Congregations in Conflict*, p. 12.
19. Becker, *Congregations in Conflict*, pp. 17-20.

In *From Culture Wars to Common Ground,* a team of practical theologians under the leadership of Don Browning and Bonnie Miller-McLemore explored the church's role in helping families make the transition from the period of the Industrial Revolution to the new postindustrial, postmodern society in which we currently live.[20] In many ways this book is an exemplar of the ways scholars carry out all four tasks of practical theology in a comprehensive research program. Here I focus on the project's empirical research and its incorporation of the empirical findings of others.

One of this team's most important findings is a shift in the model of love and moral obligation informing marriage today. While many people in their study believe that self-sacrifice characterized their parents' understanding of marital love, they are more committed to marriages characterized by mutuality.[21] Indeed, they evaluate sacrifice somewhat negatively. Moreover, love as mutuality is valued even more highly than individual self-fulfillment. This contradicts a prominent thesis of much social science over the past decade, which portrayed the "new individualism" of American culture as a major contributor to family breakdown.

At the same time, the team also called attention to the many signs of crisis in the family, drawing on a wide range of research beyond their own.[22] In the United States, more than 50 percent of all marriages end in divorce. More than 30 percent of all births are out-of-wedlock. Single-parent households are overwhelmingly headed by women (86 percent), who must cope with less than half the average income of two-parent families. Consequently, many single-parent families live below the poverty line. Not only do fathers offer little financial support, but they also spend relatively little time with their children after divorce. The long-term effects of divorce on children are striking; children of single-parent families do worse on five measures of high school performance than children of intact families.[23]

Browning and his colleagues place these trends in a broader interpretive framework, which incorporates changing cultural values, economic patterns, socialization practices, and the continuing influence of patriar-

20. Don Browning et al., *From Culture Wars to Common Ground: Religion and the American Family Debate* (Louisville: Westminister John Knox, 1997).

21. Browning et al., *Culture Wars,* pp. 8-9, 19-20.

22. Browning et al., *Culture Wars,* pp. 52-53.

23. Browning et al., *Culture Wars,* pp. 56-57.

chy. These sorts of trends are properly a part of the interpretive task of practical theology treated in the next chapter. For present purposes, it is enough to note the ways this project's empirical description of the current state of marriage and family life afford the pastoral staff in the above scenario with a perspective on events taking place in their congregation. The recent spate of divorces in their congregation is not solely due to failures on the church's part. It reflects much broader patterns of cultural and institutional change. The staff would do well to pay particular attention to the emergence of mutuality as an increasingly important ideal of marital love and moral obligation. It might explore the normative resources of the Christian tradition that could deepen this ideal and develop programs for couples and families that help them actualize mutuality in their communication patterns, parenting, and negotiation of household/career roles.

Research Design

In the previous section we examined examples of empirical research by scholars that may help interpretive guides better understand what is going on in their congregations. But many reasons exist for congregational leaders to carry out research themselves. Here are a few of the more important:

- To evaluate programs or plan new ones.
- To deepen their understanding of a crisis in the life of an individual, family, congregation, or local community.
- To develop a better understanding of the "culture" of their congregation in order to enhance their ability to lead it or to communicate more effectively in preaching, teaching, interpersonal communication, etc.
- To develop a better understanding of the local context of the congregation, including potential members and opportunities for mission.
- To enhance their understanding of different groups in the church: e.g., different age groups, long-term/new members, people holding diverse theological perspectives, and so forth.

How might leaders design research projects to accomplish one of these goals? We focus on four steps that are basic to research design: (1) clarity about the purpose of the project; (2) choice of a strategy of inquiry;

Elements of Research Design

- *Purpose of the Project* — The specific reasons for carrying out research and a clear statement of what the questions are designed to answer.

- *Strategy of Inquiry* — The particular methodology guiding a research project, connecting the methods used to the outcomes desired.

- *Research Plan* — How the project will be carried out in a specific time frame, including decisions about what or who will be investigated, who will conduct the research, and the methods to be used to gather and analyze data.

- *Reflexivity* — Reflection on the metatheoretical assumptions informing the project, including assumptions about the nature of reality, knowledge, human beings, and the moral ends of life.

---

(3) formation of a research plan and execution of it; (4) reflection on the assumptions informing a particular project.[24]

Clarity about the Purpose of Research

Clarity about the purpose of your research is an absolutely crucial first step in research design. Why do you want to carry out this project? What questions do you want to be able to answer at the end of the project? Research is carried out for many purposes.[25] Often in the academy, basic and applied research are primary. In "real world" research, evaluation and action research are more important, for the goal is to improve a program or solve a problem in a timely way.

All decisions about your research strategy and plan flow from clarity about the purpose of your project, and this is where you should begin. As a rule of thumb, you should discipline yourself to write down a clear state-

---

24. For an overview of these elements, see John Creswell, *Research Design: Qualitative, Quantitative, Mixed Methods Approaches,* 2nd ed. (Thousand Oaks, Calif.: Sage, 2003).

25. The purposes described in the text box come from Michael Patton, *Qualitative Research and Evaluation Methods,* 3rd ed. (Thousand Oaks, Calif.: Sage, 2002), pp. 213-24.

Purposes of Research

- *Basic research* — to contribute to fundamental knowledge and theory.

- *Applied research* — to illuminate a societal concern.

- *Summative evaluation* — to determine program effectiveness.

- *Formative evaluation* — to improve a program.

- *Action research* — to solve a specific problem.

ment of the purpose of your project in a short paragraph and then develop two or three research questions that you hope to answer when it is completed. For example, the purpose of your research might be to evaluate the adult education program because attendance has declined significantly over the past five years. By the end of the project you hope to answer three questions: Why have people who were involved in adult education in the past stopped participating? Who currently is participating in this program and why? What sorts of changes might attract new people to adult education?

Strategies of Inquiry

Once you have achieved clarity about the purpose of your research, you are in a position to make decisions about the strategy of inquiry that will guide your project.[26] Broadly speaking, these strategies fall into two categories: quantitative and qualitative research. *Quantitative* research gathers and analyzes numeric data to explore relationships between variables.[27] *Qualitative* research seeks to understand the actions and practices in which individuals and groups engage in everyday life and the meanings they as-

26. Creswell describes theses strategies as informed by different *traditions of inquiry,* which he describes as having a "distinguished history in one of the disciplines and [as having] spawned books, journals, and distinct methodologies that characterize its approach." John Creswell, *Qualitative Inquiry and Research Design: Choosing among Five Traditions* (Thousand Oaks, Calif.: Sage, 1998), p. 2.

27. Variables are empirical indicators of the concepts you are researching and are given two or more values. For example, the concept of gender is assigned the values male and female and of social class, upper class, middle class, and working class.

cribe to their experience. Quantitative research is especially helpful in discovering broad statistical patterns and relationships. Qualitative research is better suited to studying a small number of individuals, groups, or communities in depth.

In the recent past, advocates of quantitative and qualitative research engaged in a fierce debate. Proponents of quantitative approaches portrayed qualitative research as soft, subjective, and unscientific. Proponents of qualitative approaches portrayed quantitative research as failing to capture the meanings that inform human action and the diversity of lifeworlds. Today, this debate is largely viewed as misguided. Many researchers combine quantitative and qualitative strategies in *mixed methods* research.[28] In Chris Smith's research for *Soul Searching* (described above), he combined large-scale survey research with in-depth interviews of a number of youth. It is more helpful to view quantitative and qualitative research on a continuum.[29] At one end is *extensive* research in which the field being investigated is very broad and, thus, commonly uses quantitative strategies like surveys and statistical analysis. At the other end is *intensive* research, in which the field being investigated is very narrow but is studied in great depth. It commonly uses qualitative strategies. But there are many intermediate points on this continuum that combine quantitative and qualitative strategies in a variety of ways. Six strategies of qualitative research are described below, which may be particularly helpful to the leaders of congregations.[30] They are located near the *intensive* end of the continuum, investigating a limited number of instances or cases in depth and detail.

Life History/Narrative Research

This strategy of inquiry focuses on gathering and telling the stories of individuals. Data is gathered through conversations in which people share sto-

28. Creswell, *Research Design.*

29. Derth Danermark et al., *Explaining Society: Critical Realism in the Social Sciences* (London: Routledge, 2002), pp. 161ff.

30. An extremely helpful summary of these perspectives is found in Creswell, *Qualitative Inquiry and Research Design.* Advocacy research is found in his *Research Design,* pp. 9-11. For additional discussion of advocacy research, see also B. Atweh, S. Kemmis, and P. Weeks, eds., *Action Research in Practice: Partnerships for Social Justice in Education* (New York: Routledge, 1998).

ries of events in their lives. These are sometimes organized into life chapters or around "epiphanies" (significant events that have left their mark on the individual). Typically, information also is gathered about the setting and historical context in which the person's life story unfolds. When people are asked to share their story in an interview, almost by necessity they give greater coherence to their lives than is actually the case. Researchers, thus, listen for and draw out competing stories in people's accounts of their lives. They also give people the chance to share stories on several occasions. When using this strategy of research, it is very important for researchers to be aware that their own experience influences what they hear and the way they interpret others' stories. Therefore, they often share their interpretations with the people interviewed, giving them the chance to revise the narrative they are constructing.

Case Study Research

This strategy focuses on a single case or a limited number of cases, studied in depth for a specific period of time. Often a single individual, program, relationship, or practice within a community is studied intensively, though sometimes the community as a whole is studied (e.g., the congregation as a case). To explore a particular case in depth, researchers must rely on multiple sources of information, using a range of methods like interviews, participant observation, focus groups, or brief surveys. They develop detailed descriptions of events and activities to provide a richly textured picture of the case.

Ethnographic Research

This strategy seeks to develop a "thick" description of a cultural or social group. Researchers examine the group's observable patterns of behavior, customs, and way of life over an extended period of time, gathering information through fieldwork. They participate in the life of the group and observe its day-to-day actions. They conduct one-on-one interviews with many individuals to grasp their understanding of practices and events. They study artifacts and symbols that express group identity and history. The goal of ethnographic research is sometimes described as the creation of a cultural portrait. This offers a detailed, holistic description of a community, including specific events and patterns of practice and meaning, noting the way they hang together in a coherent whole, as well as tensions and fissures.

Grounded Theory Research

This strategy seeks to develop a theory that is closely related to the context of the phenomenon being studied. It intentionally adopts a zigzag approach to research, moving back and forth between data gathering, analysis, and reflection several times over the course of the project. This takes the form of several technical procedures and steps, summarized here for purposes of introduction. Researchers gather an initial round of data through interviews, participant observation, and document analysis and then begin to analyze what they have discovered through a process known as open coding, grouping data into an initial set of categories. Further data is gathered to "saturate" these categories, that is, until no new relevant information emerges. Researchers then reassemble their categories through a process known as axial coding in which they describe the phenomenon being studied in terms of central categories (which capture its key properties), causal categories (which capture conditions influencing the phenomenon), and strategies (the actions or interactions that result when the phenomenon is influenced by certain conditions). The goal is to form a theory grounded in the field. Theory emerges out of research rather than serving as the starting point of research designed to test it.

Phenomenological Research

This strategy seeks to describe the essence of a particular type of event or activity for a group of people. For example, it might ask: Among hospital patients, what is the essence of their experience of a caring interaction with a nurse?[31] A guiding assumption of phenomenology is the "intentionality" of consciousness, that is, that consciousness is always directed toward an object. Researchers attempt to bracket out their own preconceptions and to allow individuals' lived experience (their consciousness) of events or activities to disclose themselves. After gathering many instances of lived experience, they then analyze them to identify their common structure or

31. Creswell discusses a phenomenological study of caring by nurses in *Qualitative Inquiry,* appendix C.

"essence." After gathering many descriptions of patients' interactions with nurses, the research might say: at the heart of patients' experience of care by nurses is the nurse's willingness to be "fully present" to the patient and not to relate to the patient as one more chore to be quickly accomplished.

Advocacy Research

This strategy is grounded in an explicit political agenda and seeks to contribute to social change. It is practical and collaborative, carrying out research *with* others rather than *about* them. It often focuses on social issues currently being debated in the public domain and seeks to give voice to perspectives overlooked or misrepresented in such debates. It also focuses on issues emerging in social movements and organizations actively engaged in social transformation. The goal of research is to shape an action agenda for change. Advocacy research sometimes is the strategy of inquiry used in feminist research, AIDS studies, and race studies.

Forming a Research Plan

A research plan involves decisions about the following: (1) the people, program, or setting that will be investigated, (2) the specific methods that will be used to gather data, (3) the individuals or research team that will conduct the research, and (4) the sequence of steps that will be followed to carry out the project in a specific time frame. Inevitably, decisions about these matters involve trade-offs, determined by the constraints of time, financial resources, and the availability of those being studied.

1. *The population, program, or setting to be investigated* is largely determined by the purpose of the project. What questions do you hope to answer in the project, and who or what can provide the data you need to answer these questions? Answering this question is not always as straightforward as it might seem. Suppose you are carrying out research in order to start a financial assistance program for low-income people who face medical and other emergencies. Research on the target population of the program and persons with knowledge of social services in your area may immediately come to mind. But you may also need to observe comparable programs by other congregations, which represent "good practice" in this area, as well as leaders and volunteers in these programs. This requires

Methods of Research

- *Interviews.* Gathering verbal data by asking questions to which the interviewee responds.

- *Participant observation.* Gathering verbal and visual data by observing practices and events while participating in the setting in which they occur. The goal is to discover patterns in the ordinary interactions of people and communities and what events, activities, and symbols mean to them.

- *Artifact analysis.* Gathering written documents (bulletins, church histories, financial and membership records) and attending to objects of symbolic importance (pictures, plaques, church logos, signs). While researchers form their own interpretations of such artifacts, they also ask "insiders" what they mean to them.

- *Spatial analysis.* Attending to the location and layout of the space in which an organization is housed. This may include the sanctuary, arrangement of offices and meeting spaces, and the exterior of the building, grounds, etc.

- *Demographic Analysis.* Gathering information about a particular population, like age, income level, gender, educational level, home ownership, and employment status. This makes it possible to form a demographic profile of a group and to compare it with others.

- *Focus groups.* Gathering verbal data on a topic with a group of ten or fewer people under the guidance of a discussion leader. Focus groups commonly are homogenous in certain demographics (e.g., age level, length of membership, gender), making it easier for all to share.

careful thinking about the kind of information you need and potential sources of this information.

2. *Methods of research* are the specific procedures used to gather and record data. These methods are determined, in part, by the strategy of inquiry you have chosen for your research. Narrative history research, for example, relies on the interview method, as does phenomenological research. But some strategies, like ethnography, use many methods, like

participant observation, artifact analysis, and interviews. In such cases the constraints of time and resources often require trade-offs. The purpose of your project provides help in deciding on the most efficient methods to gather the information you need. Research by congregational leaders usually does not strive to meet academic standards of basic or applied research. It is designed to evaluate programs or solve specific problems in a timely manner. This may rule out methods that are time-consuming and costly. In short, you must think carefully about the information you truly need to carry out a valid study and the most efficient methods that will provide you this information.

3. *The individuals or research team* that will conduct the research is an important, and often vexing, issue in congregational research. Some congregations have members with expertise in leading focus groups, designing surveys, and conducting interviews. They can be a great resource in designing a project. But in many congregations, no one but the pastor has any background in research. This is not an insurmountable obstacle, but it does require training if other people are recruited to help carry out the research. Some methods of qualitative research like interviewing are easier to learn than others. Moreover, if the interviews are taped and transcribed, then the pastor will be in a position to listen to them at a later point and make judgments about their reliability. Here again, careful thinking is required to make use of the personnel available in the congregation or in neighboring institutions.

4. *The sequence of steps* in executing the research plan requires thinking through details of the project, projecting specific dates to accomplish certain tasks, and assigning roles when a team is involved. If interviews or focus groups are involved, who will recruit the participants? Where will they be held? How will they be recorded? Who will analyze the data and by what date? To whom will the findings be presented and in what manner? The clearer you are about these issues before beginning the project, the more likely you will accomplish your goals in a timely fashion. Beyond these kinds of specific questions, research projects include the following general steps.

- *Data collection.* This is the process of gathering data, using the agreed-upon methods and format. It involves decisions about how the data will be recorded. Will it be tape-recorded, videotaped, or written down like field notes?
- *Data transcription.* This is the activity of turning a recording or notes

into a written text. If transcription is involved, it is time-consuming; if people are hired, it is expensive. If resources are limited, then intermediate ways of turning data into usable texts may have to be devised. Sometimes data can be recorded in ways that are close enough to transcription for the purposes of the project. For example, if data is gathered using focus groups, then one member of the research team might lead the group while a second member records a rough transcription on a laptop computer. If individual interviews are audiotaped, then the interviewer might later listen to the tape, writing down significant themes and transcribing only key comments word for word. If a particular event or activity is videotaped, then the research team might review the tape together, pausing to discuss key insights as they occur and recording their insights as they do so. While these shortcuts do not meet the standards of publishable, academic research, they may be the only means available to congregations with limited financial resources. I believe it is better for such congregations to do "good enough" research than none at all.

- *Data analysis and interpretation.* Typically, researchers begin by reviewing all their field notes, transcripts, and interview notes to gain a sense of the whole and to spot recurrent language, issues, or themes. Researchers then begin to code the data, chunking it into smaller units for analysis and gradually forming categories that allow these chunks to be organized and compared across different data sources (e.g., different interviews, focus groups, or events). While academic researchers often use technical procedures to ensure the validity of their analysis, the key for congregational leaders is discerning patterns or themes. It is a matter of looking closely at specific chunks of data, forming categories that capture similarities and differences, and then looking again at the same or new data.

- *Performing research findings.* Researchers *do* something with the knowledge they have gained. Many academic researchers today are giving more attention to the rhetorical and performative dimensions of research reporting, especially if they try to communicate their research to a wider audience and impact public life. Some, for example, are turning to "civic journalism" or creating "performance texts" that communicate their findings in vivid and compelling ways.[32] So too,

32. For a discussion of the turn toward rhetoric and performance theory, see Norman Denzin, *Interpretive Interactionism* (Thousand Oaks, Calif.: Sage, 2001), pp. 9-20.

congregational leaders must consider carefully the audiences with whom they will share their findings and how they might "perform" their research in ways that move and motivate others to act upon their research.

Reflexivity in Research

Reflexivity in contemporary social science is the by-product of the *double crisis* of empirical research.[33] The first crisis is one of *representation*. It is no longer assumed that "facts" are formed through direct observation of phenomena. Rather, observation is theory-laden and dependent on the research practices and technologies used to gather data. This makes any direct correspondence between a phenomenon and scientific representations of that phenomenon problematic. The second crisis is *legitimation*. The classical experimental criteria used to judge the adequacy of scientific research (i.e., validity, reliability, and generalizability) are now viewed as too narrow. Such criteria are not universal. Generalizability, for example, is relatively unimportant in qualitative research, which studies a few cases in great depth and rarely makes claims that can be generalized to a broader population. Thus, it is no longer possible to legitimate scientific research by appealing to a single set of criteria. Criteria vary, depending on the kind of research being conducted and its guiding purpose.

This twofold crisis has led social scientists to become more *reflexive* about the choices and assumptions guiding their work.[34] This means that they must reflect on and articulate for others their own perspective on questions like the following: What is the nature of reality (ontology)? How is it known (epistemology)? What is the nature of science (philosophy of science)? What sorts of claims can science make and how are they justified? What social values does science serve? Contemporary researchers draw on a variety of philosophical perspectives to answer these questions. This is sometimes known as the *metatheoretical* perspective informing

33. Uwe Flick, *An Introduction to Qualitative Research*, 2nd ed. (Thousand Oaks, Calif.: Sage, 2002), pp. 9-10, 30-31.

34. Michael Crotty, *The Foundations of Social Research: Meaning and Perspective in the Research Process* (Thousand Oaks, Calif.: Sage, 2003). See also William Outhwaite, *New Philosophies of Social Science: Realism, Hermeneutics, and Critical Theory* (London: Palgrave, 1987).

their work. The Latin root *meta* means to go beyond or transcend. A metatheoretical perspective, thus, is composed of the assumptions about reality, knowledge, and science that transcend particular research projects and theories.[35] The network of beliefs and values justifies why researchers work the way they do on a particular project. In an appendix at the end of this chapter, I review several perspectives that are influential today.

Awareness of these perspectives is important to congregational leaders for two reasons. First, it helps them read the research of scholars critically, allowing them to spot background assumptions that influence the way they carry out research and their findings. Second, it helps congregational leaders to become more reflexive about their own research. If they conduct research in their congregations and community on a regular basis, it is important to move beyond simply getting the information needed to answer the research questions. They need to determine their own stance on metatheoretical issues in dialogue with perspectives currently available.

Disciplined Skills of Attending:
Describing, Observing, and Interviewing

In this chapter I have portrayed empirical research as a form of formal attending in a spirituality of presence. It involves attending to others in their particularity and otherness in a systematic and disciplined way. Such attending is one of the ways congregational leaders engage in priestly listening, entering into the lives of others to carry out ministries like intercessory prayer and preaching on the congregation's behalf. I end this discussion of empirical research by focusing on three of the most important skills of qualitative research: describing, observing, and interviewing. Each skill is a disciplined way of attending to others and is dependent on the *person* of the researcher, whose competence in attending is the instrument of research. I highlight issues coming to the fore when describing, observing, and interviewing are carried out by leaders in their own congregational setting.

35. Danermark et al., *Explaining Society,* p. 3.

Describing

Simply describing what you see and hear is more difficult than you might think. In my teaching, I have found that seminary students often combine description with interpretation and evaluation. If we take hermeneutics seriously, of course, we realize that there is no such thing as pure description. It always takes place from a particular perspective and location. Yet, it is worthwhile for students and leaders to learn the skill of attending to the words and actions of others without filtering them through interpretive and normative judgments. This is very important in the descriptive-empirical task of practical theological interpretation, which focuses on *what* is going on before reflecting on why it is going on or what ought to take place.

It is helpful to approach the skill of describing with a common distinction in qualitative research between insiders' and outsiders' viewpoints. When researchers study an unfamiliar community, they are *outsiders*. They face the challenge of gaining access to the viewpoints of insiders: the meanings people ascribe to their actions and the ways they interact with others. Most of the time congregational leaders face the opposite challenge. They are *insiders*, who already have formed perceptions of others and the meaning of congregational actions. They face the challenge of becoming outsiders who attend to people and activities with fresh eyes and ears. They must put aside their preconceived perceptions, interpretations, and judgments and adopt the viewpoint of someone who is encountering people and activities for the first time. The skill of describing is an important way of attending to others along these lines.

Describing is writing down what you see and hear, capturing the exact words and actions of others. In research, describing takes place in writing field notes, verbatim comments, process notes, and other records of what is seen and heard. The setting, sequence of events, emotions, and other relevant details are also described. Many researchers also find it helpful to describe their own subjective responses and hunches. They become an outsider to themselves, standing back and describing their own experience. Not only does this help them become aware of their own viewpoint, but it also is a source of data in its own right. This internal dialogue offers clues about matters that may need further attention. Every time you talk to Sam Griswald, for example, you come away feeling exhausted. Upon writing down one such encounter in detail, you realize that talking to Sam makes you feel under attack and slightly intimidated. What is going on here? Do others respond to Sam in the same way? How does this play out in his role as the chair of the administrative board? By describing your own subjective responses, thus, you often are led to new lines of attending.

Observing

In qualitative research, firsthand participation in the field under investigation is crucial. This takes the skill of observing. It is one thing to listen to the reports of others about the meaningfulness of the congregation's new small-group ministry and quite another to actually observe some of these groups yourself. This provides direct access to this setting, rather than relying on the selective impressions of others. It allows you to discover things that participants might not notice or might be unwilling to share.

Michael Patton describes six characteristics of good observers: (1) learning to pay attention, (2) writing descriptively, (3) recording field notes in a disciplined way, (4) knowing how to separate detail from trivia, (5) triangulating observations, and (6) recognizing the strengths and limitations of one's own perspective.[36] By triangulation Patton means observing and gathering data about a field in more than one way. This might include, for example, paying attention to the range of emotions expressed before, during, and immediately after your congregation's worship service; videotaping the service and asking a small group of participants to reflect on their experience during various parts of the service; studying written texts used in the service (bulletins, hymns); returning to the sanctuary at a later time to study its space and symbols.

Just as a tension exists between insiders' and outsiders' viewpoints in describing, a tension also exists between participating and observing. Congregational leaders often are participating in — even leading — activities and practices they might like to observe. But even when they are not, others may experience their presence as a formal leader as intrusive and disrupt their normal ways of acting. How to negotiate the tension between participating and observing, thus, is a critical issue for congregational leaders to consider. Danny Jorgensen helpfully portrays this tension in terms of a continuum of participant roles: "a complete observer, a participant-as-observer (more

36. Patton, *Qualitative Research*, p. 281.

observer than participant), an observer-as-participant (more a participant than observer), or a complete participant."[37]

Much of the time it is not possible for leaders to adopt the role of complete observer. They are members of the congregation already, and their prior participation will influence what they observe, as well as how others respond to their presence. The key, thus, is taking advantage of the other three participant roles. Adopting the participant-as-observer role (more observer than participant) may be easiest when they are observing an activity or meeting they normally do not attend. For purposes of observation, for example, they visit the women's circle, confirmation class, or AA group that meets in the church. The observer-as-participant role (more a participant than observer) may be more appropriate in settings in which they normally participate. They may be a member of a committee, for example. For the purposes of observation on a particular evening, they minimize their participation in the work of the committee and focus instead on certain aspects of group process. They may even jot down notes during the meeting and add to them immediately after it concludes. When they are a complete participant — e.g., participating in a mission trip — they must observe in the midst of participating, setting aside regular times to write up what they are observing. In my own research, I have found it helpful to supplement all these participant roles with videotaping.[38] It allows you to participate in an activity and then examine it later, stopping and replaying the tape or discussing it with others. Since more people use this medium today, it is no longer as intrusive as it once was.

Interviewing

The skill of interviewing is a very important part of attending in qualitative research. An interview is a conversation between two people in which one of the parties is seeking information from the other for a particular purpose.[39] A good interviewer is an active listener who attends carefully to

37. Danny Jorgensen, *Participant Observation: A Methodology for Human Studies,* Applied Social Research Methods Series, vol. 15 (Thousand Oaks, Calif.: Sage, 1989), p. 55.

38. I used this method extensively in studying the case study congregations written up in *The Teaching Ministry of Congregations* (Louisville: Westminster John Knox, 2005), part 2.

39. Bill Gillham, *The Research Interview,* Real World Research (New York: Continuum, 2000), p. 1. Throughout this section I draw on this work and on Patton, *Qualitative Research,* chapter 7.

the verbal and nonverbal responses of the interviewee and guides the conversation without overcontrolling it. A common mistake of novice interviewers is talking too much. They may be anxious about moving the interview along and grow impatient when the conversation is slow to start. They also may fail to appreciate the "curious potency" of silence, which provides the respondent a chance to mull over questions before answering.[40] In contrast, mature interviewers talk less and listen more. They signal their attentiveness to the other person by responding with eye contact, facial expressions, nodding, and leaning forward or backward at appropriate times. They also know how to use these actions to move the conversation along.

Two decisions prior to the conversation shape the interview: the amount of structure and the type of questions. Bill Gillham portrays the dimension of structure along the line of a continuum.[41]

The degree of structure in an interview impacts the types of questions used and the amount of flexibility in the questioning route of the interview (the order in which questions are asked). Highly structured interviews like verbal questionnaires ask closed-ended questions in a set order. Closed-ended questions offer the interviewee a set of options from which to choose: e.g., Which of the following best characterizes your experience of confirmation: deeply meaningful, somewhat meaningful, not meaningful at all? As you move toward the unstructured end of the spectrum, the questions become open-ended and the questioning route more flexible. In semistructured interviews, for example, the interviewer usually has a predetermined set of questions in a set order but is willing to depart from this order if the interviewee spontaneously moves into an area to be covered at a later point. These kinds of interviews usually include open-ended questions, which encourage the interviewees to construct their own responses, providing access to their language and meanings: e.g., Which parts of the confirmation program were most meaningful to you? Why? At the far end of the continuum, the researcher overhears naturally occurring conversations rather than carrying out a formal interview per se.

A good interviewer is skillful in steering the conversation with prompts and probes.[42] Prompts signal to the interviewee where you are in the inter-

---

40. Gillham, *The Research Interview*, p. 36.
41. Gillham, *The Research Interview*, p. 6.
42. Gillham, *The Research Interview*, chapter 6.

Structure in Interviews

UNSTRUCTURED · *Verbal observation:* overhearing others' conversations in everyday life.

| · *Natural conversations:* using informal, naturally occurring conversations to ask research questions.

| · *Open-ended interviews:* using a few key open-ended questions without a planned questioning route.

| · *Semistructured interviews:* asking both open-ended and closed-ended questions in a planned sequence, which is adapted to the emerging flow of the conversation.

STRUCTURED · *Verbal questionnaires:* asking closed-ended questions in an invariant order.

---

view. For example: "During the first part of this interview, I'm particularly interested in what you got out of the sermon." "Now, let's turn to other parts of the service. When do you feel most involved in the service, beyond the sermon?" "We have one last area to cover . . ."

Probes build on the interviewee's response and ask him or her to go further. They can take a variety of forms.[43] (1) Clarification — "I'm not quite sure what you mean by that. Tell me a bit more." (2) Justification — "You believe the use of contemporary music is ruining worship? Can you tell me why you think that's the case?" (3) Relevance — "I'm not sure how your comments about the church preschool program are related to what you said earlier about the need to bring in new people. Could you tell me how you see them as related?" (4) Examples — "Give me an example of what you mean by the pastor being heavy-handed." (5) Filling out a narrative — "After Bob and Joan's argument, how did the rest of the committee respond? What happened next?" (6) Ordering — "I'm not quite sure I've got the events in the right order. Your father first lost his job and then began to drink? Or did his drinking cause him to lose his job?"

---

43. Gillham, *The Research Interview*, pp. 46-50.

Describing, observing, and interviewing are disciplined forms of attending. When leaders use these skills in their research, they can better understand what is going on in their congregations. Such skills help them move beyond preconceived perceptions and evaluative judgments and attend closely to what others are actually thinking, feeling, and doing. They make it possible for leaders to gain a richer understanding of the culture and subgroups of their congregations, to evaluate and plan programs, to grasp the dynamics of church committees, to enter into the life stories of individuals, and many other matters. Developing these skills in concert with the capacity to design research projects is an important dimension of practical theological interpretation. It reflects a leader's willingness to attend to others with openness, attentiveness, and prayerfulness within the presence of God.

Narrative Research: Olivia Potter's Story

I began this chapter with events from the story of Olivia Potter and will end it by presenting her story in greater detail, drawing on my interviews using the life history/narrative strategy of inquiry. We will return to her story often in future chapters. In my interviews of Olivia, I drew on guidelines and questions offered by Ken Plummer in *Documents of Life 2*.[44] Before the first interview I asked Olivia to approach our conversation like a person writing an autobiography, and to write down chapter headings and events or people that stood out in each life chapter. This provided the structure for our first interview.

I later listened to the audiotape of the interview and took an initial round of notes. I was particularly interested in identifying "epiphanies" in Olivia's first telling of her story, significant events or relationships that left their mark on her life.[45] Epiphanies provide special insight into personal identity narratives and often are interpreted by people as turning-point experiences. I identified a number of epiphanies in Olivia's story and spent the second interview exploring some of them in greater depth. Below are the chapter headings Olivia used to structure her story and some of what she shared about each chapter. Quotation marks indicate her exact words.

---

44. Ken Plummer, *Documents of Life 2: An Invitation to a Critical Humanism* (Thousand Oaks, Calif.: Sage, 2001), pp. 124-25.

45. Denzin, *Interpretive Interactionism,* pp. 34-39.

Daddy's Little Girl

Olivia began our interview by showing me a picture of her as a young child standing next to her father behind a rented house in which they were living in Vermont. She was the oldest of three children (she, a brother, and a sister) and had an especially close relationship with her father as a child, a relationship she has maintained to the present. Both parents grew up just outside Burlington, Vermont. Her mother was an elementary school teacher. Her father held many different jobs as an adult — teacher, pastor, mill worker, piano tuner, choir director, and gas station attendant. But his primary role was family nurturer and caretaker. "There was kind of a role reversal in our family. My father was more emotional and did a lot of the housekeeping and letter writing. He wrote me a beautiful letter when I got married. Mom was your typical New Englander, very stoic, very quiet, not a lot of words. She was happy with her knitting. Dad did most of the talking." Throughout her high school years, Olivia's mother was the primary breadwinner, providing a regular income and health-care benefits.

As Olivia holds up the picture of her standing next to her father, she says that "they are probably just home from church or maybe on their way to church." Church was a big part of her life as a child, largely because of her father's involvement. Her father's parents both were alcoholics, according to Olivia, and he was born with both of his hands deformed — three "stubs" for fingers and a regular thumb. But he had a "voice like an angel" and, as a child, was taken under the wings of a Methodist pastor who encouraged him to use his musical gifts in the church. "This probably was his saving grace as a child." Later, in his early thirties, he attended Asbury Theological Seminary in Wilmore, Kentucky (Olivia was nine), and then briefly became the music director of a "kind of cathedral." While her father was never ordained, he worked in United Methodist churches in one capacity or another throughout his adult life.

Singing in the choir and going to church were activities Olivia took for granted as a child. The Christian faith was important in the home as well. One of Olivia's most vivid memories of childhood was "sitting in the living room and having my father say: 'We're going to have church here. We don't have to worship just in the church building.' We had lots of times when my family would read the Bible and sing. My father was always at the center of this. That's one of the reasons this chapter's called 'Daddy's Little Girl.'"

I Don't Fit In

Olivia locates the beginning of this chapter when she was sixteen. Her family moved a lot during childhood in search of job opportunities for her father — from Vermont to Connecticut to Kentucky to Georgia and back to Vermont. They also moved many times within these states. Just before Olivia entered the tenth grade, the family moved to Lyndonville, Vermont. Her mother finally "put her foot down and said, 'I'm teaching and we're staying here!'" She was in her early forties and, according to Olivia, was tired of moving. Moreover, since Olivia's parents grew up in Vermont, it felt like "coming home."

But it did not feel like coming home to Olivia. "This was the beginning of a very difficult time for me. I just didn't feel like I fit in. We moved from Warner Robins, Georgia, and I was in a huge high school there. My school in Vermont was called Central High. It had a total of five hundred students. The Georgia school had five hundred in *every grade.* You could be invisible in the larger school and I liked that. Everyone knew everyone else at Central. In Georgia, school felt easy. I came into Vermont near the top of my class. School seemed harder at Central. Maybe it's because I lost focus on school. I was more interested in trying to fit in and didn't work that hard. It was a pretty rough culture too. Most of the kids wanted to work in the mill when they graduated. The union was strong, and pay and benefits were pretty good. Not many saw the point in going on to college. And there was a lot of drinking and drugs. That's when I first started using them a lot. Mostly, I used them to fit in."

Throughout high school Olivia describes her self-confidence as taking a "big hit." "I became kind of afraid to say anything in class. Almost every teacher wrote on my report card 'Lacks self-esteem.'" Two epiphanies stand out during this period. In the eleventh grade she was in an advanced literature class studying *Moby-Dick.* Olivia struggled with the book, but her father read it with her, and "he loved that kind of symbolism." With his support, she felt she was finally beginning to catch on. One day her teacher called on her in class to give an opinion about the homework assignment. Following her response, he said to Olivia in front of the class: "I find it difficult to believe that you even read the assignment." "After that I completely shut down in all my classes. I was humiliated. Only years and years later did I feel like I had something to say in class."

Later that same year, when talking with her guidance counselor, Mr.

Boyer, about "what's next," she mentioned that she'd like to apply to Colby-Sawyer College. He responded by saying: "You're not really suitable for that kind of school." Olivia reports, "That was a really big blow to my dreams. It took me a pretty long time before I had another dream for my life, and God had a lot to do with that." Though she was admitted to Kenyon College, Olivia decided not to attend and lived at home the year after she graduated from high school. She took business classes at the high school while working part-time at a mill nearby.

During this period Olivia began an affair with a married man, Bob Marcum, who worked in the mill office. He told her he was going to divorce his wife and marry her. The relationship continued even after Olivia left home and enrolled in a two-year college to become an executive secretary. "I didn't really like the school. I didn't fit in there either. The school was about a mile from the Connecticut state line. I drove to the bars there because you only had to be eighteen to drink. The thing I was proudest of was that I could drink any guy under the table. I felt the girls at school were naive. I was sexually active, and they weren't. I spent a lot of time sitting in my dorm room listening to music because I didn't feel like I fit in." When Olivia told her mother that she and Bob were talking about moving in together after she graduated, her mother said, "You've always said that you wanted to go to New York City, and that's where you're going." She helped Olivia pack her bags. This was the beginning of the end of her relationship with Bob.

I Have Freedom Now, but I'm Wandering

One of Olivia's friends in college, Judy, was from Long Island and invited Olivia to stay with her while she looked for a job in the city. So Olivia moved to Long Island. The problem was that Judy had not gotten permission from her mother for Olivia to stay with them. When Judy was not around, her mother would drink and berate Olivia, telling her she didn't want her to stay there. "I remember calling home and telling my mother, 'This woman gets drunk, and she's mean to me' and yada yada ya. My mother said in her typical way, 'You know, Olivia, there are a lot of people in this world, and it's about time you got used to it.' Those were her exact words. This is life; deal with it! Looking back, my mother knew I wasn't happy in Vermont and wasn't going to make it there."

Olivia got a job at Bristol-Myers Squibb and moved out about three months later, living with a divorced friend in an apartment on the Upper East Side. She then worked for Dean Witter Reynolds in the World Trade Center as a legal secretary, and worked on the weekends at Gimbalds to make ends meet. What was her life like during this period? "Drinking, drinking, drinking. Happy hours. I met another man at Bristol-Myers and got involved with him. Again, sex and drinking. I broke up with him and decided that I didn't want any more of this. I was lonely. My friends would leave the city on the weekends but I'd have to stay behind to work my second job. . . . I wasn't dating anybody else. I had this gnawing feeling that there had to be something more."

At the end of this chapter in her life Olivia went to St. Petersburg, Florida, for vacation and contacted an old high school acquaintance, John Cassell, who lived there. "We partied so hard that I missed my flight back home. We decided I would move to Florida. That sounded like a great idea," she said, laughing. So I went back and quit my job. I'm twentysomething. When you've moved around a lot, it doesn't seem so hard." She laughed again.

Bondage of Self and Victimization

"So I moved in with John. There is still a lot of drinking and behavior. . . . I am searching. I put bondage of self for this chapter. Its in the *Big Book* of Alcoholics Anonymous. . . . They say the root of alcoholism is in being in bondage to self. You're so caught up in your own stuff and yourself that you can't be free. I moved in with a man who had a *serious* drinking problem." Olivia and John were married three years later. "And I'd like to say that was a *bad* idea and I kind of knew it when I married John. But I wanted to be happy." She paused, before continuing, "I think that was what my whole search was all about, about being happy. . . . The affairs that I had, the drinking, the searching . . . I wanted to be happy. We bought a house and I still wasn't happy. We even bought a boat and I still wasn't happy. And I was just thinking there's this person and he's got all these problems and so I began to think *that's* the problem. But when the marriage broke up, I still wasn't happy."

During the years Olivia and John were married a pattern began to emerge in their relationship. Every morning John would leave for his construction job and Olivia for her real estate job. But John would not return home after work. He would go out with his drinking buddies, often returning home long after Olivia had gone to bed. After a while, Olivia began to ask John to stop going out every night and be at home in time for supper. "But he never showed up. I became more demanding and angry. And the angrier I got, the more I drank. Before I knew it, I was addicted to alcohol." Finally, after one last ultimatum to John, she moved out and initiated divorce proceedings.

During this period Olivia lived for a while in a "very nice shed" outside a friend's home. While John eventually gave her their condominium, he had fallen so far behind in the monthly payments that Olivia lost it to the bank. Olivia describes her father as playing a pivotal role during this period, confronting her with the problems of her marriage and her drinking and encouraging her to go to a pastor. And Olivia did, eventually facing up to her own drinking problem and becoming involved in Alcoholics Anonymous. It was during this period that the events described at the outset of this chapter took place.

God Plucked Me out of a Dark Place

When we reached this chapter in her life, Olivia began to use religious language extensively for the first time. Here is some of what she shared. "I stopped drinking on my own and went through two periods of depression. I realized at that time that my problems weren't just about John but me. I got involved in AA working the steps. . . . I envision God plucking me out of this despair and black hole and being redeemed. I never felt good about myself until I started accepting responsibility for myself and my life." In a different interview she added: "When I was thirty-seven and started to sober up I feel that God plucked me out of this horrible situation and I got a second chance and was able to come back. I really feel like the church and my Christianity and my love for Jesus, and all that I learned as a child, came back to me, and I got to be back on track. Lots of people struggle with their alcoholism. I know if I ever feel sorry for myself that God's will for me is not to pick up or use that drug. I can't help but give service to God and to my fellow brother or sister. I feel really fortunate that that foundation never left me."

During this chapter of her life, relationships with women became very important to Olivia. She was particularly committed to an all-women's group in AA. "They reflected back to me the goodness of who I am. I was sick of sex with men and relationships that were superficial. These women let me share what was real and loved me back. They helped me stay sober and encouraged me to keep working the Twelve Step program."

Her relationship with Rev. Gains was particularly important. "We talked about my marriage and depression. She was really supportive and encouraging, a kind of mentor for me at times." Dorothy was to play a pivotal role in helping Olivia consolidate the new life she was beginning to piece together and, as we shall see, in her transition to the next chapter of her life story. The Presbyterian women of her church also played an important role during this period, providing financial support that made it possible for Olivia to take courses part-time at Eckerd College. When she initially ran into difficulty writing papers, one of the leaders of this group, a teacher, tutored her.

Two epiphanies stand out during this period. One took place in a literature course at Eckerd College, taught by a professor who was especially gifted at getting the students to engage the reading and one another. "The whole class was like Parker Palmer's teaching philosophy: We learned from one another. Dr. Johnson's English classes were really important to me. For the first time since high school, I felt I had something to say. But I was still pretty cautious, pretty quiet. We did a lot of presentations for that class, and I remember two girls stopped me in the hall after one of my presentations. They told me, 'You're a really great speaker. We never would have gotten that from your class participation.' Slowly, I spoke out more. I found my voice, and I graduated with highest honors."

The second epiphany took place at a work camp for youth. As Olivia became more involved in Rev. Gains's church, she began to serve as an adviser for the youth group. She describes this as "really important" to her for many reasons. "I was really good at the relational thing. I would eat a meal with them, check in with them, go to their events. I was really good at band in high school but my parents couldn't show up. But now I was showing up for these kids and that was healing. Back in high school was the time I started to drink a lot. I've learned that you don't grow up when you're on drugs or drinking and so I never really grew up in lots of ways. So working with the youth gave me a chance to go back and grow up from there."

Every summer Olivia would travel with the church youth to a work camp in West Virginia. Her third year there she was invited to serve as the speaker for one of the evening worship services. "We'd start off with about twenty minutes of singing. I was probably very nervous. I'd been going through a very difficult time at work . . . a lot of closings and new developments. The builders were trying to use me as a scapegoat when they didn't get their work done on time. And they were lying and cheating. It was really hard to be a Christian there. My message to the youth was about loving your neighbor as yourself, and I remember talking to them from where I was at. It is so easy to love each other at a place like this camp but not very easy back home or at school. How can they take what they're learning here back there? I also told them that it's great to love your neighbor as yourself, but what if you don't love yourself? You have to start by loving yourself, because God loves you and has something special for you to do. I got a really positive response from the kids. All week they would catch me and say, 'I really got what you were saying.' It was an affirmation for me that I had connected with them."

When Olivia returned home, she decided she wanted to quit her job and work full-time with youth in a church. She talked to Rev. Gains about her work camp experience, and Dorothy responded by saying, "It sounds like a call." As it happened, their church was looking for a new youth pastor, but Dorothy encouraged her not to take the job, saying, "I want you to get your education. You need to move on. I want you to go to Princeton Theological Seminary (PTS). That is where I went and Bruce (the senior pastor) went." Shortly thereafter, Olivia went to a youth forum sponsored by PTS's Institute for Youth Ministry and came back "really jazzed." She worked in another church as a youth pastor for a while and then applied to and was accepted at PTS.

In the Seminary but Not of the Seminary

As an entering Presbyterian student at PTS, it made sense for Olivia to take Hebrew in summer school before her first year. Almost immediately, old feelings of "not fitting in" began to resurface. Hebrew was so difficult that she would not have passed the course without the special support of the professor. When the academic year began, Olivia soon discovered that the seminary was different from what she had expected. "I came from a supportive, huggy church but found the seminary a pretty hard place to make friends. I felt different. I was older than most of the students. I was an alcoholic. I'd been out of school for a while. They seemed like kids and were coming straight from college. . . . I came here thinking that people would be open for conversations, but I found that my classmates wouldn't even make eye contact with you when they were taking a break from their studies. They were too busy and wanted to get their work done. My relationships outside of seminary were more important."

Though Olivia was in seminary, she was not really of the seminary. She jumped at the opportunity to house-sit for an extended time so she did not have to live in a dorm. She often studied in the library of Princeton University, not the seminary library. She found friends elsewhere. A Friday night, all-women's AA group became very important to her, and she attended other AA meetings during the week. "I always felt like my AA people would stop at any time to go for coffee and be there for me if I needed anything. How can people who don't even claim Jesus as their personal savior feel more like God to me than students at a seminary? I thought about this a lot during seminary and even wrote a couple of papers about it."

Olivia also got a lot out of her field education. She spent one of her summers as an intern in a dynamic inner-city church in South Boston, where she made some lasting friends. During the school year she drew on her experience as a real estate agent and became a home closer for Habitat for Humanity. She decided to take the four-year dual degree option in order to graduate with a social work degree from Rutgers in addition to a seminary degree. Her specialty during this extra year was addiction.

Return of the Prodigal

Following graduation, Olivia began working as the assistant director of a faith-based nonprofit organization that provides food, financial assistance, and advocacy in the Trenton and Princeton areas. She works directly with clients and handles the advocacy network among congregations. She is the supervisor of college students who volunteer in the organization, something she enjoys because it takes her "right back to that youth group thing, connecting with them, that I loved so much." While she remains single, she is in a serious relationship "with a good Christian man."

Near the end of our second interview she reflected on her life in terms of Henri Nouwen's *Return of the Prodigal,* a book that became important to her during seminary. "The reason I resonated with Nouwen's book is that he seemed so real to me. He put in words things that I've learned in my life. We're always searching for that outside stuff to make us happy: Maybe I'll get married and then I'll be happy. Maybe if I get a house, then I'll be happy. I have gone to distant places and then come back. God calls us to be his beloved and find our home in him. But we're always searching for the superficial outside stuff. . . . I learned from Dorothy that being in relationships — being in and for each other — is where God's found. In the morning at my work when the volunteers and staff gather in a circle to pray, I look around the circle and see the differences in ages, races, and genders. Sometimes I can smell the alcohol on one of our client-volunteer's breath. I think that God is smiling down on those people." She added softly, "That's a good place to be. I'm not really a morning person, but I love coming to work."

I was not Olivia Potter's interpretive guide when I carried out these interviews, but it would have been easy for Rev. Gains to use the life story research approach as she began to form a relationship with Olivia. Likely, she carried out some sort of clinical assessment of Olivia during their initial meeting to gauge the seriousness of her suicidal thoughts. During their second meeting, however, it would have been very helpful for Rev. Gains to gather Olivia's story in a systematic way. The life story approach is one of many ways to do that.

This sort of careful listening to individuals' stories is also useful in noncrisis situations. In my own research in congregations, I continue to be surprised at the number of people who thank me at the end of interviews. They often add that the interview was the first time in many years that someone had invited them to share their story. If congregations are to be fellowships of mutual guidance and their leaders, interpretive guides, then this sort of sharing of stories may well need to become more common. It is one more reason to take the descriptive-empirical task of practical theological interpretation quite seriously.

Appendix to Chapter One:
Metatheoretical Perspectives in Empirical Research

The following is an overview of some of the metatheoretical perspectives found in contemporary social science.

Critical Realism

The defining feature of this position is the belief that the world exists independently of our knowledge of it. There is no reason to believe, for example, that the shift from a flat earth theory to a round earth theory was accompanied by a change in the shape of the earth itself.[46] Rather, what changed was our understanding of a natural object (a planet) that exists independently of our knowledge. Critical realism, however, rejects the simple correspondence theory of truth found in naive realism. It acknowledges that the world can be known only "under particular descriptions and in terms of available discourses."[47] It holds together ontological realism, epistemological relativism, and judgmental rationality.[48] Empirical research, thus, does not claim to offer direct access to natural and social objects, for it is informed by particular (and relative) theories. Rather, empirical research interacts with theory, testing, revising, and elaborating its perspectives. It is the interaction of empirical research and theory that leads to the formation of more adequate explanations of the natural and social world.

Post-structuralism

This diverse perspective grew out of the critique of structuralism by a group of French intellectuals in the 1970s and 1980s.[49] Its proponents reject "grand," or universal, theories and narratives and are attentive to the ways language, culture, and social practices construct "reality." The accent is on

46. Andrew Sayer, *Realism and Social Science* (Thousand Oaks, Calif.: Sage, 2000), p. 11. An introduction is found in Danermark et al., *Explaining Society*.

47. Sayer, *Realism and Social Science*, p. 2.

48. For a brief discussion of these distinctions, see the introduction to Margaret S. Archer, Andrew Collier, and Douglas V. Porpora, *Transcendence: Critical Realism and God* (London: Routledge, 2004). In that book judgmental rationality "means that we can publicly discuss our claims about reality, as we think it is, and marshal better or worse arguments on behalf of those claims" (p. 2). We explore this with a communicative theory of rationality, which features argumentation, among other things. See chapter 2.

49. Stanley Grenz, *A Primer on Postmodernism* (Grand Rapids: Eerdmans, 1996). For an appreciative but critical introduction to postmodern philosophy, see Richard Bernstein, *The New Constellation: The Ethical-Political Horizons of Modernity/Postmodernity* (Cambridge: MIT Press, 1991).

local knowledge, grounded in particular histories, values, and language. Moreover, post-structuralists typically incorporate a deconstructive impulse in their work. They strive to expose the taken-for-granted assumptions and internal contradictions of established regimes of power and knowledge to make room for alternative voices and new forms of knowledge. Within this perspective empirical research is viewed as *constructing* the natural and social phenomena it investigates. It offers only one possible interpretation of phenomena, which is subject to the critique of other interpretations.[50] Empirical researchers, moreover, are obligated to make the purpose and findings of their work available to those being investigated when this involves human subjects. Many also view themselves as obligated to study marginalized people and groups in order to give voice to their perspectives in the public domain.

Pragmatism

This indigenous American philosophy emerged in the nineteenth century and has been reinvigorated in recent years by a variety of American intellectuals.[51] In the writings of John Dewey, it features contextualism. This is the belief that human beings are situated in concrete relations with the natural and social world.[52] These contexts are diverse and evolve across history, posing different problems and making available different resources with which to cope with these problems. Dewey portrays the experimental approach of empirical research and the problem-solving reasoning of everyday life as sharing the same basic structure. Both identify problems, gather information about them, explore possible courses of ac-

---

50. For excellent examples of this approach to research, see Denzin, *Interpretive Interactionism,* and Denzin, *Interpretive Biography* (Thousand Oaks, Calif.: Sage, 1989).

51. For a historical overview of pragmatism, see John Patrick Diggins, *The Promise of Pragmatism: Modernism and the Crisis of Knowledge and Authority* (Chicago: University of Chicago Press, 1994); Cornel West, *The American Evasion of Philosophy: A Geneaology of Pragmatism* (Madison: University of Wisconsin Press, 1989). Recent proponents of pragmatism are Cornel West, Richard Rorty, Nicholas Rescher, Robert Brandom, and Jeffery Stout.

52. Of John Dewey's many writings, the following are particularly important: *Experience and Nature* (New York: Dover Press, 1958), a republication of the second edition; *Democracy and Education: An Introduction to the Philosophy of Education* (New York: Free Press, 1916); *The Public and Its Problems* (Athens, Ohio: Swallow Press, 1927).

tion, enact particular solutions, and consider the consequences that follow. Both involve reflection on experience to enhance learning and to reconstruct experience toward desired ends. Empirical research, thus, contributes to a group's ability to understand, debate, and resolve the problems with which it is presently coping in a particular context.

Interpretive Social Science

This perspective has its roots in the work of German sociologist Max Weber and German philosopher Wilhelm Dilthey.[53] Weber portrayed sociology as studying social action that is purposeful. This requires entering into and grasping the meanings that shape people's actions. Dilthey argued that there are two fundamentally different kinds of science: *Naturwissenschaft,* natural science based on abstract explanation, and *Geisteswissenschaft,* human science, based on empathetic understanding, or *Verstehen.* The perspectives of Weber and Dilthey influenced a wide variety of social scientific approaches, from symbolic interactionism to ethnomethodology. Common to them all is a commitment to understanding the interpretive perspective and meanings of social actors, which cannot be gained by statistical data. The research must enter into social actors' worlds and understand them from their perspective, as well as the context in which their actions are meaningful. Interpretive social science today also gives attention to the interpretive perspective of the researcher, informed by the thinking of Gadamer and others. This interpretive perspective influences what researchers find in their research, as well as the sense they make of their findings. But if they are open to the interpretive perspectives of the research subjects along the lines of a genuine hermeneutical dialogue, then their own interpretive perspective will not predetermine their findings but may be altered by what they encounter.

53. Max Weber, *The Methodology of the Social Sciences,* trans. and ed. Edward Shils and Henry Finch (New York: Free Press, 1964); Wilhelm Dilthey, *Introduction to the Human Sciences: An Attempt to Lay a Foundation for the Study of Society and History,* trans. Ramon J. Betanzos (Detroit: Wayne State University Press, 1988).

Critical Social Theory

This term was coined during the 1930s by the members of the Institute for Social Research of the University of Frankfurt, commonly known as the Frankfurt School.[54] It expressed their interest in forming a critical theory of society. Influenced by the thinking of Karl Marx and Sigmund Freud, the members of the Frankfurt School argued that traditional social science merely describes society as it presently exists. In contrast, the purpose of a *critical* social theory is to critique and transform society, providing guidance to emancipatory movements and praxis. Critique involves identifying the way social structures and ideas systematically benefit some classes and groups of people while oppressing others. It examines social formations and practices to determine whose interests are being served. Empirical research, thus, strives to contribute to human emancipation, guided by the comprehensive perspective of a critical theory of society. It explores social relations and institutions to unmask forms of domination and to enhance resistance and human liberation.

Postpositivism

Positivism in social science is closely identified with the work of Auguste Comte, the founder of sociology, and, later, Emile Durkheim.[55] Lawrence Neuman provides a helpful definition: "Positivism sees social science as an organized method for combining deductive logic with precise empirical observations of individual behavior in order to discover and confirm a set of probabilistic causal laws that can be used to predict general patterns of human activity."[56] In positivism, the only true knowledge is scientific knowledge based on observations of the world, which yield "facts" that can

54. For an introduction, see David Held, *Introduction to Critical Theory: Horkheimer to Habermas* (Berkeley: University of California Press, 1980); Andrew Arato and Eike Gebhardt, eds., *The Essential Frankfurt School Reader* (New York: Urizen Books, 1978).

55. Auguste Comte, *Introduction to Positive Philosophy*, ed. and trans. Frederick Ferré (Indianapolis: Bobbs-Merrill, 1970); Emile Durkheim, *The Rules of Sociological Method*, trans. Sarah A. Solovay and John H. Mueller, ed. George E. G. Catlin (Glencoe, Ill.: Free Press, 1938).

56. W. Lawrence Neuman, *Social Research Methods: Qualitative and Quantitative Approaches*, 5th ed. (Boston: Allyn and Bacon, 2003), p. 71.

be turned into propositions and related to one another logically in the form of a theory, which explains the social world. Positivism was subject to severe criticisms following World War 2. Postpositivism takes this critique seriously, while continuing to affirm certain of positivism's values and methods, which are viewed as essential to good social science. It accepts the critique of positivism that knowledge, theories, and hypotheses cannot be "proved." This is especially the case when human actions and meanings are the focus of research. For some scientists, like Karl Popper, this led to a redefinition in the goal of science.[57] Science does not prove (or verify) theories and hypotheses, but rather, subjects them to rigorous testing that may falsify them. Scientific knowledge passing the tests of refutation stands a better chance of contributing to the problems of the scientific community and society generally. In social research, postpositivists remain committed to forming hypotheses and refining and falsifying such hypotheses through empirical research involving careful observation and measurement. Quantitative data and statistical analysis hold a privileged position. Moreover, objectivity in the sense of controlling for bias and subjecting research to the scientific standards of validity and reliability remain important, even as the much stronger claims to complete objectivity have been discarded, along with the goal of discovering social "laws" comparable to the "laws" of natural science.

57. Karl Popper, *The Logic of Scientific Discovery* (New York: Basic Books, 1959); Popper, *The Open Universe: An Argument for Indeterminism* (Totowa, N.J.: Rowman and Littlefield, 1982).

Chapter 2

The Interpretive Task:
Sagely Wisdom

You know, I *loved* to drink Scotch. Its funny, I always loved to exercise, and I tried to balance out my exercise with my drinking, and it
was a struggle. I was working a job at the time that had absentee own-
ers so sometimes I'd go off for lunch and never come back to the job.
But, um, with that said, when I would come home and I didn't know
where John was or whatever, I'd pick up the Scotch and start drinking. I'd think, "I'm not sure this is such a good idea." I was so angry
that it wouldn't calm me down but would elevate my mood. But, um,
hitting bottom and the depression — I had two bouts of depression
— didn't happen until after John and I broke up. . . . I gave him one
last chance, and he pulled another 3:00 A.M. gig or whatever. I remember getting all of the money I could find in his pockets and the
house, and I packed my bags and left. . . . I stayed with a friend. She
had a *really nice shed* outside her house [laughs], and I stayed there
for a while.

Olivia Potter

This excerpt reminds us of some of the problems leading Olivia Potter
to seek help from Rev. Dorothy Gains. Suppose Rev. Gains has carried
out the descriptive-empirical task, gathering information about Olivia's
present crisis and the longer story of her life. What is next? Obviously, she

hopes to guide Olivia in ways that will help her deal with her problems. This takes more than good intentions. Rev. Gains must identify the important issues with which Olivia is struggling and draw on theories that allow her to understand these issues. This is the *interpretive* task of practical theological interpretation. It calls for wise judgment on the guide's part.

Several years ago a group of twelve freshmen at a university in Oklahoma set off on a hike as part of their orientation. The hike was supposed to take only a few hours, so they did not take clothing, sleeping bags, a compass, or food. And they did not take a map. At some point the leaders disagreed about the direction they were to take at a fork in the trail, and before they knew it, the group was lost. They ended up descending into a steep gorge and became trapped. The leaders could not agree on what actions to take. Luckily, two experienced hikers in the group managed to hike out and get help. But even with the assistance of an experienced guide, it took six hours for the entire group to climb out of the gorge.

When these events were later written up in a rescue newsletter, the headline read: "Lost, No Map, Inadequate Clothing." This captures nicely what the group experienced, but it says even more about their leader-guides. Without a map they had no way of discerning the right fork to take or of correcting their mistake once they were lost. So too, interpretive guides are wise to bring with them theoretical maps when they are leading others. Such maps offer a picture of the lay of the land they are traveling and possible paths that might be taken.

Map readers must learn two skills early on. First, they must learn that "the map is not the territory," as it is sometimes put by cartographers (mapmakers). Maps portray certain features of a territory but, necessarily, leave many things out. So too, theories help us understand and explain certain features of an episode, situation, or context but never provide a complete picture of the "territory." Wise interpretive guides, thus, retain a sense of the difference between a theory and the reality it is mapping. They remain open to the complexity and particularity of people and events and refuse to force them to fit the theory. This takes wise judgment on their part.

Second, skillful map readers must learn to choose a map that is suitable for their purposes. Some maps are good for some purposes but not others. Topographical maps portray the height and depth of mountains, valleys, and plains, using contour lines that connect points of similar elevation. They are used by geologists and engineers. The meteorological maps used by television stations commonly show cities, temperatures, jet streams, and storm patterns. They help us decide what to wear on a given day and provide information about possible delays at the airport. Neither of these maps would have helped the college freshmen who got lost during orientation. They needed a trail map that portrayed the twists and turns of particular paths, as well as their length. Likewise, different theoretical maps are good for some purposes but not others. Interpretive guides, thus, must be wise in discerning which theoretical maps will be most helpful in guiding others through the territory they are entering.

A Spirituality of Sagely Wisdom

For a seminary professor like me, one of the most depressing findings of research on pastors is how little they read once they have graduated from seminary. I know firsthand how busy ministers are. There always are more responsibilities to carry out than hours of the day. Yet, I believe it is very important for congregational leaders to continue to grow intellectually. There has long been a link between the life of the mind and the spiritual life in the Christian tradition. It was no accident that monasteries were the great protectors of the liberal arts tradition of classical education after the fall of the Roman Empire. They gathered books to form libraries and served as centers of teaching and learning, and their greatest theologians portrayed intellectual growth as an integral part of the spiritual path to God.[1] Nor was it an accident that the Reformers of the sixteenth century placed so much emphasis on the teaching ministry of congregations, writing catechisms and popular literature and consistently preaching "teaching" sermons. They also helped establish educational institutions that were open to all people and viewed these schools as central to the success of their reform movement.

Loving God with the mind is an important dimension of Christian spirituality. It is necessary to emphasize this in an American context, where the church has a long history of anti-intellectualism and pragmatism. A

---

1. Portraying intellectual learning as a part of the spiritual path is found as early as Augustine, *On Christian Doctrine*, trans. D. W. Robertson (New York: Macmillan, 1958). A later example is *Didascalicon of Hugh of St. Victor: A Medieval Guide to the Arts,* trans. Jerome Taylor (New York: Columbia University Press, 1961).

learned ministry remains a worthy ideal today, as it was in the past. But perhaps, in our contemporary world, *learned congregations* are an even more important ideal. These are congregations whose members are deeply grounded in Scripture, church tradition, and theology and are willing to grapple with the questions raised by contemporary science and public life. Such communities support a thinking faith. They are all too rare in the United States and around the world.

Learned congregations need leaders for whom the love of God and the desire to learn go hand in hand. Such leaders offer their communities the gift of sagely wisdom. Many people today are no longer satisfied with leaders who preach and teach "at" them along the lines of the older, hierarchical model of pastoral authority. They want leaders whose wise guidance helps them make sense of the circumstances of their lives and world. The spirituality of such leaders is characterized by three qualities: thoughtfulness, theoretical interpretation, and wise judgment, which may be viewed along the lines of a continuum. I deal initially with the two ends of the continuum and then focus on wise judgment, which is so important to the interpretive task in congregational leadership.

A Spirituality of Sagely Wisdom

Thoughtfulness ——————————————— Theoretical Interpretation

Wise Judgment

Thoughtfulness

When we describe people as thoughtful, we usually mean one of two things: they are considerate in the ways they treat others or they are insightful about matters in everyday life. Both qualities are important to leaders' interactions with others. Treating others with consideration and kindness often involves pausing to reflect on their circumstances. This is especially necessary when we are dealing with people who are difficult. Our normal reaction is one of impatience and irritation. Thoughtfulness, in contrast, strives for insight into the particular circumstances of such people, which may even lead to kindness on our part.

Thoughtfulness also is called for in situations that bring us up short, when we are not sure how to proceed. As Josef Pieper puts it, "The person who plunges head over heels into decision and action, without proper consideration and without well-founded judgment is being imprudent in the mode of thoughtlessness."[2] Moreover, the experience of being brought up short often challenges us to deepen our thoughtfulness. A person like Olivia Potter shows up at our office. She is depressed and has a drinking problem, but we know very little about either of these things. While it may be appropriate to refer Olivia to a knowledgeable professional, this encounter may kindle a desire to learn more about depression and alcoholism. Congregational leaders come up against the limits of their understanding all the time. These are opportunities to read and learn. Do they want to continue to grow intellectually? Do they remain intellectually curious? A great deal is at stake in leaders' willingness to embrace these questions as a part of their spirituality. Thoughtful leaders make for thoughtful congregations. This is the grounding point of a spirituality of sagely wisdom.

Theoretical Interpretation

At the other end of the spectrum is theoretical interpretation. This is the ability to draw on theories of the arts and sciences to understand and respond to particular episodes, situations, or contexts. In the final part of this chapter, I offer a way of approaching such theories with wise judgment, learning from them but also criticizing them. At this point it is enough to note that my approach is based on a communicative model of rationality, which presupposes fallibilist and perspectival understandings of theoretical knowledge. By fallibilist I mean an awareness that the theories constructed by human reason offer an approximation of the truth, not truth itself. Theories are fallible and always subject to future reconsideration. By perspectival I mean that theories construct knowledge from a particular perspective, or position. Today, especially, we are deeply aware that no one perspective captures the fullness of truth and that, often, many perspectives are needed to understand complex, multidimensional phenomena.

2. Josef Pieper, *The Four Cardinal Virtues* (Notre Dame, Ind.: University of Notre Dame Press, 1966), p. 13. The book is a brilliant analysis of the cardinal virtues as portrayed in the writings of Thomas Aquinas.

What does this have to do with Christian spirituality? There is a deep-seated human need for certainty, for the one, true, right answer. Yet, a fallibilist, perspectival understanding of theoretical interpretation confronts us with the limited nature of human knowledge and reason. We must learn to live with uncertainty: the more we know, the more we realize how little we know. We must also learn to live with the tension between different perspectives, including those of theology. These are spiritual challenges. But they are not foreign to the Christian tradition. In this tradition the distinction between Creator and created has long supported the recognition that human knowledge is fallible and that perfect wisdom belongs to God alone. The biblical canon of this tradition, moreover, contains a diversity of perspectives on God and God's people, forged in different times and places. Sometimes these perspectives stand in tension with and even criticize one another, as we shall see. A spirituality of sagely wisdom, thus, puts aside the quest for certainty and the one true perspective. Loving God with the mind is a way of moving more deeply into the mystery of God and God's creation.

Wise Judgment

This is crucial to good leadership. It is the capacity to interpret episodes, situations, and contexts in three interrelated ways: (1) recognition of the *relevant particulars* of specific events and circumstances; (2) discernment of the *moral ends* at stake; (3) determination of the most *effective means* to achieve these ends in light of the constraints and possibilities of a particular time and place.

The concept of wise judgment has a long history in moral philosophy and theology, largely under the influence of Aristotle on Western Christianity. His concept of *phronesis* — translated as both "practical wisdom" and "prudence" — is practical reasoning about action, about things that change. It involves discerning the right course of action in particular circumstances, through understanding the circumstances rightly, the moral ends of action, and the effective means to achieve these ends.[3] Aristotle portrays *phronesis* as closely related to virtue, acquired through moral edu-

3. Scholars of Aristotle disagree on whether *phronesis* includes reflection on moral ends or focuses solely on the best means to achieve such ends.

cation and practice. Virtue enables persons to know and desire the right moral ends and motivates them to carry out appropriate action toward these ends. Good character and wise judgment, thus, are bound together. Moreover, since wise judgment involves the ability to sift through and evaluate particulars, it requires experience, making it rare among the young.

In classical Western Christianity wise judgment in the form of prudence is one of the cardinal virtues (along with justice, fortitude, and temperance). It is a "hinge" on which the capital virtues pivot.[4] Wise judgment, for example, is necessary to determine when an action is courageous, not reckless, and the available means to pursue courageous action in a given time and place. It also is required when choices between various goods must be made, since circumstances make it impossible to achieve them all. As a virtue, or moral capacity, rooted in the character of a person, prudence has a deep connection to spirituality. Indeed, some theologians argue that the "theological virtues" of faith, hope, and love are more important to prudence than experience. Contemporary narrative theologians, moreover, call attention to the conceptual patterns that determine what counts as virtue and to the ways the narratives and spiritual practices of different traditions shape the character and wise judgment of their members.[5]

This brief history makes it clear that wise judgment is much broader than the interpretive task of practical theological reflection alone. But it allows us to see the relationship between interpretation, moral character, and wise judgment. Drawing on theories of the arts and sciences to interpret the relevant particulars of episodes, situations, and contexts takes wise judgment and moral sense, as well as a solid grasp of the theories being used. This is a complex intellectual activity, requiring judgments about the theories most relevant to the case and their contribution to the realization of moral ends defined theologically. We will

---

4. The capital virtues include humility, liberality, brotherly love, meekness, chastity, temperance, and diligence. They often are paired with the seven capital vices, or "deadly sins": pride, avarice/greed, extravagance (later lust), envy, gluttony, wrath, and sloth.

5. Alasdair MacIntyre, *After Virtue: A Study in Moral Theory* (Notre Dame, Ind.: University of Notre Dame Press, 1981); Stanley Hauerwas, *A Community of Character: Toward a Constructive Christian Social Ethic* (Notre Dame, Ind.: University of Notre Dame Press, 1981); Gregory Jones, *Transformed Judgment: Toward a Trinitarian Account of the Moral Life* (Notre Dame, Ind.: University of Notre Dame Press, 1990).

explore the sort of cross-disciplinary dialogue this involves in a later chapter.

When people like Olivia Potter bring the raw pain and messiness of their lives to congregational leaders like Rev. Gains, they are seeking a wise interpreter of life. They hope to find a guide who is thoughtful and knowledgeable and will point them in the right direction. In Christian Scripture these qualities are closely identified with the role of sage. Here we also find leaders who are approached by others to help them with their problems and to set them on the right path. We find stories like that of two women who come to King Solomon both claiming to be the mother of the same baby, and of the rich young ruler who asks Jesus what he must do to inherit eternal life. Hence, we turn to the Wisdom tradition of ancient Israel where the sage, or wise one, is treated most extensively and, then, to the New Testament's portrait of Jesus as sage. This biblical material is neglected in most descriptions of Christ's royal office.

Israel's Wisdom Tradition

The Wisdom tradition is a rich and complex part of Hebrew Scripture.[6] Wisdom themes appear in many of its writings but do not use wisdom forms.[7] It is the marriage of form and content that distinguishes Wisdom literature, which contemporary scholars generally limit to three books: Proverbs, Ecclesiastes, and Job.[8] These books make use of wisdom genres also found in the wisdom traditions of the ancient Near East: (1) *admonitions* — short sayings offering do's and don't's in an imperative fashion (e.g., Prov. 22:24-25); (2) *sayings* — short sayings that offer advice in the form of an observation (e.g., Prov. 14:31); (3) *aphorisms* — short sayings at-

---

6. Introductions include the following: James Crenshaw, *Old Testament Wisdom* (Atlanta: John Knox, 1981); Crenshaw, *Education in Ancient Israel: Across the Deadening Silence* (New York: Doubleday, 1998); Charles Melchert, *Wise Teaching: Biblical Wisdom and Educational Ministry* (Harrisburg, Pa.: Trinity, 1998); Roland Murphy, *Wisdom Literature* (Grand Rapids: Eerdmans, 1981); Murphy, *The Tree of Life: An Exploration of Biblical Wisdom Literature* (New York: Doubleday, 1990); Gerhard von Rad, *Wisdom in Israel* (Nashville: Abingdon, 1972).

7. For example, the Joseph cycle, the first part of Daniel, and certain psalms like Ps. 104 contain wisdom ideas but do not use wisdom forms, or genres.

8. See Crenshaw's comments in *Old Testament Wisdom*, p. 19.

tributable to an individual (e.g., Matt. 10:39); (4) *instructional poetry* — poetry offering moral and theological insight, which often includes admonitions or sayings (e.g., Job 6:5-6; Prov. 2:1-12); (5) *disputation speeches* — an extended debate or dialogue in which opposing viewpoints are articulated (e.g., Job); (6) *the reflection* — a treatise that addresses a variety of topics in light of the author's experience (e.g., Ecclesiastes).[9]

The Wisdom tradition is closely identified with David's son King Solomon, who is portrayed in 1 Kings as paradigmatic of the wise king and leader. Solomon is described as praying to God for "an understanding mind to govern your people, able to discern between good and evil" (3:9, 12). He also is described as exercising wise judgment in the cases brought before him (e.g., two women claiming to be the mother of the same child, 3:16-28; cf. chapters 9–10). It is likely that Solomon's monarchy gave rise to a diverse group of "sages" affiliated with Israel's royal court: wise counselors offering advice to the king (2 Sam. 17), collectors and copiers of proverbs (Prov. 25:1), and teachers preparing young people to serve as court officials (Prov. 25:2-7; 31:1-9).[10] Sages affiliated with the court may have contributed to the creation of a written wisdom literature. By the time of Jeremiah, the sage, or wise counselor, appears to have been an established role alongside priests and prophets (Jer. 18:18).

Yet, the emergence of an official group of sages and a written wisdom literature is a relatively late development in Israel's history. Many scholars believe the origin of the Wisdom tradition lies in the use of proverbs as a form of instruction in a predominantly oral culture. As Charles Melchert notes, proverbs are often used in oral cultures that offer informal instruction in the home and during the course of everyday life.[11] They also fit naturally in the conversation of *sodh,* informal gatherings of friends who "sit together" to share their experiences and of judges who consult one another

9. Alyce McKenzie, *Preaching Biblical Wisdom in a Self-Help Society* (Nashville: Abingdon, 2002), pp. 23-24.

10. Scholars debate the evidence supporting the existence of schools in ancient Israel. For an overview see G. I. Davies, "Were There Schools in Ancient Israel?" in *Wisdom in Ancient Israel: Essays in Honour of J. A. Emerton,* ed. J. Davy, R. Gordon, and H. Williamson (Cambridge: Cambridge University Press, 1995). See also Melchert's nice summary, *Wise Teaching,* pp. 24-26.

11. Melchert, *Wise Teaching,* pp. 25-26. The following point about *sodh* also comes from Melchert, who is relying on Annemarie Ohler, *Studying the Old Testament from Tradition to Canon* (Edinburgh: T. & T. Clark, 1985), p. 168.

about the cases they are deciding. It is likely that the sage, or wise one, first appeared in this sort of oral cultural context and described people who coined and taught *meshalim,* figurative proverbial sayings.

There are five dimensions of Israel's Wisdom literature that have something to teach us about the interpretive task of practical theological interpretation. While explored briefly here, they are discussed more extensively in the sources cited in the notes to this section.

The Goal of Wisdom: The Art of Steering

The prologue of Proverbs offers the following reason for learning the way of wisdom:

> For teaching sound judgement to the simple,
>   and knowledge and reflection to the young. . . .
> Let the wise listen and learn yet more,
>   and a person of discernment will acquire the art of guidance.
>
> (1:4-5 NJB)

Learning wisdom is portrayed here as a lifelong task with something to offer the young and inexperienced, as well as the wise and discerning. The mature can learn yet more about "the art of guidance." This is an apt image of the goal of wisdom.

The Hebrew term translated "guidance" is *tahbulot,* which literally means steering. Wisdom provides a set of steering strategies with which to navigate life. As Alyce McKenzie notes, this image is associated with a method of navigating the Nile River by pulling the ropes of a boat.[12] Wisdom involves "learning the ropes," learning how to steer one's way through life. Metaphorically, it involves learning which parts of the river to avoid and where the best routes lie; it involves flexible, on-the-spot decisions when weather conditions change and discerning when it is best not to travel at all; it involves learning which provisions to take when one travels and where to stop for the night or to find help. The art of steering is a beautiful image of wise judgment, central to the interpretive task of practical theology interpretation.

---

12. McKenzie, *Preaching Biblical Wisdom,* p. 21.

The Method of Wisdom: Reflection on the Meaning of the Patterns of Nature and Human Life

Proverbs, Job, and Ecclesiastes share a common method in their approach to wisdom. They believe that nature and human life fall into discernible patterns and that careful observation of and reflection on these patterns yield insights worth knowing and handing on.[13] Wisdom, thus, refers to both a method of inquiry and the knowledge gained from this inquiry. Many of the sayings in Proverbs take the form of moral insights, portraying certain courses of action as wise and others as foolish. Yet, they often do not even mention God, simply offering insights gleaned from experience. For example:

> Whoever digs a pit will fall into it,
>> and a stone will come back on the one who starts it rolling. (26:27)

> The lazy person does not plow in season;
>> harvest comes, and there is nothing to be found. (20:4)

Moral lessons can be learned by observing the patterns of life thoughtfully.

Ecclesiastes and Job use literary forms quite different from Proverbs, genres rooted in the scholarly traditions of the sages. The conclusions they reach about wisdom are also different from Proverbs. Yet they share with Proverbs the wisdom method of inquiry, *deriving general insights from the observable patterns of nature and human life.* The interpretive task makes use of this method as well. Much can be learned by reflecting on the meaning of discernible patterns discovered by the natural and social sciences. Much can also be learned by attending to the folk wisdom of local culture in congregations and communities. Here, guides may gain insight into the ways people interpret their everyday lives and the actions they deem wise and foolish.[14]

---

13. For a succinct discussion of this point, see Kathleen Farmer, "The Wisdom Books: Job, Proverbs, Ecclesiastes," in *The Hebrew Bible Today: An Introduction to Critical Issues,* ed. Steven McKenzie and Patrick Graham (Louisville: Westminster John Knox, 1998), pp. 129-30.

14. See, especially, McKenzie, *Preaching Biblical Wisdom in a Self-Help Society.*

The Pedagogy of Wisdom: Educating for Character and Teasing Thought into Being

How does the Wisdom tradition help people acquire wisdom? It cultivates their moral character and evokes their capacity to think.[15] As we have seen, both are necessary for wise judgment. Here I focus primarily on the way Proverbs handles these two dimensions of wisdom pedagogy. Throughout this book, many sayings commend certain attitudes and actions as the way of wisdom and condemn others as the way of foolishness. The former includes hard work, self-control, integrity, courage, and humility. In contrast, the foolish person is portrayed as lazy, lacking self-control, and holding destructive attitudes toward others such as envy, dishonesty, and cruelty.[16] Proverbs is concerned not just with the memorization of pithy moral sayings but also with the shaping of lasting dispositions and virtues of good character.[17] Proverbial teachings were offered in the living context of example, practice, and actual behavior. In this way they helped people learn and desire the right moral ends and how these ends might be achieved in particular situations.

Proverbs also evokes people's capacity to reflect, cultivating wise judgment by "teasing thought into being," to borrow Melchert's apt phrase.[18] It does this in a variety of ways. One is by placing side by side or in groups proverbs offering generalizations that are contradictory. Proverbs 26:4-5 is a nice example:

> Do not answer fools according to their folly,
>   or you will be a fool yourself.
> Answer fools according to their folly,
>   or they will be wise in their own eyes.

The reader comes face-to-face with the partial nature of each of these generalizations and must discern the different kinds of situations in which

15. Melchert, *Wise Teaching*, pp. 66-67; Alyce McKenzie, *Hear and Be Wise: Becoming a Preacher and Teacher of Wisdom* (Nashville: Abingdon, 2004); McKenzie, *Preaching Biblical Wisdom*, chapter 3.

16. See McKenzie's nice summary, *Preaching Biblical Wisdom*, pp. 105-7.

17. For an especially helpful overview, see William Brown, *Character in Crisis: A Fresh Approach to the Wisdom Literature of the Old Testament* (Grand Rapids: Eerdmans, 1996).

18. Melchert, *Wise Teaching*, p. 54.

they apply. Moving between generalizations and particular situations is a key skill of wise judgment.

Likewise, many proverbs take the form of paired lines, and the reader must reflect on their relationship.[19] Are they synonymous, complementary, or antithetical? Does the second line complete, intensify, or qualify the first? Consider the different ways paired lines are related in the following proverbs:

> A generous person will be enriched,
>> and one who gives water will get water. (11:25)

> Better the poor walking in integrity
>> than one perverse of speech who is a fool. (19:1)

> Bread gained by deceit is sweet,
>> but afterward the mouth will be full of gravel. (20:17)

The reader must pause and think about the relation of these pairs. Wisdom is not simply a matter of memorizing correct answers or following conventional behavior. It takes thoughtfulness about the relationship between different interpretations of experience, the ways they are similar and dissimilar.

Finally, Proverbs evokes thinking about good timing, what Gerhard von Rad calls the "doctrine of the proper time."[20] Wise actions and words are a matter of proper timing. They must fit the circumstances. Proverbs puts it like this:

> A word fitly spoken
>> is like apples of gold in a setting of silver. (25:11)

> To make an apt answer is a joy to anyone,
>> and a word in season, how good it is! (15:23)

Ecclesiastes offers possibly the most memorable statement of this doctrine: "For everything there is a season, and a time for every matter under heaven" (3:1; cf. 3:2-8).[21]

---

19. See Melchert's helpful discussion, *Wise Teaching*, pp. 19-21.
20. Von Rad, *Wisdom in Israel*, chapter 8.
21. But see also Eccles. 3:11, where the author asks what good it served to know that everything has its proper time if human beings cannot discern God's timing.

How do we learn to interpret particular episodes, situations, and contexts with wisdom? The pedagogy of the Wisdom tradition reminds us that this is not simply a matter of learning a set of techniques. It takes good character, reflective judgment, and a sense of timing.

The Framework of Wisdom: Openness to the World in a Theology of Creation

One of the most striking features of the Wisdom literature is the virtual absence of creedal summaries and narratives of God's "mighty acts." Some scholars believe this absence places it at odds with Israel's traditions of salvation history. But many others argue (rightly, I believe) that the Wisdom literature assumes a theology of creation found throughout Hebrew Scripture (e.g., Gen. 1–2; Pss. 8; 104; Isa. 40ff.).[22] God is the author of the created world, affirms it as good, and provides it with order and form. The Wisdom literature draws out the implications of this understanding of creation for everyday life, when the "mighty acts" of God are not in view. Using the literary device of personification, it sometimes portrays Woman Wisdom as participating with God in original and continuing creation, joining in the divine ordering of life (e.g., Prov. 2–4; 8–9). Proverbs 8:22-31 is a beautiful example:

> The LORD created me at the beginning of his work,
>   the first of his acts of long ago.
> Ages ago I was set up,
>   at the first, before the beginning of the earth.
> When there were no depths I was brought forth,
>   when there were no springs abounding with water.
> Before the mountains had been shaped,
>   before the hills, I was brought forth —
> when he had not yet made earth and fields,
>   or the world's first bits of soil.
> When he established the heavens, I was there,
>   when he drew a circle on the face of the deep,
> when he made firm the skies above,

22. For a helpful historical overview of shifting evaluations of the Wisdom literature, see Farmer, "The Wisdom Books."

when he established the fountains of the deep,
when he assigned to the sea its limit,
    so that the waters might not transgress his command,
when he marked out the foundations of the earth,
    then I was beside him, like a master worker;
and I was daily his delight,
    rejoicing before him always,
rejoicing in his inhabited world
    and delighting in the human race.

This portrait of Wisdom's role in creation gives rise to a fundamental *openness to the world*, which Roland Murphy describes as a willingness to engage in "*reflection* upon the wide gamut of human experience, and a *discernment* of values therein."[23] It is based on three corollaries of a theology of creation.[24] First, all wisdom comes from God. When sages gain insight by observing and reflecting on life, they are not constructing this wisdom on their own. They are discerning a moral structure that is built into creation itself. Creation "speaks" to people wise enough to listen. Second, the fear of the Lord is the beginning of wisdom, a verse repeated more often in Proverbs than any other. This does not mean being frightened of God. Rather, it is an attitude of reverence and humility toward God, which acknowledges the fundamental distinction between the Creator and creation. It underscores the limited nature of human understanding.[25] Third, instruction in the way of wisdom is ignored at one's peril. In Proverbs, especially, this is portrayed in terms of the two paths, the way of life and the way of death. Heeding the wisdom implanted in creation leads to life; ignoring it leads to ruin and death.

The interpretive task is based on an attitude of openness to the world. It depends on a thinking faith willing to learn from the intellectual resources of contemporary culture. It is not difficult to recall examples of the

23. Roland Murphy, "The Hebrew Sage and Openness to the World," in *Christian Action and Openness to the World,* ed. Joseph Papin (Villanova, Pa.: Villanova University Press, 1970), pp. 219-44.

24. Alyce McKenzie, *Preaching Proverbs: Wisdom for the Pulpit* (Louisville: Westminster John Knox, 1996), pp. 35-37.

25. As Prov. 19:21 puts it: "The human mind may devise many plans, / but it is the purpose of the LORD that will be established" (cf. 16:1, 2, 9; 20:24; 21:30-31). Indeed, one of the biblical proverbs that continues to have widespread currency underscores this point: pride goes before the fall (Prov. 16:18; 18:12).

disastrous consequences that have followed the church's unwillingness to learn from modern science: treating alcoholics as morally weak, instead of afflicted with a disease; relating to the mentally ill as demon-possessed instead of ravaged by a disorder of the brain. At the same time, the Wisdom tradition brings a theological framework to its open dialogue with the world, and this too is important in the interpretive task. With the acceleration of scientific research, technological innovation, and the Internet, we have access to more and more knowledge. But do we really have more wisdom? The church has something to offer the world about the moral and theological ends that inform the wise use of human knowledge.

The Diversity of Wisdom: Tensions between Proverbs, Ecclesiastes, and Job

Proverbs, Ecclesiastes, and Job come to remarkably different theological conclusions about what is learned from the careful observation of the natural and human world. This is perhaps most clearly evident in their divergent attitudes toward what is often called the "act-consequence" understanding of life found in the traditional wisdom of Proverbs (also known as the doctrine of retribution). While there are exceptions, Proverbs generally asserts that human actions have consistent and foreseeable consequences.[26] The wise and just are rewarded, or perhaps better, their deeds lead naturally to health, well-being, and prosperity. Foolish and immoral actions lead naturally to disaster.[27] Today we refer to this schema as "natural consequences" and draw on it more than we might realize.[28] As parents, we teach our children the consequences that follow from smoking, drug use, and a diet of fast food. As citizens, we are concerned about the consequences of political cronyism and corruption for the future of democracy. As world citizens, we worry about the long-term consequences of global warming and the elimination of biodiversity. The act-consequence schema is a powerful interpretive tool with which to make judgments about the wise course of action.

26. Exceptions to this schema include the following: poverty is sometimes caused by injustice, not laziness (e.g., Prov. 13:23), and wealth can be gained in evil, as well as virtuous, ways (e.g., 16:8; 21:6; 28:6).

27. See, for example, Prov. 11:17; 20:21; 26:27.

28. Melchert, *Wise Teaching*, p. 33.

Yet this perspective is challenged by Job and Ecclesiastes. Qoheleth, the Hebrew name for the primary voice in Ecclesiastes, contends that consequences do not follow human actions in the manner portrayed in the acts-consequences schema. As he puts in Ecclesiastes 7:15, "In my vain life I have seen everything; there are righteous people who perish in their righteousness, and there are wicked people who prolong their life in their evildoing." The term translated "vain" literally means "vapor" or "breath" in Hebrew. As C. L. Seow notes, Qoheleth does not use this term to indicate that life is meaningless; "rather, his message is that there are no failsafe rules, no formulas that will guarantee success, nothing that one can hold on to, for everything is as ungraspable as vapor."[29] The search for absolute security is like "chasing after wind" (Eccles. 1:14; 2:11, 17, 26; 4:4; 6:9). Far from counseling resignation or despair, however, Qoheleth commends enjoyment of the transitory goods of life that come one's way and receiving them as a divine gift (2:26; 3:12-13, 22; 5:19). But the predictability and certainty of the act-consequence schema have all but disappeared.

Job also challenges the acts-consequences schema.[30] The introduction to this book makes it clear that Job has done nothing to deserve the tragedy and suffering that come upon him and his family. He rejects the counsel of his "friends," which is based on the act-consequence schema of traditional wisdom.[31] Surely, they contend, he must have done something wrong to deserve his suffering, and the wise course of action is to confess this to God. But Job's reflection on his experience tells him otherwise. Ignoring his friends, Job takes his case directly to God, filing a lawsuit that charges God with "mismanagement of the universe."[32] God, if your royal rule is truly wise, why am I suffering? When God responds, divine anger is directed against Job's *friends,* who are told: "you have not spoken of me what is right, as my servant Job has" (42:7). To Job, God speaks "out of the

29. Choon-Leong Seow, "Theology When Everything Is Out of Control," *Interpretation,* July 2001, p. 243. See also Seow, *Ecclesiastes: A New Translation with Introduction and Commentary,* Anchor Bible (New York: Doubleday, 1997).

30. See Melchert's especially helpful and provocative interpretation of Job in *Wise Teaching,* chapter 2.

31. For example, in Job 18:5, Bildad offers Job the traditional counsel of Prov. 24:20, "the evil have no future; / the lamp of the wicked will go out." Yet in 21:17, Job's experience as an innocent sufferer leads him to ask: "How often is the lamp of the wicked put out? / How often does calamity come upon them?" Likewise, in Job 7:17-19 he offers a biting parody of Ps. 8.

32. Melchert, *Wise Teaching,* p. 83.

whirlwind," reminding him that the purposes of the Creator cannot be fully grasped by human creatures. But Job's question about his own suffering and, by implication, the suffering of creation is left dangling. This represents a radical challenge to the acts-consequence schema. Arguably, Job raises the question with which Israel will struggle throughout its exile and return: If you are righteous, God, why am I suffering? Job yearns for a redemptive wisdom. He cannot find it in the wisdom of creation.

We have, then, a diversity of perspectives within the Wisdom literature. This, too, is analogous to the interpretive task. It is dangerous to absolutize any one interpretive perspective and to apply it indiscriminately to all circumstances. Wise interpretation is deeply contextual. It must fit the particular circumstances it seeks to understand and explain. What counts as wise interpretation in one context is foolishness in another.[33]

Jesus Christ: God's Hidden Wisdom Revealed

The Wisdom tradition continued to develop during the intertestamental period in apocryphal books like the Wisdom of Solomon and Ecclesiasticus, or the Wisdom of Jesus Son of Sirach.[34] Perhaps more important for our purposes is the way this tradition began to cross-fertilize with prophetic and apocalyptic traditions.[35] This contributed to the devel-

---

33. Many scholars believe that Proverbs is directed to a stable social context in which the collective wisdom of parents and elders continued to provide guidance across generations. Seow portrays Ecclesiastes as directed to a postexilic context characterized by a high degree of social and economic instability, with great opportunities to gain wealth, power, and status, and equally great possibilities of losing them overnight. See *Ecclesiastes*, pp. 23-36, and "Theology When Everything," pp. 238-43. While the social context and date of Job are extremely difficult to determine, some argue that it too seems to address the socioeconomic changes of the Persian period, which called into question the traditional values of Israel's wisdom. It was no longer clear that wise conduct and material prosperity and good health went hand in hand. For a discussion of the difficulties in identifying the social context and date of Job, see Carol A. Newsom, "The Book of Job: Introduction, Commentary, and Reflections," in *The New Interpreter's Bible: A Commentary in Twelve Volumes*, vol. 4 (Nashville: Abingdon, 1996), pp. 319-28.

34. See Melchert's helpful discussion of these books in *Wise Teaching*, chapter 4, and that of Ben Witherington III, *Jesus the Sage: The Pilgrimage of Wisdom* (Minneapolis: Fortress, 1994), chapter 2.

35. See Witherington's comments, *Jesus the Sage*, pp. 158-59, 163, 201.

opment of new wisdom forms, like the narrative *meshalim,* or parable, and to a new theological framework in which God's hidden wisdom about the resolution of suffering, evil, and oppression is viewed eschatologically. Within this new understanding of wisdom, a seer or apocalyptic sage is sometimes portrayed as gaining access to the divine wisdom in a vision, which discloses the secret of God's royal rule over history and nature.

It is against this background that we can best make sense of the New Testament's portrait of Jesus as a sage, whose words and actions manifest God's royal rule.[36] His utterances and actions are those of an eschatological sage, who brings "near" the kingdom of God (Matt. 3:2; 4:17). Of the sayings of his teaching and preaching, 70 percent take the form of wisdom utterances such as aphorisms, parables, beatitudes, and riddles.[37] Likewise, his actions often are parabolic: eating with tax collectors and sinners, healing on the Sabbath, forgiving an adulterous woman, and overturning the tables of the money changers in the temple. Clearly, Jesus as sage is not a simple continuation of the older Wisdom tradition. He does not merely offer insights based on observation of the natural world within a theology of creation. Rather, he seeks to disclose God's royal rule, which is breaking into the present through his ministry. Indeed, he is the very embodiment of God's Wisdom.

As an eschatological sage, Jesus offers wisdom of a counterorder, designed to help his listeners imagine God's royal rule in new ways. His teachings often reorient hearers through a process of disorientation and subvert wisdom themes like prosperity and health by reversing the ways they traditionally were portrayed.[38] A brief sampling of his teachings makes this apparent. *Parables* like equal pay for unequal work (Matt. 20:1-15), the Good Samaritan (Luke 10:30-35), and the prodigal son (Luke 15:11-32) upend the expectations of listeners so they might imagine God's royal rule in new ways. So too, Jesus' *beatitudes* reverse the moral calculus of the acts-consequences schema, telling the poor, outcasts, and oppressed that they are the special beneficiaries of God's loving care and that their plight will be rectified in God's kingdom (Luke 6:17-26). Likewise, Jesus' *aphorisms* often address particular situations in ways that are paradoxical

36. Thus, I follow here those scholars who view Jesus in relation to the development of Israel's Wisdom traditions during the intertestamental period, not as a Greco-Roman cynic. See Witherington, *Jesus the Sage,* chapter 3.

37. Witherington, *Jesus the Sage,* pp. 155-56.

38. Witherington, *Jesus the Sage,* pp. 161-74.

and shocking: e.g., "It is easier for a camel to go through the eye of a needle than for someone who is rich to enter the kingdom of God" (Mark 10:25); "Those who try to make their life secure will lose it, but those who lose their life will keep it" (Luke 17:33); "Whoever wishes to be great among you must be your servant" (Matt. 20:26).

But the New Testament portrays Jesus as more than a sage who teaches subversive wisdom. It portrays him as God's Wisdom in person, drawing on images and themes of Woman Wisdom, the personification of Wisdom in Israel's Wisdom literature.[39] As early as Paul (e.g., 1 Cor. 8:6; cf. Col. 1:15-20), there are indications that the church was constructing wisdom Christologies to describe Christ's relationship to his Father, his preexistence, his role in creation, his lordship over the cosmos, and his pre-eminence in the new creation.[40] Among the Gospels, Matthew and John develop the most extensive wisdom Christologies.[41] They portray Jesus as Wisdom incarnate, who reveals God's secret Wisdom (see especially Matt. 11; John 1:1-18), and the disciples as those who take Wisdom's yoke upon themselves and learn from him.[42]

39. For discussion of the New Testament's appropriation of the theme of Woman Wis-dom, see Jack Suggs, *Wisdom, Christology, and Law in Matthew's Gospel* (Cambridge: Har-vard University Press, 1970); Celia Deutsch, *Lady Wisdom, Jesus, and the Sages: Metaphor and Social Context in Matthew's Gospel* (Valley Forge, Pa.: Trinity, 1996); Witherington, *Jesus the Sage*, chapter 4.

40. See James Dunn's discussion in *The Theology of Paul the Apostle* (Grand Rapids: Eerdmans, 1998), pp. 267-68; Dunn, *Christology in the Making: A New Testament Inquiry into the Origins of the Doctrine of the Incarnation* (London: SCM, 1980), pp. 179-83. Likely, Paul and the author of Colossians are drawing on elements of early Christian tradition, formed prior to their particular letters. The appropriation of wisdom motifs to reflect on Jesus, thus, was a very early development in the Christian community.

41. Raymond Brown, S.S., *The Gospel according to John (i-xii)*, Anchor Bible (Garden City, N.Y.: Doubleday, 1966), pp. cxxii-cxxv; Witherington, *Jesus the Sage*, pp. 341-80; Witherington, *John's Wisdom: A Commentary on the Fourth Gospel* (Louisville: Westminster John Knox, 1996).

42. The parallels between Sir. 6:19-31 (a popular intertestamental wisdom book) and Matt. 11:28-30 are striking. The former reads, in part: "Come to her [Wisdom] like one who plows and sows"; put your "neck into her collar. / Bend your shoulders and carry her"; "Come to her with all your soul, / and keep her ways with all your might"; "For at last you will find the rest she gives"; "Then her fetters will become for you a strong defense, / and her collar a glorious robe. / Her yoke is a golden ornament." In Matthew Jesus is portrayed as saying: "Take my yoke upon you, and learn from me; for I am gentle and humble in heart, and you will find rest for your souls. For my yoke is easy, and my burden is light." As

In Christ, Job's longing for a redemptive wisdom finally receives its answer. God in Christ enters fully into the suffering of creation, culminating in his crucifixion at the hands of the wise political and religious leaders of the day. In Christ's resurrection from the dead, God's redemption of a sinful and suffering creation stands revealed. The resurrected Christ is the first-born of the new creation. With the consummation of God's royal rule, creation will be transformed: the suffering will be healed, the captives set free, and the outcasts welcomed home. Those who live already in the sphere of God's royal rule will open themselves to possibilities of transformation that anticipate God's promised future. They will be guided by a redemptive wisdom that may place them at odds with the wisdom of the world. In the present age, this wisdom is hidden from those without eyes to see or ears to hear. As Jesus puts it, "I thank you, Father, Lord of heaven and earth, because you have hidden these things from the wise and the intelligent and have revealed them to infants" (Matt. 11:25). Paul carries this theme forward in his theology of the cross near the beginning of 1 Corinthians:

> For the message about the cross is foolishness to those who are perishing, but to us who are being saved it is the power of God. For it is written,
>
> > "I will destroy the wisdom of the wise,
> >   and the discernment of the discerning I will thwart."
>
> Where is the one who is wise? Where is the scribe? Where is the debater of this age? Has not God made foolish the wisdom of the world? . . . For God's foolishness is wiser than human wisdom, and God's weakness is stronger than human strength. . . . He is the source of your life in Christ Jesus, who became for us wisdom from God, and righteousness and sanctification and redemption. (1 Cor. 1:18-20, 25, 30)

Witherington notes: "In Sirach, it is clearly Wisdom's yoke the disciple is to put on, and in Matthew it is Jesus'/Wisdom's yoke." *Jesus the Sage*, p. 205. Across the New Testament, wisdom themes are used to describe God and Jesus on the one hand, and the disciples who have placed themselves in the yoke of Jesus' wisdom, which might be grouped into the following categories: (1) God's wisdom: Rom. 11:33; 16:27; Rev. 7:12; (2) Christ as wisdom: Mark 6:2 par.; Luke 2:40, 52; 7:35; 10:21; Col. 2:3; (3) the disciples' wisdom: Matt. 7:24ff.; 10:16; 13:54; Luke 21:15; Acts 6:3, 10; 1 Cor. 6:5; 12:8; Eph. 3:10; 5:15; Col. 3:16; James 1:5; 3:13, 17; Rev. 13:18; 17:9; (4) wisdom of creation rejected: Rom. 1:22.

What are the implications of our examination of Jesus as sage and Wisdom incarnate for the interpretive task? It qualifies our reliance on experiential, creation wisdom alone. While the church continues to learn in the wisdom way, reflecting on the meaning of the discernible patterns of life, it places such knowledge in a new and different theological context: the redemptive wisdom of Christ. This wisdom has strong elements of reversal and subversion, pointing to the counterorder of God's royal rule. It directs what is learned from worldly wisdom toward moral and theological ends discerned in Wisdom incarnate, Christ Jesus.

The leaders of learned congregations, thus, face a challenge. How can they remain open to the world and learn from the knowledge it offers, while placing this knowledge in a theological context based on the redemptive Wisdom of Christ? This is the challenge of cross-disciplinary dialogue, examined in the following chapter. We lay the groundwork for this dialogue in the remainder of the present chapter by exploring a communicative model of rationality. Rationality is portrayed as a special form of communication in which people offer reasons to others for their position, inviting their critical scrutiny and dialogue. A framework is offered that allows interpretive guides to learn from the knowledge of the arts and sciences, while reminding them that such knowledge is fallible and grounded in a particular perspective. It does not provide the fullness of wise judgment.

Theory in a Communicative Model of Rationality

Let us begin by returning to the case of Olivia Potter. If you were in Rev. Gains's position and had gathered information about Olivia's present crisis, you would now face the task of interpreting what you discovered. The "art of steering" in your relationship with Olivia involves *theoretical interpretation* of her problems and the ability to guide her in ways that take account of the particulars of her present situation and life history. We move thus to the far end of the continuum of sagely wisdom, focusing on issues that come to the fore as we draw on theories of the arts and sciences to carry out the interpretive task. Let us focus on one issue that likely came to the fore in your reading of Olivia's life story: alcoholism. It is a part of her family history and marriage, and Olivia has engaged in drinking behaviors that might be interpreted as those of an alcoholic.

Criteria of Alcoholism

- compulsive, repetitive alcohol use, often in ritualized ways

- tissue tolerance: over time, increasing amounts of alcohol are required for the desired effects

- withdrawal symptoms (ranging from restlessness and irritability to severe hangovers) when alcohol is no longer used

- increasing dependence, both psychological and physiological, on alcohol

- craving for alcohol and obsessive thinking about drinking

- loss of control: the inability to stop once drinking has begun, and loss of control over alcohol's effects

---

The wise interpretive guide relies on more than intuition to decide if Olivia is appropriately interpreted as an alcoholic. He makes an assessment based on criteria of alcoholism found in the literature,[43] and decides whether alcoholism is the most pressing issue in Olivia's current crisis. There may be other issues at stake, but this is where he will focus his attention initially. As the mental health and addiction literature make clear, it will be difficult to deal with other problems Olivia might face until she has begun to deal with her addiction to alcohol. The interpretive guide now must draw on theories of alcoholism to guide his dialogue with Olivia and, more generally, with his congregation. A variety of theoretical "maps" could be used. As we explore various theories of alcoholism, it will become clear that this phenomenon is interpreted in many different ways today. Thoughtful leaders, thus, must sift through a variety of theories and discern those that offer the best arguments and will be the most helpful in Olivia's circumstances. It is not as simple as finding the one true theory and then applying it to her situation. It takes wise judgment on the leader's part.

Leaders can better judge theories if they view them in terms of a communicative model of rationality. This model contains three basic elements.

---

43. These are offered by James Nelson, *Thirst: God and the Alcoholic Experience* (Louisville: Westminster John Knox, 2004), p. 37.

First, it views reason as a special form of communication in which people offer *arguments* for a particular set of claims. We all make assertions in our everyday lives. It looks like rain. Volvos are the safest cars on the road. Most of the time we make such assertions and move on. But sometimes we are asked for more. Rationality is the activity of offering good reasons to support our assertions, especially when others challenge them or ask us to unpack what they mean. Scholars are obligated to subject their arguments to the assessment of a competent community of peers.[44] Rationality, thus, is a form of communication in which people offer reasons to others in support of their assertions.

Each of the theories examined below attempts to persuade us to accept its interpretation of alcoholism. These theories offer evidence and other reasons to support their claims. We may be persuaded by their argument or remain unconvinced. But we cannot simply reject a sound argument as stupid, irrational, or devoid of reason altogether. In a communicative model of rationality, the process of argumentation does not necessarily lead to consensus.[45] Often, rational dissensus is the outcome. Parties agree to disagree. But they are clearer about the reasons for their differences and may have revised their original position because they engaged in rational communication with others. This sort of rational dissensus is evident in the theories of alcoholism examined below. There is no single "consensus" theory of alcoholism. Theoretical interpretation by the interpretive guide, thus, involves assessing the relative strength of competing theories.

Second, forming and communicating good reasons for one's claims always are grounded in a particular perspective, or position.[46] In rational communication, all people who argue for a particular set of assertions do not share one universal perspective. The influence of perspective will be

44. Harold Brown, *Rationality* (London: Routledge, 1990).

45. Jürgen Habermas, who develops one of the most important theories of communicative rationality, does argue that consensus is the goal of rational communication. See *Theory of Communicative Action,* vol. 1, *Rationality and Rationalization,* trans. Thomas McCarthy (Boston: Beacon Press, 1984). I follow here Nicolas Rescher's critique of Habermas in *Pluralism: Against the Demand for Consensus* (Oxford: Clarendon, 1995). See also Stephen Toulmin, *The Uses of Argument* (Cambridge: Cambridge University Press, 1958).

46. In addition to Rescher, cited immediately above, for a range of feminist perspectives on this issue, see Sandra Harding, *Whose Science? Whose Knowledge? Thinking from Women's Lives* (Ithaca, N.Y.: Cornell University Press, 1991); Seyla Benhabib, *Situating the Self: Gender, Community, and Postmodernism in Contemporary Ethics* (New York: Routledge, 1992); Donna Haraway, *Cyborgs, Simians, and Women* (New York: Routledge, 1991).

evident in the theories of alcoholism examined below. Drawing on the perspective of psychology, some argue that alcoholism is best understood in terms of personality deficits or family dysfunction. Others argue that it is profoundly influenced by the dynamics of gender, arguing from the perspective of feminist social theory. Still others adapt the perspective of medicine, arguing that alcoholism is best interpreted as a disease. Each of these theories, thus, makes its case from a particular point of view, and the wise guide will do well to attend to this perspective.

Third, theories in a communicative model of rationality are viewed as *fallible.* They are subject to reconsideration, especially in the exchange of reasons with others who raise questions. Rational communication, thus, requires epistemic humility. People may argue passionately for their point of view, but in the end, unless they are willing to reconsider their position in light of the perspectives of others, they have not really entered into the process of rational communication. They must put at risk their own point of view to gain a closer approximation of the truth. Theoretical interpretation by the interpretive guide, thus, requires a willingness to enter the tension between various theories, recognizing that they all are fallible. Just as the proverb user confronted contradictory generalizations and faced the challenge of discerning the situations in which they applied, so too does the contemporary guide confront competing theories and must discern their usefulness in different situations. She may even discover that the problem she faces is multidimensional and is helpfully illumined by a variety of perspectives.

As you explore competing theories of alcoholism, you will do well to begin forming your own assessment of these theories. Which do you find most persuasive? What sort of help might they offer in guiding Olivia Potter or your congregation? In the final section, a framework is offered that might help you assess theories in a systematic manner.

Theories of Alcoholism

Alcoholism Is a Disease

This theory uses a medical model to interpret alcoholism, informed by new research on the human genome. It portrays alcoholism as a disease: "the condition has a clear biological basis; is marked by identifiable signs and symptoms; shows a predictable course and outcome; and the condition or its manifestations are not caused by volitional acts."[47] The disease theory of alcoholism is prominent in Alcoholics Anonymous.

Recent mapping of the human genome has given rise to research that is attempting to identify the genetic basis of alcoholism. Genes do not "cause" alcoholism any more than they cause any other specific form of behavior. Rather they *predispose* people to alcohol addiction if they begin to consume alcohol on a regular basis. This is similar to the way genes predispose some people to gain weight, even if they consume only normal portions of food. Some research has found evidence for genes influencing susceptibility to alcoholism on chromosomes 1 and 7, with weaker evidence for a gene on chromosome 2.[48] Most researchers do not believe that a single gene will explain alcoholism; rather, the interaction of a number of genes makes people susceptible to alcohol addiction.[49]

The theory of a genetic predisposition toward alcoholism receives additional support from twin and adoption studies.[50] This research has found that when one identical twin is an alcoholic, the other twin is likely to be an alcoholic as well. This is not the case with fraternal twins, who do not share identical genetic material. Likewise, adoption studies have found that adopted children with an alcoholic, biological parent are far more likely to become alcoholics than adoptees without alcoholism in their families of origin.

The disease theory of alcoholism draws our attention to several dimensions of Olivia's life story, especially the presence of alcoholism in her family history. Both of her father's parents were alcoholics, and Olivia suspects that her father's deformed hands may have been the result of his mother's drinking while she was pregnant. An important practical implication of

47. D. C. Lewis, "Addiction: A Disease Defined," *Research Update* (Hazelden Institute), August 1998, p. 1.

48. Karen Balkin, ed., *Alcohol: Opposing Viewpoints* (San Diego: Greenhaven Press, 2004), p. 64.

49. The single-gene theory is sometimes found in the media. For example, great coverage was given to Blum and Noble's research on the allele of the dopamine receptor gene. See K. Blum et al., "Association of the A1 Allele of the D2 Dopamine Receptor Gene with Severe Alcoholism," *Alcohol* 8, no. 5 (1991): 409-16. This was later challenged by J. Gelernter, D. Goldman, and N. Risch, "The A1 Allele at the D2 Dopamine Receptor Gene and Alcoholism," *Journal of the American Medical Association* 269, no. 13 (1993): 1673-77. Their research received much less media coverage.

50. A. C. Heath, "Genetic Influences on Alcohol Risk: A Review of Adoption and Twin Studies," *Alcohol Health and Research World* 19, no. 3 (1995): 166-71.

this theory is the importance of helping people like Olivia understand that they have a lifelong, genetic vulnerability to alcoholism. Any alcohol will be too much alcohol. This also may be a worthwhile topic for preaching and teaching, as part of a broader attempt to make abstinence from alcohol a viable identity in the congregation.

Alcoholism Is a Psychological Disorder

This is not a single theory but a cluster of theories. They are grouped together because they all draw on the discipline of psychology to understand alcoholism.

The Individual Characteristics and Social Competence Theory of Alcoholism

This theory draws on cognitive psychology and social learning theory. Drug use and alcohol use are viewed as by-products of certain psychological characteristics, like low self-esteem, high anxiety, shyness, and low impulsive control.[51] People use drugs and alcohol to cope with certain deficits in their social functioning. To overcome shyness or anxiety, for example, they use alcohol to fit in or to lower their inhibitions in social situations. This theory directs our attention to the many times Olivia reports "not fitting in" during adolescence and adulthood. Alcohol eased her anxiety with peers and helped her cope with low self-esteem during adolescence. These are personal characteristics that a guide might need to address in counseling or a support group.

A Developmental Theory of Alcoholism

This theory focuses on adolescence as a stage of life in which vulnerability to drug and alcohol use is heightened, with potential long-term conse-

---

51. R. B. Millman and G. J. Botvin, "Substance Use, Abuse, and Dependence," in *Developmental-Behavioral Pediatrics,* ed. M. Levine et al., 2nd ed. (New York: W. B. Saunders, 1992), pp. 451-67. See also G. E. Barnes, "The Alcoholic Personality: A Reanalysis of the Literature," *Journal of Studies on Alcohol* 40 (1979): 571-634; Stanton Peele, "Personality and Addiction: Establishing the Link," in *Alcoholism: Introduction to Theory and Treatment,* ed. D. A. Ward, 3rd ed. (Dubuque, Iowa: Kendall-Hunt, 1990), pp. 147-56.

quences.[52] Young people who begin drinking before the age of fifteen are four times more likely to develop alcohol dependence than people who do not drink until twenty-one or older.[53] Adolescence is a time of many psychological changes, including psychosexual maturation, cognitive advances, identity formation, and increased reliance on the peer group. These kinds of developmental issues make teens vulnerable to drug and alcohol use. This is especially true if they are part of a peer group that uses drugs and alcohol recreationally, as was Olivia. Research indicates a common progression in drug and alcohol use, often beginning with experimental and recreational use of alcohol and cigarettes, moving to marijuana, and only later progressing to drugs with opiates and hallucinogens.[54] If alcohol remains the drug of choice, then this progression may move from recreational to heavy to addictive drinking in which alcohol is the center of a teen's existence and shuts down his or her psychological development. This theory, thus, draws our attention to the vulnerability of teens and to the stage of life when heavy drinking begins. In Olivia's case, this was late adolescence, and she might need guidance toward developmental tasks that were not accomplished during this period. Indeed, she describes her work with church youth as giving her the chance to go back and work on certain issues left hanging when she began to use drugs and alcohol regularly. At the congregational level, this theory underscores the importance of educating families and youth leaders to recognize the early signs of drug and alcohol dependence to prevent experimental and recreational use from progressing to more serious problems.

52. Peter Monti, Suzanne Colby, and Tracy O'Leary, *Adolescents, Alcohol, and Substance Abuse: Reaching Teens through Brief Interventions* (New York: Guilford Press, 2001); Katherin Ketcham and Nicolas Pace, *Teens under the Influence: The Truth about Kids, Alcohol, and Other Drugs — How to Recognize the Problem and What to Do about It* (New York: Ballantine Books, 2003).

53. These statistics draw on a report by the National Institute on Alcohol Abuse and Alcoholism: "Age of Drinking Onset Predicts Future Alcohol Abuse and Dependency," found at www.nih.gov.

54. Robert Coombs and Douglas Ziedonis, *Handbook of Drug Abuse Prevention: A Comprehensive Strategy to Prevent the Abuse of Alcohol and Other Drugs* (Boston: Allyn and Bacon, 1995), p. 22.

The Dysfunctional Family Theory of Alcoholism

This theory posits a relationship between dysfunctional family systems and increased incidence of drug and alcohol abuse.[55] In his research on the families of seventy-six adult alcoholics, for example, the pastoral theologian Howard Clinebell found forty-four families that likely could be described as dysfunctional and twenty-seven with a moderate degree of dysfunctionality. He identified four destructive patterns of parenting in these families: "heavy-handed authoritarianism, success-worship, moralism, and overt rejection."[56] More recent research, moreover, has found that adults who abuse drugs like alcohol are far more likely to engage in acts of domestic violence and child abuse.[57] It also reveals that the victims of abuse as children often turn to alcohol and other drugs later in life.[58] Among women who abuse alcohol, between 60 and 70 percent were sexually or physically abused as children or experienced violence in their families.[59] This theory, thus, leads us to take very seriously parent education, support of abused women, and intervention in families with an alcoholic parent where signs of domestic violence or sexual abuse are present.

55. For an excellent discussion of the whole topic of abuse from a theological and social science perspective, see James Poling, *The Abuse of Power: A Theological Problem* (Nashville: Abingdon, 1991).

56. Howard Clinebell, *Understanding and Counseling Persons with Alcohol, Drug, and Behavior Addiction,* revised and enlarged edition (Nashville: Abingdon, 1984), p. 60.

57. For a global perspective on violence against women, see "Population Reports: Ending Violence against Women," available at http://www.vawnet.org. Accessed June 2006. For a summary of research on the relationship between substance abuse and violence against women, see Larry Bennett, "Substance Abuse and Women Abuse by Male Partners," available at www.vawnet.org. Accessed June 2006.

58. A study by the National Center on Addiction and Substance Abuse found that children of substance-abusing parents were almost three times as likely to be abused and more than four times as likely to be neglected than children of parents who were not substance abusers. Other studies suggest that an estimated 50 to 80 percent of all child abuse cases substantiated by Child Protective Services involve some degree of substance abuse by the child's parents. Cited at www.preventchildabuse.com/abuse.htm. For a critical overview of research on this topic, see Paul Mullen and Jillian Flemming, "Long-Term Effects of Child Sexual Abuse," www.aifs.gov.au/nch/issues9.html#alc.

59. "Alcoholism," in *The Reader's Companion to U.S. Women's History,* www.college.hmco.com/history/readerscomp/women/html/wh_001100_alcoholism.htm. Accessed July 2006.

Cultural Theories of Alcoholism

Here, too, several different theories are clustered together. They draw on the perspectives of anthropology, sociology, and gender studies to call attention to the effect society has on patterns of drinking.

Drinking Culture Theory

This perspective argues that problem drinking and alcoholism are influenced by the cultural patterns and attitudes of a society toward drinking. Societies in which moderate drinking is integrated into everyday life (e.g., drinking wine with meals) develop cultural norms in which alcohol is treated with respect.[60] Parents teach their children to drink, model drinking in moderation, and condemn drunkenness as a form of weakness. Indeed, some research has found that moderate alcohol consumption may actually have a beneficial effect on health.[61] In the so-called French paradox, researchers found that while the French have a diet high in saturated fats and cholesterol, they have one of the lowest rates of coronary heart disease in the Western world.[62] Apparently, regular consumption of red wine prevents damage to their arteries caused by a high-cholesterol diet.[63]

In marked contrast, other societies foster a drinking culture that centers around binge drinking. Drinking to excess is socially acceptable at special times and places (e.g., parties, sporting events, and bars).[64] During these "time out" periods, conduct normally not permitted is viewed as temporarily okay, the effect of alcohol, and not the way a person normally behaves (e.g., sexual permissiveness, wild behavior). In a culture of binge drinking, alcohol use is a mark of maturity. Young people are taught to

60. See the introduction to the Transaction edition of Norman Denzin, *The Alcoholic Society: Addiction and Recovery of the Self* (New Brunswick, N.J.: Transaction, 1993).

61. One study is available online at www.hsph.harvard.edu: "Study Finds Frequent Consumption of Alcohol Linked to Lower Risk of Heart Attack in Men" (Harvard School of Public Health, 2003). It was reported in the *New England Journal of Medicine*, January 9, 2003.

62. This research is summarized in Balkin, *Alcohol*, pp. 15-16.

63. Studies of health-care workers in the United States, Great Britain, and Denmark have found similar positive effects of moderate alcohol consumption. Balkin, *Alcohol*, pp. 18-20.

64. Balkin, *Alcohol*, pp. 21-25.

drink by peers, not parents, often in situations involving at-risk behaviors. People who binge-drink on a regular basis have *more* health problems than nondrinkers, such as strokes, cirrhosis, and esophageal cancer.[65] They also tend to smoke more, have poorer diets, and are more likely to be involved in traffic accidents and violent acts.

This theory directs the interpretive guide's attention to the sort of drinking culture characterizing Olivia's peer group during high school, college, and young adulthood in New York City. This was a culture of binge drinking in which alcohol was associated with sexuality, growing up, having fun, and fitting in. Few, if any, models of moderate drinking were available.

Gender Construction Theory of Alcoholism

Research indicates that alcoholism is gendered in significant ways.[66] In the United States, men drink almost twice as much as women and are two times more likely to be heavy drinkers. Over 90 percent of people arrested for drug and alcohol violations are men. They are three times more likely than women to be in substance abuse programs and five times more likely to be diagnosed as alcohol dependent. Two-thirds of all men in treatment programs relapse within their first year, and only 20 percent stay sober for five years.

While more men are alcoholics than women, the incidence of alcoholism among women has been increasing over the past thirty years in the United States. Women tend to move into addictive drinking later in life than men. Moreover, heavy drinking by women is often *preceded* by depression.[67] Women who are depressed are 2.6 times more likely to engage in heavy drinking.[68] The heaviest drinking rates are found among women who are divorced, separated, or never married. As noted above, moreover,

---

65. The principal researcher of one such study, George Davey-Smith, professor of epidemiology at the University of Bristol in the United Kingdom, is interviewed by Natasha Mitchell online. See "Alcohol Consumption and Mortality," *Health Report*, July 5, 1999; available at Australian Broadcasting Corporation Online; www.abc.net.au/rn/talks/8.30/helthrpt/stories/s33704.htm.

66. The following statistics come from Nelson, *Thirst*, pp. 79-80, 108.

67. Donald Goodwin, *Alcoholism: The Facts* (Oxford: Oxford University Press, 2000), p. 78.

68. Goodwin, *Alcoholism*, p. 78.

women who abuse alcohol and other drugs frequently experienced sexual or physical abuse as children or grew up in families with domestic violence.

The gender construction theory of alcoholism argues that these different profiles of men and women alcoholics reflect socialization practices and cultural patterns by which male and female identities are constructed. A helpful perspective on the relationship between male identity and alcoholism is offered by James Nelson in *Thirst: God and the Alcoholic Experience*.[69] Nelson argues that cross-cultural research identifies a common core in male identity: the need to prove one's power, maturity, and worth by enduring hardship and distress. In many cultures this is ritualized in rites of passage. But even in cultures without such rites, the need to prove oneself by enduring hardship is a key dimension of male identity, resulting in "chronic insecurity" and "emotional isolation." Men turn to alcohol to relieve the stress this creates and to numb feelings of not measuring up. Alcohol also is a "masculinity booster," offering temporary feelings of power and camaraderie, allowing men to break out of their emotional isolation. As the statistics cited above indicate, male identity appears to create many barriers to successful recovery, like a man's willingness to admit that he is not in control of his drinking.

Stephanie Brown, Claudia Bepko, and Jo-Ann Krestan argue that female identity creates very different patterns of alcohol abuse.[70] Bepko and Krestan say the "code of goodness" structuring female conduct and relationships includes moral norms like the following: be unselfish and of service to others, make relationships work, and be competent without complaint. This creates unbalanced relationships in which many women do too much for others at their own expense. They are overly responsible, making it difficult for them to assert their own needs and leaving them vulnerable to difficulties in relationships. These kinds of gender-specific issues are evident in Olivia's life story: her vulnerability to relational difficulties and depression, her tendency to accept too much responsibility and blame for the problems in her marriage, and her ongoing struggle to de-

69. Nelson, *Thirst,* chapter 5.

70. Claudia Bepko and Jo-Ann Krestan, *Too Good for Her Own Good: Breaking Free from the Burden of Female Responsibility* (New York: HarperCollins, 1990); Bepko, *The Responsibility Trap: A Blueprint for Treating the Alcoholic Family* (New York: Free Press, 1985); Bepko, ed., *Feminism and Addiction* (Binghamton, N.Y.: Haworth Press, 1993); Stephanie Brown, *A Place Called Self: Women, Sobriety, and Radical Transformation* (Center City, Minn.: Hazelden, 2004).

velop a clear sense of self. Many women turn to alcohol to cope with these kinds of gender-specific issues. Moreover, Stephanie Brown argues that women face a special challenge in recovery. Often, this is not a matter of retrieving a self that has been buried during addiction but of constructing a more fully developed self for the first time.[71]

The Social Drama Theory of Alcoholism

This theory is found in the work of Norman Denzin, who draws on symbolic interactionism to portray active alcoholism and recovery as two distinct social dramas. Denzin developed this theory on the basis of extensive research on people participating in Alcoholics Anonymous and treatment programs based on the AA model.[72] He calls the *social drama of active alcoholism* "a merry-go-round named desire," which is composed of three acts.[73]

Act 1, the Alcoholic Situation. While alcoholics commonly believe they are in control of their drinking, their behaviors indicate this is not so, repeatedly creating crises at home or work. Significant others with whom they interact are forced into an alcohol-centered relationship, characterized by sharply contrasting experiences: e.g., emotional violence and sexual intimacy, failure to show up for work and heartfelt apologies. These relationships are constantly going up and down and around and around in circles without getting anywhere, like people on a merry-go-round. Family members, coworkers, and friends often intercede on the alcoholic's behalf and attempt to control his or her drinking. They may inadvertently fall into patterns of enabling and codependency.

Act 2, Violence and the Merry-Go-Round of Trouble. This act begins

---

71. Brown, *A Place Called Self,* chapters 6, 7, and 8.

72. Denzin, *The Alcoholic Society,* and Denzin, *Interpretive Interactionism,* 2nd ed. (Thousand Oaks, Calif.: Sage, 2001). The latter provides an account of methods used in the former. See also "Interpretive Interactionism," in *Beyond Method,* ed. G. Morgan (Beverly Hills, Calif.: Sage, 1983). *The Alcoholic Society* pulls together in a single volume two books originally published separately: *The Alcoholic Self* (Beverly Hills, Calif.: Sage, 1986) and *The Recovering Alcoholic* (Beverly Hills, Calif.: Sage, 1986). Denzin also published during this period *Treating the Alcoholic* (Beverly Hills, Calif., 1986). In *The Alcoholic Society* he draws on the theory of the emotions developed in *On Understanding Emotion* (San Francisco: Jossey-Bass, 1984).

73. Denzin, *The Alcoholic Society,* chapter 6.

with a serious crisis: an eruption of violence beyond emotional attacks or behaviors that exposes the alcoholic's condition to others (e.g., a DUI, inadequate job performance, or drunkenness at a holiday dinner). An escalation of mutual hostility and alienation gradually takes place, as family, friends, and coworkers are confronted with the seriousness of the alcoholic's problem. Often alcoholics are painfully aware of the damage their drinking is causing but are unable to stop their drinking.

Act 3, Collapse and Surrender. Three factors are pivotal in precipitating this act: (1) withdrawal of support from significant others; (2) collapse of alcoholics' world of interaction; (3) surrender, which involves "an admission of alcoholism, acceptance of this fact, and an inner surrender to this situation."[74] Alcoholics have now "hit bottom."

Denzin describes the *social drama of recovery* in three acts as well.

Act 1, Sobriety. This act overlaps act 3 of the drama of active alcoholism. Having hit bottom, the alcoholic now reaches out for help. Since Denzin's research focused on people involved in AA or treatment programs using the AA model, this involves attending an AA meeting and admitting publicly for the first time that he or she is an alcoholic who is powerless over this drug. The alcoholic begins the struggle of remaining sober.

Act 2, Becoming an AA Member. Recovering alcoholics become regulars at AA meetings where they learn how to maintain sobriety on a daily basis. They begin working the twelve-step program, reading key AA texts like *The Big Book,* and connecting with an AA home group and sponsor. These teach them a language of emotions with which to talk about buried feelings that are part of their illness and have been numbed for many years by alcohol.[75] They also learn to acknowledge the spiritual dimension of their recovery, which involves surrendering to a higher power, facing up to the harm they have done others, receiving forgiveness, and learning to value serenity, or inner peace.

Act 3, Two Selves. Through regular and prolonged participation in AA, individuals are integrated into its social network, becoming a sponsor, temporary chair of meetings, and participant in regional meetings. They participate numerous times in AA's storytelling practices. *The Big Book* contains forty-four model stories of people who have traveled the path to recovery. In AA meetings individuals practice grafting their personal sto-

---

74. Denzin, *The Alcoholic Society,* p. 141.
75. Denzin, *The Alcoholic Society,* p. 208.

ries onto these models and overhear others telling their stories along these lines. This storytelling articulates the transition between two selves: "the old drinking self of the past . . . and the new nondrinking self of the present and future."[76] A kind of "doubling" takes place in which storytellers describe their former, alcoholic self and the new self they are struggling to become.

Denzin cautions against using his description of the social dramas of active alcoholism and recovery to interpret people in a mechanical fashion.[77] Individual life stories are unique. Yet, social drama theory provides the interpretive guide with a framework to interpret Olivia's story. Olivia seems to have moved into act 1, the Alcoholic Situation, after her marriage to John. His drinking and erratic behavior led her to try to control his drinking, leaving her frustrated and escalating her own drinking. As Olivia's troubles intensified, she moved into act 2. Her marriage breaks up; she lives in a shed; the bank forecloses on her condominium; she begins to leave work at lunch to drink and not return. Yet, she responds when her father encourages her to seek help, moving into act 3, and then the social drama of recovery. She confides in Pastor Gains, attends AA, and stops drinking. Working the twelve-step program, she begins to accept her powerlessness over alcohol, the bondage to self it causes, and her need to surrender to a higher power, describing God as "plucking" her out of a dark place and placing her on a new path. She uses the patterns of AA model stories to tell her life story, constructing double selves: the "prodigal" Olivia who used alcohol to cope with the loneliness of "not fitting in" and the "homecoming" Olivia who copes with these feelings by depending on others who support her growing independence and abstinence from alcohol.

Analyzing and Assessing Theories in the Interpretive Task

We now have before us a variety of theories of alcoholism. Our primary goal in the interpretive task is to draw on theories of this sort to better understand and explain particular episodes, situations, and contexts. In the present case, we are attempting to interpret Olivia Potter's alcoholism and to gain help in our work with her. Our interpretation of alcoholism, more-

76. Denzin, *The Alcoholic Society*, p. 310.
77. Denzin, *The Alcoholic Society*, p. 177.

Theories of Alcoholism

- Medical theory: Alcoholism is a disease
- Psychological theories
  - individual characteristics and social competence
  - developmental
  - dysfunctional family systems
- Sociocultural theories
  - drinking culture
  - gender construction
  - social drama

---

over, has implications for our leadership in congregations. Different interpretations of alcoholism point us in somewhat different directions, as indicated in the summary of each theory. Interpreting alcoholism as a disease may lead us to work hard at making abstinence from alcohol a viable identity in our congregation; interpreting it in terms of drinking culture theory may lead us to emphasize models of drinking in moderation in the home, social situations, and the church.

A great deal is at stake, thus, in deciding which theories we find most persuasive. This requires careful analysis and assessment. A communicative model of rationality, which includes argumentation, perspectivalism, and fallibility, opens up three forms of analysis and evaluation of theories: (1) the model, or root metaphor, a theory uses and the conceptual field built on this model; (2) the disciplinary perspective a theory uses and the level of reality this discipline addresses; (3) the soundness and strength of a theory's argument(s).

1. *Identify and assess the model, or root metaphor, of a theory and the conceptual field built on this model.* This form of analysis and assessment draws on recent discussion of the metaphorical nature of knowing and the role of models, or root metaphors, in organizing the conceptual field of a theory.[78] It reminds us that theories as rational communication always

78. Max Black, *Models and Metaphors* (Ithaca, N.Y.: Cornell University Press, 1962). See also Mary Hesse, *Models and Analogies in Science* (Notre Dame, Ind.: University of Notre Dame Press, 1966), and Ian Barbour, *Myths, Models, and Paradigms: A Comparative Study in*

work from a particular *perspective*. Metaphor analysis is an important way of gaining insight into this perspective.

A metaphor proposes analogies between a familiar area of life and another area that is less familiar. When the congregation is described as a body, for example, a metaphor is being proposed: the interrelated functioning of different parts of the human body is being used to understand a community whose diverse members and groups are organically related to one another. This metaphor makes a comparison by similarity-in-difference. Congregations are similar to bodies in some ways: their various parts are interconnected; problems in one part may influence the whole. But congregations are different from bodies in other ways: their parts are not connected by a central nervous system; massive failure in one part (e.g., the brain or heart) does not automatically lead to the death of a congregation. The key point is that metaphors bring together two fields in similarity-in-difference.

An important insight of contemporary philosophy of science is the role of metaphorical knowing in science and other forms of scholarship.[79] Here metaphors are usually described as *models* or *root metaphors*. As Sallie McFague puts it, "a model is, in essence, a sustained and systematic metaphor."[80] Theories are based on models in which a familiar area of life is used to understand a less familiar area.[81] Similarities with the familiar area are noted (the positive analogy), as well as differences (the negative analogy). Sometimes certain points of comparison are left open (the neutral analogy), which allows the exploration of new features of a phenomenon at a later point.

In the disease theory of alcoholism, for example, the medical model of a disease is used to understand alcoholism. This suggests certain lines of

---

Science and Religion (New York: Harper and Row, 1974). The concept of root metaphors was first developed by Stephen Pepper in *World Hypotheses* (Berkeley: University of California Press, 1942). This book has been underappreciated in the discussion of models and metaphors.

79. Two of the earliest and most influential contributors to this discussion were Black, *Models and Metaphors*, and Hesse, *Models and Analogies in Science*.

80. Sallie McFague, *Metaphorical Theology: Models of God in Religious Language* (Philadelphia: Fortress, 1982), p. 67.

81. Barbour, *Myths, Models, and Paradigms,* chapter 2. For a very helpful discussion of the relationship between metaphor and theory, see Mark Johnson, *The Body in the Mind: The Bodily Basis of Meaning, Imagination, and Reason* (Chicago: University of Chicago Press, 1987).

comparison. Alcoholism, like a disease, is an impairment of normal bio-logical functioning (positive analogy). Disease is sometimes caused when the host is invaded by a pathogenic agent (negative analogy). Or it can be caused by dysfunctions of organic mechanisms that are inherited (positive analogy). Diseases are identified by their symptoms and developmental course (positive analogy). Some diseases like diabetes can be treated with drugs like insulin (negative analogy).

A very different model informs social drama theory. Here, human in-teraction is compared to a play in a theater. Like a play, interaction between alcoholics and other people is organized around certain roles and scriptlike patterns (positive analogy). Plays are performed in acts, which develop the dramatic action (positive analogy). The ending of a play is known by the actors in advance (negative analogy). Actors distinguish be-tween the characters they play and their everyday personalities and rela-tionships (neutral analogy).

Models, or root metaphors, thus draw on a familiar area of life to un-derstand an unfamiliar area. They play an especially important role in the context of scientific discovery, giving rise to new insights and lines of re-search. Viewing alcoholism as a disease, for example, generated new in-sights about this phenomenon. Alcoholism is best interpreted not as a fail-ure of willpower, but as a genetic vulnerability, with organic causes, symptoms, and a developmental course. This "discovery" opened up new lines of research.

But models continue to play an important role beyond the context of discovery. They provide direction in carrying out research and in forming a full-blown theory. Viewing alcoholism as a disease, for example, gave rise to research on the genetic basis of alcoholism and twin studies. It also has led to certain theories that attempt to explain how a genetically based sus-ceptibility to alcohol addiction is triggered in people's lives. On the basis of the disease model, thus, a theory develops a conceptual field, a set of con-cepts related to one another in a systematic way. Such concepts attempt to explain alcoholism as a disease.

When analyzing a theory, thus, it is helpful to begin by identifying the model on which it is based and then to map the conceptual field built on this model. Conceptual mapping typically begins by identifying the basic concepts of a theory, the concepts setting forth the core features of the model. Subsidiary concepts that elaborate these basic concepts are then identified, noting the relationship of one concept to another. For example, in Bepko and Krestan's gender construction theory of alcoholism among women, the model is the building of identity through social interaction and group membership. Some of the most basic concepts that explain how this construction takes place are socialization, identity formation, and the internalization of moral codes. The concept, code of goodness, elaborates the moral code into which women are socialized. This, in turn, is elaborated with the concepts of overresponsibility and unbalanced relationships that describe the effects of the female code of goodness on women. This conceptual field is used to explain patterns of alcohol addiction among women.

Identifying the model of a theory and mapping the conceptual field based on this model are important forms of analysis. They enable interpretive guides to draw on a theory's concepts with integrity in their interpretation of a phenomenon like alcoholism. When Olivia Potter reports numerous instances of "not fitting in" in her life story, for example, this is interpreted quite differently within the conceptual fields of the theories we have examined. In the developmental theory of alcoholism, it is interpreted as a sign of life-cycle tasks that were not accomplished during adolescence, when Olivia began to use drugs and alcohol on a regular basis and shut down her development. In gender construction theory, relational difficulties like not fitting in are often interpreted as especially threatening to women, who are socialized into relational identities. Such difficulties sometimes are a source of depression, which, among women, frequently *precedes* problem drinking. The very same feature of Olivia's life story, thus, is interpreted in different ways within the conceptual fields of these two theories. Mapping the conceptual field, thus, is critical to your ability to use a theory in appropriate ways.

Metaphor analysis and conceptual mapping also allow you to take an important first step in assessing theories. They enable you to identify the "familiar" area of life on which the root metaphor of a theory is based. You are then in a position to ask questions like: How adequate is the medical analogy proposed by disease theory or the theater analogy proposed by social drama theory? What sorts of things does this perspective help me see? What sorts of things does it leave out? To answer these kinds of questions, you will need to take note of the disciplinary perspective in which the model and conceptual field are located. This leads us to the second form of analysis and evaluation.

2. *Identify the disciplinary perspective a theory uses and the level of life this*

discipline addresses. In a communicative model of rationality, theories are viewed as forms of rational communication with others. When you read a book or hear a lecture that offers a theory, it is important to recognize that you are entering the middle of a conversation that has been taking place for some time. It is like stepping into the hallway of your dorm and suddenly finding two of your friends in the midst of a heated argument. How do you make sense of what the argument is about? When you enter the middle of a theoretical argument between scholars, one of the ways of figuring out what the argument is about is to pay attention to the *disciplinary perspective* the speaker is using to make her case. This is the *field,* or discipline, in which the argument is taking place. All the theories of alcoholism examined above develop their arguments from the perspective of a particular field. The disease theory draws on the disciplinary perspective of medical science, especially as this field is informed by the field of genetics. We examined several theories drawing on the disciplinary perspectives of psychology and sociology/anthropology, respectively. Why is it important to identify the disciplinary perspective in which a theory develops its argument? Most basically, this allows you to identify the *level of reality* the disciplinary perspective of a theory is most helpful in understanding.

Throughout this book I use the concept of the web of life to portray the broad scope of practical theological interpretation. This portrays systems as nestled within systems. Disciplines typically address one system located at one level of life. They do not explain all systems at all levels. This is sometimes described in terms of a *stratified model of life.*[82] Reality is composed of interconnected systems located at different levels, or strata, of life. This model was developed to account for the world as an emergent order. In the evolution of the universe, new strata of life have emerged from preexistent levels with new properties, structures, and forms of complexity. The universe can be viewed as a hierarchy of emergent systems with different levels of complexity, moving from inorganic life to organic life to conscious life to social systems.[83]

---

82. Stratified models of reality are found in the following: Nancey Murphy and George Ellis, *The Moral Nature of the Universe: Theology, Cosmology, and Ethics* (Minneapolis: Fortress, 1996); Roy Bhaskar, *A Realist Theory of Science* (Hassocks, Sussex, U.K.: Harvester Press; Atlantic Highlands, N.J.: Humanities Press, 1978); Michael Polanyi, *The Tacit Dimension* (Garden City, N.Y.: Anchor Books, 1966).

83. For an excellent summary of this perspective, see Murphy and Ellis, *Moral Nature,* chapter 2.

In a stratified model of life, thus, systems located at different levels have different structures, properties, and forms of complexity. We cannot explain one level of life in terms of another level. Each level has its own integrity. The disciplinary perspectives of different fields address a particular level of life. We have seen this in the theories of alcoholism examined above. The disease theory addresses the organic level of life, which focuses on the functioning of bodily systems. Psychological theories of alcoholism focus on the human psyche, or mind, including consciousness, the unconscious, the emotions, the personality, and the myriad ways this field explains the psychological functioning of human beings. Sociological and anthropological theories focus on the level of groups and societies, exploring the ways social structures and cultural patterns shape human beings. Identifying the disciplinary perspective of a theory, thus, allows you to recognize the level of life it addresses. If systems are nestled in systems within the web of life, a discipline typically addresses one system located at one level. Why is this important? There are two basic reasons.

First, it allows interpretive guides to assess the scope and limitations of a particular theory. Psychological theories, for example, are not going to tell you much about social institutions and broad cultural patterns. This is not the level of life they address. Rather, they are helpful in explaining the human psyche. The explanatory scope of a theory is limited by its disciplinary perspective, which is clearly recognized in the perspectivalism of a communicative model of rationality. A theory is good for some purposes but not for others. It explains one system or level of life but not all. This helps the interpretive guide to spot and avoid forms of *reductionism*. This takes place when a theory appropriate to one system or level is used to explain the whole. Either explicitly or implicitly, the theory claims a phenomenon is "nothing but" the particular form of explanation offered. Alcoholism is "nothing but" a person's genetic susceptibility or "nothing but" socially learned behaviors. This sort of reductionism is more common than you might think, and interpretive guides will do well to reject it. In practical theological interpretation, they affirm the complexity of systems nestled in systems within the web of life.

The second reason this is important is that it points the interpretive guide to *multidisciplinary* forms of thinking and dialogue. This is the use of the theories of several disciplines to interpret complex, multilayered systems and problems that are multidimensional. Alcoholism is a multilayered and multidimensional phenomenon, and it will take the theories of more than one discipline to understand it. The disease theory directs our attention to the organic level; psychological theories, to the level of an individual's personality, development, and family history; sociocultural theories, to the social level where cultural patterns, gendered identities, and social dramas operate. Theories of different disciplines are needed to understand and explain different levels or dimensions of alcoholism. This is the heart of multidisciplinary thinking.

This raises an important question: How might the theories of different fields be related to one another with integrity? Here the danger is not reductionism but *easy eclecticism,* using theories in a haphazard fashion without any consideration of how they are appropriately related to one another. It may be helpful to examine an example of multidisciplinary thinking that does *not* fall prey to an easy eclecticism and provides a clear picture of how various theories of alcoholism might be related to one another.

In *Thirst: God and the Alcoholic Experience,* James Nelson draws on various disciplines to interpret alcoholism.[84] He argues that the disease theory is primary because it draws our attention to the genetic factors increasing the risk of alcoholism. But he does not believe that genes *predetermine* alcoholism; rather, they *predispose* people to alcohol addiction. Nelson portrays psychological and cultural theories as accounting for *contributing* factors that interact with this genetic vulnerability at different levels of reality. The individual characteristics and social competence theory, for example, calls our attention to psychological factors that may lead people to turn to alcohol to bolster confidence in social situations, ease stress, or enhance self-esteem. Many people with these personal characteristics, however, do not become alcoholics, even if they drink. The genetic vulnerability of only some individuals is "triggered" when they begin to drink to cope with psychological issues. Nelson portrays the gender theory of alcoholism along similar lines, giving special attention to the ways male identity *contributes* to alcoholism. While many men turn to alcohol to cope with the burden of proving themselves, this "triggers" only among some men an inherited vulnerability to alcohol addiction.

In Nelson's multidisciplinary interpretation of alcoholism, priority is given to disease theory, and psychological and gender theories provide contributing factors. This is not the only way these theories might be related to one another. But it underscores my basic point. Interpreting a phe-

84. Nelson, *Thirst,* pp. 39-41.

nomenon like alcoholism with multidisciplinary thinking involves attending to the relationship of the various theories being used, moving beyond simple eclecticism. This is complex. It is best to start by identifying the discipline in which a theory is located and the level of reality it addresses. Only when you have done this for several theories that address different levels of reality will you be in a position to ask how they are related to one another. You get real help in starting this process by spotting the model, or root metaphor, of a theory. This provides important clues about the level of reality that a theory addresses and the ways it portrays natural or social systems at that level.

3. *Identify and evaluate the central argument(s) of a theory.* In a communicative model of rationality, theories are viewed as attempting to persuade us to accept certain assertions about a phenomenon like alcoholism.[85] They make an argument or a series of interconnected arguments in support of a particular way of understanding and explaining this phenomenon. Learning to identify and evaluate the argument(s) of a theory is a key task of the interpretive guide. If theories provide you with a "map" of the territory you are entering, you need to make sure the map is accurate and appropriate for the journey you are taking.

Arguments take two basic forms. *Dialectical* arguments take the form of point/counterpoint.[86] Assertions are made; they are challenged by others; a defense is offered in which good reasons for these assertions are brought forward. Persuasion rests on the ability to respond to the challenges raised by others with reasons deemed compelling. In the point/counterpoint pattern of dialectical arguments, this is sometimes described as the force of the better argument. *Dialogical* arguments take the form of collaborative give-and-take.[87] Assertions are put forward more tentatively,

85. The model of argumentation developed here is dependent on Stephen Toulmin. See his *The Uses of Argument.* For a clear introduction to his theory and the ways arguments are shaped by the fields in which they occur, see Stephen Toulmin, Richard Rieke, and Allan Janik, *An Introduction to Reasoning,* 2nd ed. (New York: Macmillan, 1978). See also Nancey Murphy, *Reasoning and Rhetoric in Religion* (Valley Forge, Pa.: Trinity, 1994).

86. James Freeman, *Dialectics and the Macrostructure of Arguments: A Theory of Argument Structure* (New York: Foris Publications, 1991).

87. William Isaacs, *Dialogue and the Art of Thinking Together* (New York: Currency Press, 1999); Linda Ellinor and Glenna Gerard, *Dialogue: Rediscover the Transforming Power of Conversation* (New York: Wiley, 1998); Ronald Arnett and Pat Arneson, *Dialogic Civility in a Cynical Age: Community, Hope, and Interpersonal Relationships* (Albany: State University of New York Press, 1999).

A Model of Arguments

- *Claims* are assertions put forward for public acceptance.

- *Grounds* are the support offered for these claims, including facts, evidence, and good reasons.

- *Qualifiers* indicate an argument's relative strength and specify the conditions under which it applies; often used are terms like "necessarily," "probably," or "possibly."

- *Warrants* are the rules or principles that create a bridge between the particular claims that are made and the particular grounds offered in support.

- *Rhetorical strategies* are the strategies of communication used to persuade a particular group to accept the argument on a particular occasion or in a particular forum (e.g., journal, book, seminar, committee meeting).

---

inviting additional input; they are elaborated and supplemented by others. Persuasion rests on cumulative insights emerging out of the dialogue. It is not a matter of "winning" the argument but of arriving at a closer approximation of the truth by reasoning together collaboratively. It is common to find both forms of argumentation in a single theory. The author may argue dialectically against the claims of other theories or rebut criticisms of his own position. But in dialogical fashion, he may also build on and elaborate theories with which he agrees.

To evaluate the argument(s) of a theory, it is helpful to work with a model of the different parts of an argument. These commonly include the following: claims, grounds, qualifiers, warrants, backing, and rhetorical strategies. *Claims* are "assertions put forward publicly for general acceptance."[88] The dysfunctional family theory of alcoholism, for example, makes three claims: (1) an alcoholic parent may give rise to pathological patterns in a family system; (2) children experiencing physical or sexual abuse in a dysfunctional family system are more likely to become alcohol-

---

88. Toulmin, Rieke, and Janik, *An Introduction to Reasoning*, p. 29.

ics later in life; (3) if children experience certain styles of parenting, like authoritarianism, they are more likely to become alcoholics at a later point. The disease theory makes a different claim, asserting that only certain individuals are predisposed to alcoholism because of an inherited genetic vulnerability.

In both of these theories the claims are supported by *grounds*, the particular facts, evidence, or research providing reasons for accepting their assertions. Clinebell, for example, carried out research on adult alcoholics in which he identified the incidence and degree of dysfunction in their families. This was high, he argued, supporting the claim of a link between adult alcohol dependence and the experience of pathological family systems during childhood. The disease theory marshals four grounds to support its claim: (1) while many people drink, a much smaller percentage become addicted to alcohol; (2) alcoholism shares many characteristics of other diseases like diabetes, asthma, and cancer; (3) advances in genetic research have begun to reveal the genetic basis of certain diseases, making it plausible that this also is true of alcoholism, as some research has begun to suggest; (4) twin and adoption studies indicate that susceptibility to alcoholism is rooted in the genetic inheritance of the family of origin, not in family patterns.

Assessing the adequacy of the grounds in support of an argument's claims is important. For example, Clinebell does not examine a group of nonalcoholic adults to determine the incidence and degree of family dysfunction in this population. Is it possible that alcoholics and nonalcoholics have similar rates of family dysfunction? He also claims that certain styles of parenting like authoritarianism contribute to alcoholism later in life but does not carry out or cite research on authoritarian parenting in support of this claim. How would we know if children raised in authoritarian families have a higher rate of alcoholism than those raised in "permissive" families? While the grounds supporting his claims are suggestive, they do not allow us to answer these kinds of questions.

Clinebell, however, does *qualify* his argument. *Qualifiers* indicate an argument's relative strength and specify the conditions under which it applies. They comprise terms like "necessarily," "probably," and "possibly." Such terms indicate how strong the claims and supporting evidence are considered to be. Clinebell explicitly qualifies his argument about authoritarian parenting, stating that if his interviews were repeated today, "authoritarianism probably would be far less common," and a "dominant theme would be a lack of loving parental authority expressed in firm limit-setting and caring discipline."[89] He locates his research in a particular historical setting and indicates that his claim about the link between authoritarian parenting and alcoholism probably would need to be revised in the present context.

The grounds of an argument are linked to its claims by *warrants*. These are principles or rules that create a bridge between the particular claims being made and the particular grounds offered in support. Sometimes grounds are offered that have no real connection to the claims. Consider an example offered by Del Ratzsch: "A national sensationalist tabloid once published the theory that the wife of a famous entertainer was the descendant of aliens. A key piece of evidence supporting the theory was that the lady had slightly lower than average blood pressure. Now lower than average blood pressure is indeed empirical data, but there is no reason to connect it with alien ancestry. Real science requires that there be some *rational* connection between explanatory theory and empirical data."[90] A warrant tells us why "grounds of *this* sort should be used to support a claim *of this sort*."[91] In this example the empirical grounds may be true, but no legitimate scientific warrant connects them to the claim that the wife is a descendant of aliens.

Different fields and disciplines warrant their claims in different ways. Law, for example, warrants legal arguments by appealing to statutes and precedents. Suppose a jury is presented with incontrovertible evidence that a woman shot a man dead. Indeed, she admits that she killed him. Will the jury necessarily find her guilty of murder? What if this man broke into her house in the middle of the night and attempted to rape her? In many states the statute of self-defense justifies her action and is well supported by precedents. In legal arguments, thus, grounds are linked to claims on the basis of statutes and precedents. They provide the rules or principles by which a legal argument is warranted. In contrast, scientific experiments in a laboratory are commonly warranted by the principle of replicability. This means that the outcome of a particular experiment will occur again if it is replicated by another investigator. Obviously, this way of connecting grounds to claims would not work in the legal case of an attempted rape, which must apply existing laws to unique events.

---

89. Clinebell, *Understanding and Counseling*, p. 61.
90. Cited in Murphy, *Reasoning*, p. 13.
91. Murphy, *Reasoning*, p. 14.

When assessing theories of alcoholism in different fields, thus, it is important to recognize that warrants may vary markedly from one field to another. For example, Denzin's social drama theory is based on his interviews of individual alcoholics and their family members in which they were asked to share their lived experience of alcoholism and recovery. He then extracted a general pattern from these many interviews that captures the common features of their interaction over time. This way of linking specific instances of lived experience to its "essence" is a warranting procedure used by the phenomenological tradition of social science. In contrast, twin studies supporting the disease theory are warranted by the mathematical rule of statistical probability, in which characteristics found in a representative sample are generalized to a broader population. Mathematical data about the incidence of alcoholism is gathered and compared across two discrete groups, identical and fraternal twins. The higher rate of alcoholism among identical twins warrants a genetic explanation, since they share identical genetic material and fraternal twins do not.

Warrants not only vary from field to field, they also vary *within* the same field. Why? The answer is found in a fourth element of arguments: *backing*. This is the argument behind the argument. It is the whole body of knowledge and practice that can be brought forward to support a specific argument, including its patterns of warranting. Commonly, scholars assume this broader framework of concepts and practices, especially in dialogical arguments with people who share their perspective. But sometimes their framework is challenged, and they must bring forward the backing that supports their claims, grounds, and principles of warranting. Today, scholars in the same field regularly presuppose different backing.

Within the field of gender studies, for example, remarkably different theories of gender identity are present. As we have seen, the gender construction theory of alcoholism portrays male and female identities as rooted in the socialization practices and cultural patterns of society. Scholars informed by sociobiology challenge this framework. They argue that most significant gender differences are rooted in the evolutionary heritage of the human species and are "hardwired" into the genetic codes of male and female human "animals." Gender differences are not just a result of socialization practices, which can be altered by social transformation. In the face of this challenge, those arguing within a gender construction framework must bring forward their backing. They must attempt to rebut sociobiology's challenges and justify their research program.

Within the theories of alcoholism we have examined, it is not difficult to discern potential challenges of this sort based on different forms of backing, the argument behind the argument. The high incidence of alcoholism among women who experienced physical or sexual abuse as children raises questions about the disease theory. Is it really true that abused women become alcoholics because of a genetic vulnerability? Are they not better interpreted as coping with posttraumatic stress? Indeed, disease theory might be challenged as an example of the dominance of the medical model in contemporary society and as drawing attention away from the reality of violence against women in patriarchal societies.

These sorts of arguments can grow quite heated. For this reason, it is important to attend to a final dimension of an argument, *rhetorical strategies*. As used here, rhetoric focuses on the strategies used to make a particular argument convincing to a specific group of readers or listeners on a particular occasion. These strategies include appeals to reason, emotions, examples, and the personal character or credibility of the speaker/writer.[92] Rhetoric should not be viewed pejoratively. By their nature, arguments attempt to persuade. The effective use of rhetorical strategies to this end is a sign of a scholar's skill and good judgment. But rhetoric is only one part of an argument, not the whole. It is important, thus, to assess the entire argument of a theory and not to be persuaded solely by its rhetorical effectiveness.

This sort of "whole argument" evaluation is done by assessing an argument's *soundness* and *strength*. Is the argument *sound*? This assesses the connections between its various parts.[93] Are its claims supported by sufficient and relevant grounds that are warranted in a manner that could be justified if necessary? In a sound argument the different parts hang together and make a coherent case for its claims. What is the *strength* of the argument? Evaluating the strength of an argument is not as simple as deciding that a theory is true or false. Rather, it is a matter of judging the relative strength of the argument(s) on which it is based, locating it on a continuum ranging from very weak to very strong. On the whole, for example,

92. For an overview of Aristotle's contribution to classical rhetoric, see George Kennedy, *Classical Rhetoric and Its Christian and Secular Tradition from Ancient to Modern Times* (Chapel Hill: University of North Carolina Press, 1980), pp. 60-82. For a detailed discussion see Eugene Garver, *Aristotle's Rhetoric: An Art of Character* (Chicago: University of Chicago Press, 1994).

93. Toulmin, Rieke, and Janik, *An Introduction to Reasoning*, pp. 27, 81-82.

you might find Clinebell's argument about family dysfunction and alcoholism relatively weak but still believe that it offers insights that may be worth exploring or are better substantiated elsewhere. It is not a matter of labeling his theory false but of assessing the relative strength of argument(s) on which it is based.

In a communicative model of rationality, judgments about the strength of an argument involve entering into the debate and dialogue of relevant audiences, people who are qualified to assess the reasons a theory offers and its contribution to life. How persuaded are these audiences by the argument? I believe it important for interpretive guides to take seriously the rational assessments of two audiences. One is a community of competent scholarly peers, members of the same field in which the theory is located. Most of us, for example, do not have the expertise to make technical judgments about the genetic basis of alcoholism. But we can enter into debate and discussion of these claims by people who are competent in genetics. Only then will we be in a position to make up our own minds about the relative strength of the claim that alcoholism is a disease rooted in a genetic vulnerability.

A second audience relevant to interpretive guides is the community of practical theologians. This includes scholars writing academic practical theology, but also congregational leaders with expertise in practical theological interpretation. How persuasive do they find the argument of a theory? What reasons do they give for their evaluation? Sometimes these reasons may be theological. Some may find the gender theory of alcoholism persuasive because it is consonant with their understanding of Christ as liberator, which compels them to give special attention to the victims of social oppression. Others may find the disease theory persuasive because it is analogous to their understanding of sin, a condition in which people are captive to forces beyond their control. Sometimes the reasons offered by this audience are not primarily theological, but rather focus on the usefulness of a theory in guiding a congregation. Some leaders may find the developmental theory of alcoholism persuasive because it has helped them recognize the special vulnerability of adolescents to drug use and has motivated them to create programs designed to prevent recreational alcohol use from turning into a serious drinking problem. Other leaders may find the drinking culture theory persuasive because it has helped them realize that moderate drinking may be the best antidote to binge drinking, leading them to develop programs that model this approach in the home, peer group, and church. The wise guide, thus, assesses the strength of a theory by listening carefully to the theological insights of others and to the reasons why other congregational leaders have found it useful.

Toward the Normative Task

We began this chapter by quoting Olivia Potter, and her situation has figured prominently in this chapter. You were asked to enter imaginatively into the position of Rev. Dorothy Gains, who served as Olivia's interpretive guide. Drawing on theories of the arts and sciences, we gave special attention to Olivia's alcoholism and the importance of using theoretical maps to guide Olivia and your congregation wisely. As Olivia's interpretive guide, however, you now face a new task. How might you interpret her situation theologically? How might you guide her dialogue with the normative resources of the Christian tradition? All that you have learned about alcoholism will contribute to your answer to these questions. Yet, as the leader of a Christian congregation, you must take the further step of drawing on the beliefs and practices of this community in your ministry with Olivia. This is the normative task of practical theological interpretation.

CHAPTER 3

The Normative Task:
Prophetic Discernment

I was first introduced to the normative task of practical theological interpretation while an intern in clinical pastoral education (CPE) at
Norwich State Hospital, a psychiatric institution in Connecticut. In my
CPE experience, extensive use was made of the case study and verbatim
methods in which we wrote up particular episodes, or "critical incidents,"
and cases in our work with patients. Theological reflection on these incidents and cases was an important part of our reporting and discussion.

I remember quite vividly one incident I wrote up that year. I had been
working on the adolescent unit for three weeks. This was a closed (locked)
unit because it had a number of youth with drug and alcohol problems
who were sent to Norwich under court order. Working with families was
often a part of the treatment plan. I had been asked to work closely with
Mark Chastain, who had a long history of problems at school, including
drug use, truancy, and violent outbursts. I visited Mark most days and felt
we were beginning to form a relationship of mutual trust. I met with his
family for the first time in one of the offices outside the adolescent unit
used by chaplains; Mark was also present.

After they had settled in, I excused myself to use the restroom located
next door and was gone for only a few minutes. When I returned, the
mother, father, and sister were there, chatting pleasantly with one another.
"Where is Mark?" I asked.

The father answered, "He told us he needed to go to the bathroom. I'm sure he'll be back in a second." As the seconds turned into minutes, it became clear what had happened. Mark had walked out of the office, down the stairs, and out of the building. He would not be found by the police for two weeks, with major repercussions for the adolescent unit. As I sat there waiting for him to return, a sinking, shameful feeling began to grow in my stomach. I can still recall that feeling to this day.

When I wrote up this incident for my group, more than a few issues came to the fore. What I remember most is the way our CPE supervisor, drawing on family systems theory, artfully framed the incident in terms of boundary issues — a lack of appropriate boundaries within Mark's family and in my relationship with him. Naively, I had assumed we were building a relationship of mutual trust. I treated him with respect and expected him to reciprocate in kind. It never occurred to me that he might run away and that I needed to set limits in our relationship or to teach his family how to set limits.

I also remember the way my supervisor moved the discussion to a theological level, using a Lutheran understanding of the law and gospel to explore theological dimensions of this incident. He pointed out that I was confusing communication of the gospel with being nice. This probably had more to do with my "need to be needed" than with offering a word and relationship of grace to this very confused adolescent. I also had not thought much about the role of the law in helping people recognize their wrongdoing or in restraining their inclination to harm themselves and others. Mark was going to need clear, consistent boundaries in his life, distinguishing appropriate and inappropriate behavior, if he was ever to turn away from his self-destructive behavior. At present, he was captive to his need to con others for his own immediate gratification.

This was not a pleasant experience. But it was one from which I learned a great deal. More than I realized at the time, I was beginning to learn two skills that would prove important to my ministry and my career as a scholar. First, I was learning how to engage in interdisciplinary thinking, the task of bringing two fields into conversation. My CPE supervisor modeled this, bringing family systems theory of therapeutic psychology into dialogue with a theological perspective on law and gospel. Second, I also was learning how to develop a normative theological perspective in ways appropriate to practical theology.

In this chapter I portray the normative task of practical theological interpretation along three lines, which were present in my CPE group's reflection on the Mark Chastain incident. The first is a style of theological reflection that I call here *theological interpretation:* the use of theological concepts to interpret episodes, situations, and contexts, including those in which we are actors. In this case our supervisor introduced the concepts of law and gospel into the group's discussion, which proved helpful in interpreting the issues at stake in this incident.

A second way of approaching this episode normatively was largely implicit in the group's discussion: the use of ethical norms to reflect on and guide practice. We came close to developing this sort of normative perspective in our reflection on boundary issues and on my description of my relationship with Mark as one of mutual trust. In retrospect, I believe we might have better discussed these issues in terms of an ethic of equal regard, a perspective in which all human beings are viewed as having equal moral worth and dignity.[1] In psychiatric hospitals, it entails that patients should not be treated as "objects" but as persons worthy of our respect. Perhaps this moral intuition informed my attempt to build a relationship with Mark based on mutual trust and respect. Yet, I ignored many issues that might have come to the fore if this ethical norm had guided my relationship with Mark.

Mark was ordered by the courts to Norwich because he had violated certain laws designed to protect the rights and dignity of other people. He was in possession of drugs at school and was suspected of dealing them to younger peers. He had threatened several of his teachers with physical harm. An ethic of equal regard affirms Mark's moral worth, but it also reminds us that in relationships and communities respect must be mutual and balanced fairly. It does not serve as license to con others or do them harm. After Mark returned to Norwich, I came to realize that his capacity to empathize with other people and to take their perspectives was severely impaired. Forming appropriate limits in our relationship and helping Mark learn to take the perspectives of teachers he threatened and younger peers he sold drugs to would have been worthy goals in my work with him. While this normative perspective would not tell me how to accomplish

---

1. An ethic of equal regard is found in the writings of many people, including Don Browning, *A Fundamental Practical Theology: Descriptive and Strategic Proposals* (Minneapolis: Fortress, 1991), chapter 7; Gene Outka, *Agape: An Ethical Analysis* (New Haven: Yale University Press, 1972); Louis Janssens, "Norms and Priorities in a Love Ethics," *Louvain Studies* 6 (1977): 207-38.

these goals (the pragmatic task), it would help me determine what I *ought* to try to accomplish.

A third way of approaching this episode normatively was central to the group's discussion. It emerged as we attempted to think through the role of a chaplain in a psychiatric hospital. Our supervisor was especially helpful in offering examples of *good practice* by chaplains who had related to adolescents like Mark in the past. They worked as part of a therapeutic team that set treatment goals and strategies in a collaborative fashion. They also took seriously their role as the representative of a religious tradition in their relationship with patients. Unfortunately, I did not check out the wisdom of taking Mark off the adolescent ward with other members of the treatment team. Nor was I clear about my role as a chaplain in working with his family. Over the course of my internship, hearing stories of good practice by others and reading cases of good practice by my peers provided normative guidance in my work as a chaplain.

In short, three approaches to the normative task are open to the interpretive guide. We explore this further in three steps. We begin by locating the normative task in the prophetic office, described here in terms of prophetic discernment. We then examine in greater depth each of the three approaches to the normative task described above. We conclude by exploring models of cross-disciplinary dialogue in which practical theology as a normative discipline is brought into conversation with other fields.

Prophetic Discernment

The prophetic office in ancient Israel is best understood in terms of this community's covenant with God. When Israel strays from covenant fidelity, the prophets announce God's Word to the people, reminding them of God's gracious actions in the past and of their promise to live as God's people. The prophetic word articulates two futures: the immediate future in which Israel faces the judgment of God and imminent disaster, and the furthest future when God will turn to Israel in mercy, renewing the covenant and delivering it from the disaster that has befallen it.[2] The prophets announce God's word of judgment and hope.

2. John Bright, *Covenant and Promise: The Prophetic Understanding of the Future in Pre-Exilic Israel* (Philadelphia: Westminster, 1976), p. 15.

For good reason, we think of prophets as God's messengers. God speaks; the prophet listens and then utters a prophetic oracle on God's behalf. The prophetic office, thus, is grounded in divine disclosure. While this is true, it also is clear that the prophets played an active role in shaping the message they delivered. They drew on particular theological traditions in Israel and addressed specific social conditions, events, and decisions before this community at a given point in its history. Abraham Heschel describes the "shaping role" of prophecy: "The prophets . . . did not simply absorb the content of inspiration, they also claimed to understand its meaning, and sought to bring such meaning into coherence with all other knowledge they possessed."[3] It is appropriate, thus, to describe the interplay of divine disclosure and human shaping as prophetic discernment. The prophetic office is the discernment of God's Word to the covenant people in a particular time and place.

The theological dimension of prophetic discernment becomes clear if we recall two understandings of the covenant that were present in Israel during the period of classical prophecy.[4] One is the promissory covenant in which God makes certain unconditional promises to Israel and asks the recipients to trust these promises. This pattern is found in God's promise to Abraham to give him a land, posterity, and blessing (Gen. 12:1-3; 18:17-19; 22:15-18), which is repeated to Isaac and Jacob. At a later point this pattern is used to portray God's promise to David. God chose Mount Zion as the seat of his earthly rule and David as his designated king. In an everlasting covenant, he promises that David's dynasty will never end. While kings are expected to rule justly and will be chastised for failing to do so, no conditions are attached to God's promise that the Davidic line will be eternal. The second understanding of the covenant is conditional and closely associated with the Sinai covenant. In this pattern the saving actions by which God liberated Israel from bondage in Egypt are rehearsed to remind the people that their very existence depends on God. The covenant is one in which God promises to be Israel's God and Israel promises to be God's people, obeying the commandments God has given them under the threat of penalty.

The prophets draw on these traditions in announcing God's word, often to counter popular or official theologies of the covenant that they viewed as

---

3. Abraham J. Heschel, *The Prophets*, 2 vols. (New York: Harper Torchbooks, 1962), 2:2.

4. Jon Levenson, *Sinai and Zion: An Entry into the Jewish Bible* (San Francisco: Harper and Row, 1985); Bright, *Covenant and Promise,* chapters 1–2.

misleading the people. The classical prophets of the northern kingdom, Amos and Hosea, draw on the pattern of the Sinai covenant, in part to counter the popular belief that the obligations of this covenant could be met by sacrifice and cultic observance alone. Addressing a relatively affluent nation, Amos critiques its way of life in which the poor are oppressed and cheated while the upper classes are pampered. Hosea addresses a dying nation and compares Israel's covenant infidelity to an unfaithful wife. In both prophets, Israel's failure to obey the obligations of the covenant is portrayed as placing it under God's judgment, with disaster sure to follow.

In contrast, Isaiah draws on the promissory Davidic covenant, in part to counter the royal ideology of the temple and the court, as well as the popular belief that God's promise to David meant that Israel would always be safe from other nations. Isaiah portrays the near future of Judah as one of impending calamity because of the king's unwillingness to trust God's promises instead of his own political calculations. He also portrays the furthest future as one in which a faithful remnant would emerge, David's line restored (Isa. 9:1-7; 11:1-9), and creation healed:

> Then the eyes of the blind shall be opened,
>   and the ears of the deaf unstopped;
> then the lame shall leap like a deer,
>   and the tongue of the speechless sing for joy.
> For waters shall break forth in the wilderness,
>   and streams in the desert. (35:5-6)

Jeremiah lived when the young ruler of the southern kingdom, Josiah, was attempting to move the community away from the official ideology of the Davidic covenant and back to the law-based conditional covenant, prompted by the discovery of a copy of Deuteronomy. While it is uncertain how Jeremiah viewed Josiah's reforms, it is clear that he too was deeply critical of popular and official versions of the Davidic covenant in which God's presence in the temple was viewed as ensuring Judah's safety (Jer. 7:4). But Jeremiah also believed that external reform was not enough. He called for an inner commitment to God's covenant stipulations "from the heart" (4:4, 14; 9:26). He portrayed the new covenant of the furthest future as surpassing the old, as a covenant in which God would forgive the sins of the people and write the law upon their hearts (31:31-34).

As this brief overview makes clear, prophetic discernment involves both divine disclosure and the human shaping of God's word. The prophets draw on specific theological traditions to critique popular and official theologies and the way of life justified by these theologies. They interpret theologically very specific social conditions, events, and choices before the covenant community at a particular moment in time.

Jesus the Prophet: God's Word

The New Testament draws on the prophetic traditions of Israel in a variety of ways. Jesus is portrayed as similar to the prophets of old, announcing God's word to the people. There are many indications that this is how he was popularly understood, as one like Elijah or Jeremiah (Matt. 16:14). It is telling that his disciples on the road to Emmaus describe him as "a prophet mighty in deed and word" (Luke 24:19; cf. 7:16). But the New Testament portrays Jesus as more than a prophet. He is the fulfillment of prophetic hope, the furthest future to which the prophets pointed: the Messiah in the line of David, one with authority to reinterpret the covenant stipulations and call the people to obey them from the heart, the inaugurator of a new covenant, and the agent of salvation promised by Isaiah, when "the blind receive their sight, the lame walk, the lepers are cleansed, the deaf hear, the dead are raised, and the poor have good news brought to them" (Matt. 11:5).

In short, Jesus does not merely serve as the messenger of God's words; he is God's Word. But what does this mean? And what does it entail for prophetic discernment by congregational leaders? It means that Christ Jesus is the full and unsurpassable revelation of God. We are not to look for other words from God alongside of or in competition with this Word. Prophetic discernment is the task of listening to this Word and interpreting it in ways that address particular social conditions, events, and decisions before congregations today. Such discernment is a matter of divine disclosure and theological interpretation in the face of popular or official theologies that may be leading the world toward disaster.

A Spirituality of Prophetic Discernment

As in prior chapters, I begin here by drawing attention to qualities of life in the Spirit and only then move to the more formal dimensions of the work of interpretive guides. This is conceptualized on a continuum.

A Spirituality of Prophetic Discernment

Sympathy —————————————————————— Theological and Ethical Interpretation

Discernment

Sympathy is human participation in God's pathos, God's suffering over the life of the covenant people and creation as a whole. We cannot understand what is meant by sympathy without first grasping the concept of divine pathos. This concept was originally articulated in the writings of Abraham Heschel and developed subsequently by Jürgen Moltmann and Walter Brueggemann.[5] Heschel's description is worth quoting in full:

> To the prophet . . . God does not reveal himself in an abstract absoluteness, but in a personal and intimate relation to the world. He does not simply command and expect obedience; He is also moved and affected by what happens in the world, and reacts accordingly. Events and human actions arouse in Him joy or sorrow, pleasure or wrath. . . . [M]an's deeds may move Him, affect Him, grieve Him or, on the other hand, gladden and please Him. This notion that God can be intimately affected . . . basically defines the prophetic consciousness of God.[6]

Among the classical prophets, Jeremiah offers some of the most profound descriptions of God's suffering over the covenant people in anger, disappointment, compassion, mourning, and longing:

> What wrong did your ancestors find in me
>   that they went far from me? (2:5)

> Let my eyes run down with tears night and day,
>   and let them not cease,
> for the virgin daughter — my people — is struck down
>   with a crushing blow,
>   with a very grievous wound. (14:17)

---

5. Heschel, *The Prophets;* Jürgen Moltmann, *The Crucified God: The Cross of Christ as the Foundation and Criticism of Christian Theology* (New York: Harper and Row, 1974), pp. 270-72; Walter Brueggemann, *The Prophetic Imagination* (Philadelphia: Fortress, 1978), chapter 3.

6. Heschel, *The Prophets,* 2:3-4.

I have forsaken my house,
    I have abandoned my heritage;
I have given the beloved of my heart
    into the hands of her enemies. (12:7)

The prophetic word is born in "a fellowship with the feelings of God, a *sympathy with the divine pathos*."[7] As Walter Brueggemann puts it, the prophetic imagination involves "the embrace of pathos," bringing to speech God's suffering over the waywardness and plight of the people.[8]

Jesus weeps over the hard-heartedness of Jerusalem. But he offers more than words about God's suffering; he is God suffering in solidarity with the suffering of creation. He acts with compassion toward the sick, social outcasts, and the unworthy. He suffers the pain of those who stand up to unjust social systems, even to the point of torture and execution. He suffers the death of all finite existence. As God's Word, Christ is divine pathos incarnate.

Leaders who would discern God's Word must begin by opening themselves to divine pathos. They must identify sympathetically with God's suffering over the sin, pain, and evil of creation. This will take the strengthening power of the Holy Spirit. Our natural tendency is to turn away from suffering and to shield ourselves with the protective ideologies of "court and temple," which rationalize the pain of creation. Prophetic discernment arises when those who have the "first fruits of the Spirit" groan inwardly with the groaning of creation, with "sighs too deep for words" (Rom. 8:22-23, 26). The words of grace and hope that leaders have to offer emerge from their sympathetic identification with God's Word, who entered fully into the suffering of creation and redeemed this condition.

Discernment is the activity of seeking God's guidance amid the circumstances, events, and decisions of life. To discern means to sift through and sort out, much as a prospector must sift out the dross to find nuggets of gold. It also means to weigh the evidence before reaching a decision, much as a judge listens to all evidence in a case before reaching a verdict. In early Christianity Paul encouraged his congregations to develop practices of discernment with which to weight the words of the prophets, to test the spirits, and to make decisions and settle disputes in the community. Over

---

7. Heschel, *The Prophets*, 1:26.

8. Brueggemann, *Prophetic Imagination*, chapter 3; "embrace of pathos" is part of the title of this chapter. Cf. pp. 53-61, 86-95.

the course of Christian history, various practices of discernment have been developed by different Christian communities. These practices are important to the work of interpretive guides. They offer a disciplined way of seeking God's guidance and sorting out what ought to be done in particular episodes, situations, and contexts.

Since many different patterns and practices of discernment have emerged in Christianity, it may be helpful to explore one example of prophetic discernment. Here I draw on Lisa Dahill's portrait of discernment in Dietrich Bonhoeffer's life, especially his decision to return to Germany right before World War 2 and to join an underground resistance movement that attempted to assassinate Hitler, costing Bonhoeffer his life. Discernment, as described in Bonhoeffer's writings and embodied in his life, involves two basic movements.

"The first move of discernment for Bonhoeffer," Dahill writes, "is simply the admission that, in reality, we don't know."[9] Discernment begins when we put aside our self-confidence and certainty about what we ought to do. We might travel several paths, and it is not clear which we should take. This requires humility and trust on our part. The second movement is actively seeking God's will. Bonhoeffer grounded this active seeking in three practices of discernment that he taught and lived throughout his life: (1) scriptural listening: attending daily to the living Word, which comes to us through the study and prayerful reading of Scripture; (2) confession and radical truth-telling: opening our hearts to trusted friends, who may save us from self-deception and help us distinguish God's guiding voice from other voices; (3) loving and being loved: discipleship as loving others in personal relationships and communities is a grounding point and focus of discernment; it is here that we learn to recognize Christ in the concrete other, especially those who suffer present-day crucifixions of poverty, violence, and oppression.[10]

Bonhoeffer is a profound example of a basic point. The normative task of practical theological interpretation is grounded in the spirituality and prac-

9. Lisa Dahill, "We Do Not Know What to Do, but Our Eyes Are on Thee," *Lutheran*, April 2005, p. 28. See also, Dahill, *Truly Present: Practicing Prayer in Liturgy* (Minneapolis: Fortress, 2005); Dahill, "Reading from the Underside of Selfhood: Bonhoeffer and Spiritual Formation," in *Minding the Spirit: The Study of Christian Spirituality*, ed. Elizabeth Dryer and Mark Burrows (Baltimore: Johns Hopkins University Press, 2004), pp. 249-66; Dahill, "Probing the Will of God: Bonhoeffer and Discernment," *Spiritus: A Journal of Christian Spirituality* 1, no. 2 (Fall 2001): 42-49.

10. Dahill, "We Do Not Know," p. 28.

tices of discernment. How will congregational leaders be able to sort out the words to offer to suffering others, the sermon to preach, or the lesson to teach, unless they first have admitted that they do not know what they are to say and do and, in humility and trust, actively seek God's guidance? Practices of discernment, thus, are crucial to the work of the interpretive guide. They provide a point of connection between God's Word of judgment and grace in Christ Jesus and the specific social conditions, events, and decisions for which congregational leaders provide normative guidance day by day.

Theological and ethical interpretation is the most formal dimension of the normative task. Just as attending in the descriptive task opens out to empirical research and sagely wisdom in the interpretive task, to dialogue with theories of the arts and sciences, so too the normative task opens out to forms of theological and ethical reflection. In discerning what we ought to do in particular episodes, situations, and contexts, we will do well to use an explicit approach to forming and assessing norms. This is the focus of the following section, which returns to the three approaches to normativity described in the first part of this chapter.

Theological and Ethical Interpretation

Theological Interpretation

The first approach is theological interpretation. This style of theological reflection is widely used in practical theology, Christian ethics, and political theology. It differs from other forms of theological reflection. Christian biblical studies, for example, focuses on the interpretation of biblical texts and dogmatic theology, on the systematic relationship between church doctrines. While informed by these fields, theological interpretation focuses on the interpretation of *present* episodes, situations, and contexts with theological concepts. While this approach to normativity is found in a number of contemporary practical theologians, here I explore the writings of H. Richard Niebuhr, who has influenced practical theologians like James Fowler and Charles Gerkin.[11] Niebuhr not only provides us with an

---

11. James Fowler, *To See the Kingdom: The Theological Vision of H. Richard Niebuhr* (Nashville: Abingdon, 1974); Charles Gerkin, *Prophetic Pastoral Practice: A Christian Vision of Life Together* (Nashville: Abingdon, 1991), pp. 56-58, 61-62, 69-70.

example of theological interpretation, but he also offers reasons for adopting the approach and a comprehensive theory of divine and human action that guides the focused interpretation of particular events.

Theological Interpretation in H. Richard Niebuhr

In *The Responsible Self* Niebuhr develops a "Christian moral philosophy" in which the answer to the "ought" question, What shall I do? is portrayed as dependent on answering a prior question, What is going on?[12] Niebuhr argues that the moral life is best characterized in terms of *responsibility,* not obedience to moral laws or commands (deontology) or pursuit of a telos, or end, which guides our activities (teleology).

Niebuhr portrays responsibility as composed of four elements, informed by an interdisciplinary dialogue with the sociological perspective of symbolic interactionism. (1) All our actions are *responses* to action upon us. (2) Our responses are shaped by our *interpretation* of these actions, which place particular episodes, situations, and contexts in larger wholes. (3) Our responses are temporal in nature, stretching backward to the history of prior interaction and anticipating responses to our present action in the future; responsibility, as such, involves *accountability* to others for the consequences of our actions within a context of ongoing interaction. (4) Our responses are shaped by the *community of interpretation* with which we identify; this community provides us with schemas of interpretation and ongoing dialogue with other moral selves.

The task of the moral life from this perspective is to respond to events in ways that are *fitting.* Niebuhr draws out the implications of this understanding of responsibility for the Christian community, offering the following general guideline: "God is acting in all actions upon you. So respond to all actions upon you as to respond to his action."[13] This does not mean that God causes all events to take place, which would subvert the contingent freedom and otherness of creation and, ultimately, make God responsible for evil.[14] Rather, God is acting to effect the divine purposes in and through human and natural events.

12. H. Richard Niebuhr, *The Responsible Self: An Essay in Christian Moral Philosophy* (New York: Harper and Row, 1963), p. 60.

13. Niebuhr, *The Responsible Self,* p. 126.

14. See James Nelson's sensitive interpretation of this point in *Thirst: God and the Alcoholic Experience* (Louisville: Westminster John Knox, 2004), pp. 155-58.

In *The Meaning of Revelation,* Niebuhr focuses on the church as a community of interpretation and the ways its interpretation of present events draws on the revelatory events of God's prior action in Israel, Jesus Christ, and the early church. "By revelation in our history, then, we mean that special occasion which provides us with an image by means of which all the occasions of personal and common life become intelligible. . . . [I]t illuminates other events and enables us to understand them. . . . Through it a pattern of dramatic unity becomes apparent with the aid of which the heart can understand what has happened, is happening and will happen to selves in their community."[15] Niebuhr compares revelation to the experience of reading a difficult book and suddenly coming upon a "luminous sentence" that throws light on the whole, rendering it intelligible.[16] He also likens it to the decisive scene of a drama that illumines the entire course of dramatic action that is unfolding.[17] The church as a community of interpretation offers its members images, concepts, and narratives that school their imaginations and nurture the capacity to interpret God's action in the events of their lives and world.

Niebuhr wrote a series of short articles that are particularly nice examples of his approach to theological interpretation: "The Grace of Doing Nothing" (1932), "War as the Judgment of God" (1942), and "War as Crucifixion" (1943).[18] We will examine here only the second article, exploring what it might teach us about the theological interpretation of contemporary events.[19]

Niebuhr's Theological Interpretation of World War 2

"War as the Judgment of God" appeared in the *Christian Century* the year after the bombing of Pearl Harbor and the entry of the United States into the war. The purpose of the article, Niebuhr writes, is to address the "question of God's action in this war." Obviously, many individuals and nations

---

15. H. Richard Niebuhr, *The Meaning of Revelation* (New York: Macmillan, 1941), p. 80.

16. Niebuhr, *The Meaning of Revelation,* p. 68.

17. Niebuhr, *The Meaning of Revelation,* p. 94.

18. H. Richard Niebuhr, "The Grace of Doing Nothing," *Christian Century* 49 (1932): 378-80; "War as the Judgment of God," *Christian Century* 59 (1942): 630-33; "War as Crucifixion," *Christian Century* 60 (1943): 513-15.

19. All quotations in the succeeding section come from pages 630-33 of Niebuhr, "War as the Judgment of God."

were acting in the war, but Christian and Jewish interpretation of history "centers on the conviction that God is at work in all events, and the ethics of these monotheistic communities is determined by the principle that man's action ought always to be response to divine rather than to any finite action." To interpret the war as the judgment of God is "to stand where Isaiah stood when he discerned that Assyria was the rod of divine anger and where Jesus stood when he saw in the crucifixion not Pilate's or the Jews' activity but that of the Father."

Niebuhr begins by ruling out certain ways to interpret the war as God's judgment that Christians were using at the time. He is particularly critical of dualistic interpretations. These portray God's judgment as falling solely on the Allies' enemies but not on them, or on the common sin of all of humanity while affirming the "relative rightness of democracy in opposition to totalitarianism." Such dualisms render Christians "di-theists" worshiping two gods, "the Father of Jesus Christ and our country, or Him and Democracy." Country and democracy are values of a high order, but only if they are under God. As "rivals of God, they are betrayers of life."

In contrast to these sorts of dualistic interpretations, Niebuhr argues that to interpret the war as the judgment of God means three things. First, it means that we must abandon any notion that God's judgment is simple vengeance for past sin, seeking "to restore the balance between men by making those suffer who have inflicted suffering." This is the case for two reasons. The suffering of the war falls most heavily on the innocent, "on all the children, wives and mothers, humble obedient soldiers, [and] peasants on the land." Moreover, God's judgment is always redemptive, seeking to bring the guilty to repentance and to transform their ways. Judgment as vengeance is not adequate to the God revealed in Jesus Christ.

Second, God's judgment cannot be identified with the "relative rightness or wrongness of the various groups involved." When Isaiah portrayed Assyria as the rod of God, he was *not* affirming this nation's moral righteousness or the rightness of its cause. Rather, he was interpreting Assyria as an instrument of God's judgment, as executing the divine will. In the present war, Niebuhr argues, God's judgment falls on all parties and cannot be used to justify either side.

Third, God's judgment in the war is that of the "one and universal God" who is sovereign over every dimension of life. It is not "the judgment of a Lord of the spiritual life, or of a Lord of religious life, or of a Christian Lord over Christian life." To confine God's judgment to the religious sphere, while leaving political activity "essentially unrepentant, self-confident action in the defense of our values," is to misinterpret the sovereign God's rule over *all* of life.

The article concludes by describing three ways Christians might respond to the war in a fitting manner when interpreted along these lines. First, they will abandon the habit of putting themselves in God's place and passing judgment on themselves and their enemies. Rather, they will simply perform the duty they are given to perform "in view of what [they] have done amiss and in view of what God is doing." The fitting response to the Axis invasion of neighboring countries and the genocide of the Jews is to intervene on behalf of those who are suffering.

This leads to a closely related second point. Christians must abandon all attempts to justify their actions or those of their nation by identifying their cause with God's. This sort of self-aggrandizement inevitably involves self-deception. In the lead-up to the war, self-centeredness characterized the actions and policies of *all* sides. For a long time the Western nations stood by idly in the face of the "crucifixion of the Jews and China" and the smaller countries of central Europe. Niebuhr links this point to the first: "If we accept God's judgment on our self-centeredness we cannot respond to it by persisting in actions of self-defense and by fighting the war for the sake of protecting our selves or our values instead of for the sake of the innocent who must be delivered from the hands of the aggressor."

Third, a fitting response to God's judgment in the war must be hopeful and trusting. Christians must refuse to give up on those they oppose in the war and must act with hope that this tragedy can be redeemed. They will respond by aligning themselves with the redemptive intent of God's judgment, working to bring good out of the evil of the war.

God's Judgment and Theological Interpretation of Contemporary Events

As a kind of thought experiment, let us imagine how Niebuhr might use this understanding of judgment to interpret contemporary events, beginning with the war on terror. Like the article, he might start by correcting certain forms of interpretation that have become widespread among many American Christians since 9/11. He might challenge dualistic interpretations that view the war on terror as a conflict between good and evil or between Christian democracy and Islamic theocracy. This too easily allows us to blame *them* while letting *us* off the hook. Niebuhr might even be willing to risk interpreting Osama bin Laden as "the rod of God," without affirming his moral righteousness or the rightness of his cause. God is judging the hedonism, materialism, and political arrogance of the Western nations, which leave so many young Arab men trapped in cycles of poverty and political corruption, the breeding ground of terrorism.

We can continue this thought experiment by asking how Niebuhr might interpret the events surrounding hurricane Katrina. As in war, suffering from the hurricane fell hardest on the innocent, on the poor, elderly, and black, on those without the money and means to evacuate. They were crucified in their innocent suffering like the Jews of World War 2. The Christian word to those in such suffering is a word of divine compassion, of a God who entered fully into innocent suffering on the cross at the hands of the political and religious establishment of his day. God is suffering in solidarity with the innocent victims of the hurricane and is seeking to redeem these tragic events.

How might Niebuhr apply his understanding of God's judgment to these events? Perhaps he would call attention to the ways the hurricane exposed the sins of a way of life driven by consumerism and self-seeking materialism. In the past, natural disasters like hurricanes were commonly interpreted as forms of natural evil. Today, however, a clear distinction between natural and moral evil is no longer so easy to make, for industrial and technological systems have radically altered the environment in which human beings and other species live. It is likely that global warming already is increasing the intensity of hurricanes as the temperature of the oceans rises.[20]

Moreover, Niebuhr might caution us against allowing God's judgment to be assimilated to the "blame game" of partisan, political infighting. Katrina exposed the long-standing indifference of both political parties to

20. See the various studies of Kerry Emanuel available at http://wind.mit.edu/~emanuel/cvweb/cvweb.html. Cf. P. J. Webster et al., "Changes in Tropical Cyclone Number, Duration, and Intensity in a Warming Environment," *Science* 309, no. 5742 (2005): 1844-46. Webster's articles are available at http://webster.eas.gatech.edu/onlinepapers.html#2005. These studies find that the number of hurricanes over the past three decades has remained relatively constant or even declined slightly. But the number of hurricanes of increased intensity (category 4 or 5) has risen. These studies attribute this to the higher temperature of the ocean's surface, which increases the amount of water taken up into the hurricane as it is gathering strength.

the plight of the poor, which resulted in a systematic miscalculation of their needs in the face of a hurricane of such magnitude. It exposed the sins of political cronyism resulting in such an inept initial response and of political trade-offs leading to the neglect of the levee system surrounding New Orleans. But Niebuhr likely would remind us that God's judgment has a redemptive intent. We must respond with hope that this disaster might open up the possibility of national repentance and reconsideration of how we are allocating our resources as a country.

Theories of Divine and Human Action in Theological Interpretation

In "War as the Judgment of God," Niebuhr primarily uses a single theological concept to interpret the historical events of World War 2. James Fowler and James Gustafson have drawn attention to the comprehensive theory of divine and human action that is found across his writings as a whole.[21] This sort of theory is an important part of theological interpretation, though it often lies in the background of focused interpretation of specific events. In Niebuhr's theory of divine and human action, he balances the Christian affirmation of monotheism, the oneness of God, and its affirmation of the Trinity, the threeness of God. He tends to associate Christian monotheism with the themes of God's universality and sovereignty: God is acting in all actions upon us. This is balanced by three distinct patterns used to interpret God's action in the world and fitting forms of human response.[22]

The first pattern focuses on *God the redeemer*. God in Christ loves the world with covenant fidelity and enters fully into the suffering of creation, especially the suffering of the innocent. God's redemptive intent encompasses divine judgment, seeking to bring good out of evil. The fitting human response is one of gratitude and trusting faith. This rules out all attempts to justify ourselves by exaggerating our moral righteousness and

---

21. Fowler, *To See the Kingdom;* James Gustafson, introduction to *The Responsible Self,* pp. 6-41.

22. Typically, the patterns of redemption, creation, and providence are not identified *exclusively* with one member of the Trinity in Christian theology, although it is not unusual to discuss them *primarily* in terms of the Son, Father, and Spirit. Moreover, the trinitarian dimension of Niebuhr's discussion of these patterns is undeveloped and, some would argue, absent altogether. I am making the modest claim of a latent trinitarianism in his thought.

refusing to acknowledge our sinfulness. It also leads us to align ourselves with God's desire to bring good out of evil. This pattern informed Niebuhr's interpretation of World War 2 in the article examined above.

The second pattern focuses on *God the creator,* the source and valuer of all being. As creation's author, God is of a qualitatively different order than creation. Yet this very Creator God affirms the goodness of creation, bestowing worth and dignity on all forms of life. The fitting human response is to acknowledge God alone as God, ruling out our idolatrous tendency to put some finite value or cause in God's place. It also leads us to affirm the sanctity of God's creatures, who are not to be turned into objects and exploited for human purposes. In human communities, it leads us to acknowledge that all human beings are created in God's image and are to be treated with respect in personal relationships and with justice in the social order.

The third pattern focuses on *God the governor and sustainer of life,* commonly portrayed as God's providential care of the world. God orders and preserves creation through both impersonal systems and personal relations, while respecting creation's contingent freedom. The fitting human response is to care for the ordering processes and structures that sustain life, working to align them with God's purposes. This calls for moral discernment of God's will within the particular events of life and the broader processes of continuing creation.

This brief description of Niebuhr's thought does not do justice to its richness and complexity. I offer it, however, as an example of a *comprehensive theory of divine and human action* that lies behind more focused theological interpretation of particular events like war. Niebuhr's approach to theological interpretation and the general patterns he employs are only *one* way this approach to normativity might be carried out.

Liberation theologians, for example, give greater priority than Niebuhr to the interpretive patterns of exodus and Christ the liberator, who defied the political and religious authorities of his day to heal and set free the outcasts, poor, and unclean.[23] Drawing on the analytical tools of

23. For an example of an account of divine and human action in which exodus is prominent, see Gustavo Gutiérrez, *A Theology of Liberation: History, Politics, and Salvation* (Maryknoll, N.Y.: Orbis, 1973), pp. 153-78. For one that focuses on Christ as the concrete embodiment of the history of divine salvation and on the "history of the human responses to the divine proposal" (p. 41), see Leonardo Boff, *Jesus Christ Liberator: A Critical Christology for Our Time* (Maryknoll, N.Y.: Orbis, 1978).

critical social theory, they attempt to expose the structures of political and economic oppression that are operative today.[24] A church that interprets the present context with the revelatory patterns of the exodus will join those who are struggling under Pharaoh's yoke and will give themselves to the "signs and wonders" by which the oppressed are led to freedom. It also will stand where Christ stood, taking the side of those who are most vulnerable.

Theological interpretation, thus, can draw on theories of divine and human action that are quite different from Niebuhr's. He is offered as one example of this approach, which includes two activities: (1) the theological interpretation of particular episodes, situations, and contexts in the present; (2) the use of a comprehensive theory of divine and human action that guides more focused forms of theological interpretation.

Ethical Interpretation

A common criticism of Niebuhr's perspective serves as a transition to the second approach to the normative task of practical theological interpretation. Some critics charge Niebuhr with failing to give adequate attention to *ethical principles, rules, and guidelines* in the moral life.[25] Such norms can play an important role in guiding human choices and actions, as we have seen in our discussion of Mary Jo James and Mark Chastain.

Ethical Norms in Don Browning

Among contemporary American practical theologians, Don Browning has given perhaps the most sustained attention to the importance of ethical

---

24. The forms of Marxist critical social theory used by liberation theologians are somewhat different from that described in the appendix to chapter 1, which focused on the Frankfurt School. Liberation theologians are interested in theories that expose the economic dependency of the South on the North and the ways religion often serves as an ideology to justify and mask this relationship. As such, they are interested in the "liberation of theology" as well as economic and social liberation. See Juan Luis Segundo, *The Liberation of Theology*, trans. John Drury (Maryknoll, N.Y.: Orbis, 1976); José Míguez Bonino, *Doing Theology in a Revolutionary Situation* (Philadelphia: Fortress, 1975), chapters 5–8.

25. See the critique offered by James Gustafson, *Ethics from a Theocentric Perspective: Theology and Ethics*, vol. 1 (Chicago: University of Chicago Press, 1981), pp. 53-56.

norms in practical theological interpretation.[26] Like Niebuhr, he is offered here as an *example* of this approach to the normative task. Browning is particularly interesting because he elaborates certain features of Hans-Georg Gadamer's understanding of hermeneutics. In the introduction we noted Gadamer's pivotal role in the widespread recognition of the hermeneutical dimension of scholarship. Gadamer spelled this out in his concept of a hermeneutical experience, portrayed along the lines of a circle including preunderstanding, the experience of being brought up short, the interplay and fusion of horizons, and the emergence of new understanding that is applied to contemporary life. Browning calls attention to a feature of Gadamer's work that is often underappreciated. Application does not merely occur at the *end* of interpretation but is present from the beginning and influences it throughout.[27]

In everyday life, for example, interpretation is set in motion when events and relationships bring us up short and require us to sort out how best to proceed. The school has just called to let us know that our child is sick, but we are leading an important meeting in thirty minutes. Figuring out how to cope with this situation will influence every interpretive strategy we consider. Can we reach our spouse on the phone? Might a trusted neighbor go to the school and pick up our child? Will the school discharge our child to this neighbor? Can we reschedule the meeting or does it include people from out of town? Concern for application does not merely come at the end of interpretation but animates it throughout.

Browning draws out two very important implications of this insight for practical theology. First, if application influences interpretation from the beginning, then practical theological interpretation is best understood along the lines of a *practice-theory-practice* model. It begins when some dimension of our present practice becomes problematic. A sermon elicits an angry response from several members of our congregation. Attendance of confirmation classes is spotty, even though we communicated clear expectations that it should be regular if the confirmands want to be confirmed. These kinds of problematic situations in present practice set in motion the

---

26. Don S. Browning, *The Moral Context of Pastoral Care* (Philadelphia: Westminster, 1976); Browning, *Religious Ethics and Pastoral Care* (Philadelphia: Westminster, 1983); Browning, *A Fundamental Practical Theology*.

27. Browning, *A Fundamental Practical Theology,* p. 39.

process of practical theological interpretation and influence it throughout. Application is not merely a tack-on.

This leads to a second elaboration of Gadamer offered by Browning. The concept of application draws attention to the fact that our present practices are filled with values and norms. We expect confirmands to attend most classes because we believe that confirmation is a big step in their lives. Yet this norm may not be shared by the confirmands or their families. They may value participation in sports and other extracurricular activities, which often conflict with confirmation classes. Present practice, Browning argues, is saturated with values and norms of this sort, which often are in conflict. This is why he believes that it is so important for the interpretive guide to develop ethical principles, guidelines, and rules in the normative task of practical theological interpretation. It is not a matter of importing ethics into the problematic situations of present practice; values and norms already are a part of present practice.

In his most recent writing, Browning draws on the work of Paul Ricoeur to describe the role of ethical norms in a practice-theory-practice model of practical theological interpretation. In *Oneself as Another,* Ricoeur offers a three-part account of the moral life: (1) the identity-shaping ethos of a moral community that is embodied in its practices, narratives, relationships, and models; (2) the universal ethical principles that a moral community uses to test its moral practices and vision and to take account of the moral claims of others beyond this community; (3) the *phronesis,* or practical moral reasoning, that is needed to apply moral principles and commitments to particular situations.[28] Ethical reflection with universal ethical principles is particularly important, for it allows moral communities to test their present practices and norms against universal ethical principles. Do they regard the moral worth of others as equal to their own? When the interests of their community conflict with the interests of others, are they committed to procedures that are fair and open to all parties? Can they enter sympathetically into the perspectives of groups that are different from themselves? These sorts of ethical tests are impor-

---

28. Paul Ricoeur, *Oneself as Another* (Chicago: University of Chicago Press, 1992). For an especially helpful interpretation of Ricoeur's model, see Johannes van der Ven, *Formation of the Moral Self* (Grand Rapids: Eerdmans, 1998), and Don Browning, "The Family and Moral and Spiritual Development," in *Developing a Public Faith* (St. Louis: Chalice, 2003), chapter 13. See also Richard Osmer, *The Teaching Ministry of Congregations* (Louisville: Westminster John Knox, 2005), chapter 10.

tant. In situations of moral conflict, human beings are likely to put the interests of their families and local communities above those of other people. Moreover, their moral practices and interpretations may not be adequate to the particular circumstances of the members of their own community.

Domestic Abuse and Ethical Reflection

Let us see how this model might be used in a specific situation. In earlier chapters we followed the story of Olivia Potter, which took us far into the field of alcoholism and addiction. One of the especially dark sides of alcoholism is the high rate of physical and sexual abuse in families with alcoholic fathers. As we saw in chapter 2, Norman Denzin identifies a common pattern in such families, the "merry-go-round named desire." This is particularly insidious in situations of abuse. Spouses and children often experience the ups and downs of emotional, physical, and sexual violence, on the one hand, and of heartfelt apologies, affection, and intimacy on the other.

Olivia Potter did not experience abuse as a child; nor was her husband physically violent toward her. Let us, thus, imagine a situation in which an adult woman in our congregation shares with us that her husband has grown increasingly violent as his drinking has escalated. How might Browning's appropriation of Ricoeur's model guide practical theological interpretation in this situation? It begins by calling our attention to moral norms that may already be present in this situation. Often, pastors and Christian friends tell the victims of domestic violence to "hang in there" and keep their marriage intact for "the good of the children." They sometimes appeal to the norm of sacrificial love to support this advice. Jesus told us to take up our cross and follow him. Coping with her alcoholic husband is the particular cross this woman has to bear. Likely, this norm comes from stories about Jesus and from practices in which sacrificial giving is held up as a moral ideal. This is common in stewardship campaigns, marriage education, and preaching on the Lord's Supper and Good Friday. Jesus sacrificed for us, so we are to sacrifice for one another.

Browning argues that the norm of sacrificial love — embedded in the narratives and practices of many congregations — must be subjected to ethical tests, the second part of Ricoeur's model. Is this norm adequate to the Christian tradition? Does it provide the interpretive guide with an appropriate normative perspective on the merry-go-round named desire in which physical violence is present? Browning's answer to these questions is no! In various writings he develops an alternate understanding of Christian love in an *ethic of equal regard*. We touched on this perspective briefly in the discussion of Mark Chastain.

An ethic of equal regard is grounded in the narratives of creation and Christ's ministry that point to the inherent dignity and worth of all human beings. In stories of creation, human beings are portrayed as created in God's image and, thus, as worthy of respect in personal relations and of fair treatment in social institutions. In narratives of Christ's ministry, he is portrayed as telling his disciples no less than eight times, "You shall love your neighbor as yourself," and to follow the Golden Rule. Building on these stories, Browning argues that the ethical principle of agapic love is the most important norm found in Christian Scripture. However, he criticizes that strand of the Christian tradition that portrays agapic love primarily in terms of self-sacrifice and self-denial. Rather, the logic of the *imago Dei* and of Jesus' call to love our neighbor as ourselves is better captured in an ethic of equal regard. In this ethic the worth and dignity of our neighbor are equal to — not greater or less than — our own. It portrays love as mutuality in personal relations in which respect for oneself and respect for others are balanced. It also affirms the fair treatment of people in social relations and institutions. Self-sacrifice, thus, is not the *primary* form love takes. Rather, it is the special effort required in a sinful and finite world when mutuality and fairness become unbalanced. In such circumstances, sacrificial effort is needed to bring damaged relationships back to mutuality or to return unjust institutions to fair treatment.

Applying the ethical norm of equal regard to the particular circumstances of the woman who turned to the interpretive guide for help calls for *phronesis,* the third part of Ricoeur's model. This involves exploring her situation in all its particularity and complexity. But such moral reasoning would be guided by an understanding of love in which violence by an alcoholic spouse is seen as a violation of the woman's inherent dignity. It violates the mutual respect that ought to characterize loving relations. As Browning puts it:

> I hold that the love ethic of equal regard has crucial relevance for
> domestic violence. Not only should this ethic restrain all violent acts
> in the name of mutual respect, but it should function to empower
> the weak to demand that they be treated as ends — as children of

God — and never as means or objects of exploitation. The love ethic of equal regard is not an ethic for the submissive, weak, and downtrodden. . . . [I]t is an ethic of empowerment that can undergird the demands for equal respect expressed by women, minorities, and exploited children.[29]

This example highlights the role of ethical reflection in the normative task of practical theological interpretation. General principles like equal regard and more concrete guidelines and rules orient leaders to the moral issues at stake in episodes, situations, and contexts. They provide guidance in determining the goals that ought to be pursued in particular circumstances.

Good Practice and Normative Reflection

A third approach to the normative task of practical theological interpretation focuses on *good practice*. Good practice provides normative guidance in two ways: (1) it offers a model of good practice from the past or present with which to reform a congregation's present actions; (2) it can generate new understandings of God, the Christian life, and social values beyond those provided by the received tradition. Since our primary focus is on the second, a few introductory comments about the way good practice may serve as a normative model are necessary.

Models of good practice offer congregations help in imagining how they might do things better or differently. Often these models are found in other congregations. By reputation, for example, some churches are known to be exceptionally strong in youth ministry, spiritual direction, mission, small groups, or some other ministry. By observing these churches, leaders gain a concrete picture of what good practice looks like, as well as resources that might be used in helping their congregation move in this direction. Too often, congregations rush headlong into starting new programs without taking the time to gain guidance from others. Observing good practice in other congregations is a powerful source of normative guidance.

Sometimes, models of good practice are retrieved from the past. An example is the recovery of the adult catechumenate in many contemporary

29. Don Browning, "Domestic Violence and the Ethic of Equal Regard," in *Equality and the Family: A Fundamental Practical Theology of Children, Mothers, and Fathers in Modern Societies* (Grand Rapids: Eerdmans, 2007), p. 378.

churches. This was sparked by liturgical and practical theologians who called attention to the integrated bundle of practices characterizing initiation into the church in the third through fifth centuries. In the catechumenate of that period, new members were offered far more than a quick trip through denominational history or polity. They participated in liturgical rites, catechesis, exorcism, prayer, and moral practices. Initiation was a lengthy process that helped new members break with their former lifestyle and begin practicing the Christian way of life. The retrieval of the adult catechumenate, thus, has provided contemporary congregations with a model of good practice, and many began to reform their approach to initiation, drawing on programs developed by their denomination, especially in the Roman Catholic Church, the Evangelical Lutheran Church in America, and the Episcopal Church.[30]

In short, good practice from the present or past can serve as a normative model offering guidance to contemporary congregations. It helps leaders imagine what their congregation might become, as well as providing resources and guidelines with which to move it in the desired direction. Alongside this role of good practice in the normative task is another, in which present practice is the generative source of new understandings of God, the Christian life, and social values. Here, good practice is more than a model; it is epistemic. It yields knowledge that can be formed only through participation in transforming practice. Like previous sections, I explore here an *example* of this approach to normativity, Elaine Graham's *Transforming Practice*.[31]

Transforming Practice in Elaine Graham

One of the most prominent characteristics of our postmodern context is a lack of consensus over values. In the United States this is most apparent in conflicts over abortion and gay rights. But it extends to issues that receive

30. Jane Carew, *Making Disciples: A Comprehensive Catechesis for the RCIA Catechumenate* (Huntington, Ind.: Our Sunday Visitor, 1997). For a description of the catechumenal approach in the Evangelical Lutheran Church in America, see *Welcome to Christ: A Lutheran Introduction to the Catechumenate; Welcome to Christ: A Lutheran Catechetical Guide;* and *Welcome to Christ: Rites for the Catechumenate.* All were published in 1997 by Augsburg Fortress Press.

31. Elaine Graham, *Transforming Practice: Pastoral Theology in an Age of Uncertainty* (Eugene, Oreg.: Wipf and Stock, 1996).

far less attention in the media. Should young adults, who are marrying later in life, engage in sexual relations outside of marriage? How important is it for both fathers and mothers to take part in child rearing, and what implications does this have for their careers? How far should society go in tinkering with the genes of plants, animals, and human beings? There is no consensus about how these questions should be answered or the basic values that ought to guide such answers. While fundamentalist and conservative religious communities often offer answers they believe are based on eternal and transcendent values, many people are deeply skeptical of their claims. Even members of the same religious tradition are skeptical of fundamentalists' claim to draw on values that are grounded in an eternal, metaphysical account of human nature or social reality. Is it really true, for example, that women are "by nature" subordinate to men and ought to raise children, not work, and not be allowed to serve as pastors of congregations or as leaders in public life?

In *Transforming Practice*, Elaine Graham argues that practical theology must face up to the challenges of a postmodern context characterized by a high degree of pluralism, fragmentation, and skepticism. It is a context of uncertainty in which it is no longer possible for theology to build on a consensus of values in society. Nor can theology take for granted the authority of traditional sources and norms of the church. It must find new ways of developing truth claims and values that will be persuasive to a skeptical postmodern world.

Graham develops an approach to normativity that focuses on *transforming practice.* She is especially interested in transforming practice that can help the church and society move beyond the oppressive legacy of patriarchy, which defines human nature *androcentrically,* assuming that maleness and masculinity are the norm. Graham argues that normativity must be approached *reflexively,* not prescriptively, as dialogue and reflection on the practical wisdom emerging in communities of transforming practice. As she puts it: "Principles of truth and value are not to be conceived as transcendent eternal realities, but as provisional — yet binding — strategies of normative action and community within which shared commitments might be negotiated and put to work. Ethics and politics therefore become processes and practices, rather than applications of metaphysical ideals."[32] Over the course of her book, Graham develops

32. Graham, *Transforming Practice,* pp. 6-7.

three central arguments about transforming practice in the Christian community: (1) transforming practice generates new knowledge and values that cannot be formed in any other way; (2) such practice is oriented to human freedom and love and struggles to overcome structures of domination, including the oppression of women; (3) transforming practice discloses God and offers a model of transcendence that is compelling to many people in our postmodern context.

Transforming Practice as Epistemic

Graham develops her understanding of transforming practice by entering into a dialogue with two European sociologists, Anthony Giddens and Pierre Bourdieu. Both develop the concept of practice to move beyond a problem that has vexed contemporary sociology: how to conceptualize the relationship between structure and agency. Structure points to the way social institutions shape people's lives. For example, as modern societies began to industrialize, work was separated from the family. Typically this meant that men left home to work in factories or offices while women stayed home to take care of young children. This division of labor impacted the social roles, identities, and life chances (e.g., educational opportunities, financial independence, legal standing) of men and women in markedly different ways. *Structure*, thus, indicates the impact of social institutions on people's lives. *Agency* points to the active role individuals and groups play in interpreting their experience and their freedom to respond to social institutions in a variety of ways. While industrial societies structured the division of labor in families along certain lines, many families modified and even resisted this pattern. In some, for example, women worked outside the home as factory workers, teachers, and professionals. In farming families, work remained rooted in the home and relied on the contributions of all members.

Sociologists have struggled to conceptualize the relationship between structure and agency. Many sociologists, like Karl Marx and Emile Durkheim, have placed so much emphasis on the structuring power of social institutions that little agency appears to remain. Others, like George Mead and Alfred Schütz, have so emphasized agency that the structuring power of institutions appears to fade into the background. In different ways, Anthony Giddens and Pierre Bourdieu develop the concept of practice to respond to this issue, portraying practice as "mediating" structure and agency.

Both acknowledge that social institutions structure human life in powerful ways. But they also affirm that social structures depend on the agency of human actors to reproduce them in the practices of everyday life. For example, students move through seminaries in a wide variety of ways. Some simply follow the prescribed curriculum; others try to get out of required courses by substituting college courses or their prior work experience. Some attend chapel regularly; others never attend. Some are full-time students who live in campus dorms; others commute to school from congregations they are serving and are part-time students. In short, students engage the seminary as a social institution in a wide variety of ways. They develop very different practices of seminary education. While they confront the preexistent patterns of the seminary, they exercise agency in how they engage these patterns, reproducing, modifying, or transforming them in their own practices as students.

Both Giddens and Bourdieu portray practice as a point of mediation between structure and agency. One of the ways Giddens describes this is his portrait of social actors as "knowledgeable." As they participate in social institutions like a seminary, they gradually build up knowledge and skills that allow them to reflect on this institution and make choices about how they will engage it. Drawing on this knowledge, they forge practices that reproduce, modify, or resist the social patterns they face. Bourdieu portrays social institutions as inculcating a *habitus* in their participants, enduring knowledge, values, dispositions, and skills. This *habitus*, however, is not all-determinative; rather, it is a source of creative agency and strategies of action that people use to form their own goals and shape their own particular practices of work, family life, and education while seminary students. In short, Giddens and Bourdieu portray practice as the dialectical interplay of structure and agency. Institutions structure human life in powerful ways, but social agents have the capacity to engage these institutions in different ways, reproducing, modifying, and transforming them.

Graham draws on Giddens and Bourdieu to make four points about gender practices.[33] First, human nature is not an eternal, ontological "given" but is socially constructed by a particular constellation of practices that is operative in a given sociohistorical context. This calls into question any attempt to portray the "nature" of women and men on metaphysical grounds, as grounded in ultimate reality or in "orders of creation" established by God. Gendered identities, roles, and relationships are constructed through a net-

---

33. Graham, *Transforming Practice*, pp. 104-5.

work of social practices. They are not a matter of innate or ontological differences between females and males. Second, while social structures shape human actors in powerful ways, human beings possess agency in the ways they engage these structures. While acknowledging the power of institutionalized patterns of gender, Graham affirms the place of choice, doubt, and resistance in response to the current network of gendered practices. Third, while practices often reproduce institutional structures, they also are a potential source of transformation of these structures, generating new forms of knowledge, values, and social patterns. In Christian communities that are struggling to overcome the social structures of patriarchy, nonsexist and transforming practices of family life, friendship, congregational life, and public commitment are a potent source of new understandings of God and the Christian life. Fourth, the transforming practice of new forms of gender identity and relationships is one of theology's most important sources for constructive work. It offers theology knowledge and norms that go beyond the received tradition and embody new ways of being the church amid the struggles of a particular time and place. Theology is a second step, both grounded in and guiding transforming practice.

Transforming Practice in Feminist Theology

Graham undertakes the second step of theological reflection by developing a feminist theology of transforming practice. She grapples with some of the most difficult questions that communities of transforming practice face. How do they avoid the trap of relativism? If such communities no longer can appeal to absolute, metaphysical norms, how do they form norms that sustain commitment and hope in the struggle for social transformation? What criteria might such communities use to assess their practice? Graham responds to these questions in three ways and, in the process, develops three criteria with which to assess transforming practice.

First, she locates transforming practice within a commitment to the Christian praxis of freedom and love. Here she follows the lead of liberation theology in which "all values, sources, and norms are understood as validated and generated in purposeful action *(praxis)* toward liberation."[34] As such, one criterion with which to make judgments about transforming practice is its contribution to liberating praxis, defined as "transforming

---

34. Graham, *Transforming Practice*, p. 114.

activity marked and illuminated by Christian love."[35] While this does not provide specific norms to guide particular actions, it does give guidance about the basic intent of transforming practice. Such practice contributes to the struggle both inside and outside the church to liberate people from social and economic oppression. Good practice is liberating. Many innovative practices in the church fail this test.

Second, Graham links this precommitment to liberating praxis to contemporary feminism, which gives special priority to *women's experience* in the reconstruction of social practices shaping gender. In a patriarchal, androcentric world, Christian communities must do more than reproduce gendered social patterns; they must make space for women's experience and leadership in an effort to form new practices of gender identity, relationships, and roles. This is an expression of the church's commitment to the praxis of Christian freedom and love.

Graham issues a very important cautionary note about women's experience in transforming practice. Congregations must not "essentialize" women's experience, that is, assume that *one* form of experience represents what *all* women want and need. Women's experience is diverse, reflecting the intersection of gender with race, ethnicity, culture, and economic circumstances. A second criterion emerges from this discussion. Practice is transforming to the extent that it takes account of women's experience in the struggle to forge new patterns of gender in the church but does not absolutize the particular insights and norms that emerge. This is closely related to Graham's next point.

Third, since the diversity of women's experience makes it impossible to posit a single norm for all transforming practice, such norms must emerge reflexively out of particular, local practices that embody new patterns of gender in a specific Christian community. Authentic practice opens up a space for conversation in which people reflect on the values and meanings that are emerging out of their experience. This allows them to distill, articulate, and criticize what they have come to know and value. It is a matter of consolidating the practical wisdom that is gained through transforming practice. For example, many couples today are struggling to form more egalitarian marriages, which balance fairly each person's career and the responsibilities of child rearing and household maintenance. Such couples could learn a great deal from one another if they came together to reflect

35. Graham, *Transforming Practice*, p. 132. Graham is quoting Gustavo Gutiérrez here.

on their common goals and problems. They would glean practical wisdom from their experience and discover norms that are helpful in building egalitarian relationships.

Such norms are not imposed from the outside. They emerge out of transforming practice and speak to those who are engaged in such practice. They are binding and authoritative because they are life-giving. While Graham affirms the importance of norms formed in this way, she also contends that it is important that they be viewed as provisional. They are situated in the particular experience and practice of specific people and communities. They disclose some values and insights while foreclosing others.[36] The practical wisdom of couples attempting to build egalitarian marriages, for example, may have very little to offer single women, who are struggling on their own to hold together work, child rearing, and relationships with others. The norms of transforming practice, thus, must be grounded in a commitment to alterity. This is the willingness to encounter "otherness" in the form of other communities and individuals whose experience of transformation may be different from one's own. A third criterion of transforming practice, thus, is the extent to which it supports the reflexive formation of norms out of the practical wisdom of a community while remaining committed to alterity.

In Graham's approach to normativity, thus, transforming practice is pivotal. It is the generative source of new knowledge, values, and social patterns. She offers three criteria with which to guide and assess transforming practice in the church: (1) Does it contribute to human liberation as an expression of the Christian commitment to freedom and love? (2) Does it attend to women's experience without "essentializing" this experience? (3) Does it support the reflexive consolidation of practical wisdom emerging out of practice, within a commitment to alterity? Near the end of her book, she draws on these criteria to assess several examples of feminist transforming practice.

Transforming Practice as Disclosing God and as a Model of Transcendence

In Graham's approach the normative task of practical theological interpretation is situated squarely in the midst of transforming practice and seeks

---

36. Graham, *Transforming Practice,* pp. 162-64.

to draw on and deepen the insights and values it generates. Moreover, it is inherently a corporate activity. While interpretive guides may play an important role in facilitating reflexivity in their congregations, this involves communication and reflection by the entire community to gather the practical wisdom of all.

Near the end of her book, Graham gathers together some of the theological themes that inform her understanding of transforming practice. Two are especially important. First, transforming practice discloses God. It makes available knowledge and understandings of God that cannot be found in any other way. Indeed, transforming practice not only discloses God to the community of faith but also serves as a "medium, sign, and witness" of God's presence to the world.[37] Second, when the transforming practice of a congregation embodies alterity, it serves as a model of transcendence in our postmodern world. As Graham writes: "The process of going *beyond* the situated and concrete in the encounter with the Other may also serve as a metaphor for the human experience of the transcendent. It speaks of an encounter with transcendence and authentic faith at the very point of loss of certainty and self-possession: divine activity and presence are encountered in the mystery of alterity."[38]

Summary

Three approaches, thus, are available to the interpretive guide in carrying out the normative task of practical theological interpretation. These approaches are not mutually exclusive. It is common for an interpretive guide or practical theologian to use a combination of all three.

The Normative Task and Cross-Disciplinary Dialogue

Several years ago I traveled to South Korea. I had received much advice from my Korean students: be sure to try bee bim bap and bulgogi; watch out for this kind of kimchi. One piece of advice I received from everyone was to be sure to visit the Namdaemun Market, one of the largest markets in the world. Established in 1414, the market spreads across ten acres of

37. Graham, *Transforming Practice*, p. 205.
38. Graham, *Transforming Practice*, pp. 206-7.

Three Approaches to Normativity

1. *Theological Interpretation:* using theological concepts to interpret particular episodes, situations, and contexts, informed by a theory of divine and human action.

2. *Ethical Reflection:* using ethical principles, rules, or guidelines to guide action toward moral ends.

3. *Good Practice:* deriving norms from good practice, by exploring models of such practice in the present and past or by engaging reflexively in transforming practice in the present.

winding alleys and comprises over one thousand shops, stalls, and street vendors. I even read about the Namdaemun Market in my guidebook before the trip.

Near the end of my first week in Korea, I had a day to visit some of the cultural sites in Seoul. I ended up in Namdaemun in the middle of the afternoon when it is busiest. The sights, sounds, and smells were truly amazing. After wandering in and out of shops and alleys for several hours, I had no idea how to return to the place where I had entered the market and my subway stop was located. It was time to get out my guidebook and see if it could help me. I had read this book in advance, but now, in the middle of my journey through Namdaemun, the landmarks it described and alleyways it named took on a different meaning.

We, too, have wandered in and out of different tasks and theories in this book. It is time to get out our "guidebook" and make sense of some of the landmarks we have seen. Many times I have called attention to the importance of cross-disciplinary dialogue in practical theology. It has come to the fore in each of the tasks of practical theological interpretation. Let's begin by recalling some of the landmarks we have encountered.

In the descriptive-empirical task, it emerged as we considered the formal attending of priestly listening, in which many strategies of inquiry and methods of research are used by the interpretive guide. Obviously, the purpose of a particular research project influences the strategy and methods that are used. But how is this purpose determined? Advocacy research strives to contribute to social change; ethnographic research strives to contribute to a better understanding of the lived experience of the members of a community. In choosing one of these strategies instead of the other, theological considerations may play a role. Those committed to emancipatory praxis of liberation and feminist theologies may believe that advocacy research should take priority over other approaches. Others may be led to ethnographic research by a theology of the priesthood of all believers, which emphasizes the understanding and ministries of the entire congregation. In short, the diversity of empirical research strategies and methods confronts interpretive guides with certain choices, and theological considerations may play a role in guiding these choices. This requires cross-disciplinary dialogue.

The interpretive task draws on the arts and sciences to better understand and explain particular episodes, situations, and contexts. While the sagely wisdom of interpretation is open to the world and reflects on the meaning of the discernible patterns of nature and human life, it also draws on the redemptive wisdom of Jesus Christ, the embodiment of God's royal rule. This also requires cross-disciplinary dialogue. How is the worldly wisdom of the arts and sciences appropriately related to the Wisdom of God?

In the present chapter we have seen many examples of cross-disciplinary dialogue in the exemplars of each approach to normativity. H. Richard Niebuhr enters into a conversation with symbolic interactionism in forming the concept of responsibility. Liberation theologians draw on critical social theory to expose contemporary forms of oppression and to concretize the task of liberation in a particular social context. Don Browning enters into a dialogue with the philosophical hermeneutics of Hans-Georg Gadamer to develop a practice-theory-practice model of practical theology and with the moral philosophy of Paul Ricoeur to conceptualize the role of universal ethical principles in the Christian life. Elaine Graham engages sociologists Anthony Giddens and Pierre Bourdieu and various feminist thinkers to develop her understanding of transforming practice. In each exemplar of the normative task, thus, there are clear indications that cross-disciplinary dialogue is involved.

The same will also be true in the following chapter, which examines the pragmatic task. Knowing what we ought to do and how to do it are not the same, and we often receive help with the latter by engaging action sciences like education, psychotherapy, social work, communication studies, and organization theory. This too involves cross-disciplinary dialogue.

It is not too much to say that practical theology as an academic field and practical theological interpretation by congregational leaders are inherently cross-disciplinary in nature. This entails two things. First, practical theology is a form of *theology*. It is not social science "lite." It uses the concepts, methods, and sources of theological discourse to develop a constructive theological perspective. Second, practical theology brings this perspective into dialogue with other fields, including other theological disciplines (i.e., biblical studies, church history, dogmatic theology, and ethics) and the arts and sciences.

Cross-Disciplinary Dialogue in a Communicative Model of Rationality

In chapter 2 we laid the groundwork for reflection on cross-disciplinary dialogue by exploring a communicative model of rationality. In this model rationality is viewed as a special form of communication in which people offer reasons to others in support of their assertions. Building on this perspective, we can offer the following definition: *cross-disciplinary dialogue is a special form of rational communication in which the perspectives of two or more fields are brought into conversation.* This dialogue takes four forms.[39]

Intradisciplinary dialogue focuses on the conversation between various perspectives within a single field. In virtually all disciplines today, more than one viable, theoretical approach is present. In contemporary psychology, for example, psychoanalysis, cognitive psychology, feminist psychology, social learning theory, and evolutionary psychology are viable positions, to name but a few. Even within a particular school of psychology, moreover, a range of positions often is present. Contemporary psychoanalysis, for example, contains perspectives based on classical instinct theory, object relations theory, and self psychology. In intradisciplinary dialogue, interpretive guides enter into the debate and discussion of a single field and form judgments about the perspective they find most persuasive on grounds *internal* to that field.

Interdisciplinary dialogue brings the perspectives of two fields into con-

---

39. I draw here on my article, "A New Clue for Religious Education in a New Millennium? Cross-Disciplinary Thinking and the Quest for Integrity and Intelligibility," in *Forging a Better Religious Education in the Third Millennium*, ed. James Michael Lee (Birmingham, Ala.: Religious Education Press, 2000).

versation. In practical theological interpretation, this commonly is the perspective of academic practical theology and another field. In Christian education, for example, this may involve a theological perspective on the teaching ministry that is brought into conversation with another field, such as developmental psychology or cultural anthropology.

Multidisciplinary dialogue brings a number of fields into conversation simultaneously. This is prompted by the recognition that many disciplines are needed to comprehend systems nestled within systems and problems that are multidimensional. In the previous chapter, this sort of conversation was described with a stratified model of reality, in which the theories of different fields address different levels of the web of life. Various theories were viewed as interpreting different levels of alcoholism.

Metadisciplinary dialogue is a conversation about the nature of a discipline, a conversation often found in the philosophy of science, the sociology of knowledge, and rhetoric/argument theory. What constitutes a discipline epistemologically, sociologically, and rhetorically? In our postmodern intellectual context, the very notion of a discipline has come under serious scrutiny. Given the radical pluralism found in many disciplines, does it continue to make sense to say these diverse perspectives belong to the same field? What is the relationship between knowledge and power, and how does this get played out in institutional carriers of the disciplines? Contemporary metadisciplinary dialogue takes these questions seriously, setting forth the status of the disciplines as forms of knowledge, intersections of power, and forms of rational communication. It articulates assumptions guiding cross-disciplinary work at other levels.

In short, cross-disciplinary dialogue can take a variety of forms. Here I focus on models guiding the dialogue between theology and other fields in interdisciplinary and multidisciplinary conversations. A model, or root metaphor, we can recall, draws on a familiar area of life to understand an unfamiliar area, noting similarities and differences. In contemporary theology three models have emerged to picture the dialogue between theology and other fields: correlational, transformational, and transversal. There is diversity, moreover, within each model.

Correlational Models of Cross-Disciplinary Dialogue

Correlational models portray the dialogue between theology and other fields as one of *mutual influence.* Correlation in science is a way of analyzing statistical data to demonstrate the relationship between two or more forces. In chapter 2 this method was used a number of times to describe the relationship between drinking and other phenomena. Women experiencing depression, for example, are 2.6 times more likely to have a serious drinking problem. Women experiencing abuse during childhood are more likely to be addicted to alcohol later in life. There is a correlation between depression or abuse and drinking patterns, a relationship of mutual influence.

When used as a model of dialogue, the quantitative dimensions of scientific correlation drop away (negative analogy). Rather, what is emphasized is the way a genuine dialogue is a conversation in which the parties enter into a mutually influential relationship (positive analogy). The parties listen closely to one another and build on each other's comments. The subject matter and flow of the conversation are codetermined. When extended to rational communication, these features of correlation are primary. As parties offer reasons for their positions, their dialogue partner listens to them carefully and respectfully. Even when they disagree, their rational exchange is codetermined. The questions raised by one party are taken seriously and responded to by the other.

In the correlational model of cross-disciplinary dialogue, theology listens carefully to other disciplines and learns from them. It may even revise traditional beliefs or practices in light of their insights. Some contemporary theologians, for example, have revised the doctrine of creation to take account of evolutionary theories of the universe, placing more emphasis than the tradition on God's creative involvement in continuing creation. But theology also contributes to this dialogue. While learning from contemporary theories of evolution, for example, Jürgen Moltmann argues that theology must teach our modern, scientific culture to see the world as God's creation and not merely as nature, as a world in which all beings have their own sanctity and integrity and are not merely objects to be exploited for human purposes.[40] In the correlational model of theology's dialogue with other fields, thus, the conversation is one of mutual influence and critique, not a one-way monologue. In contemporary theology, three variations of the correlational model have emerged: the method of correlation, the revised method of correlation, and the revised praxis method of correlation.

The *method of correlation* is closely identified with the work of Paul

---

40. Jürgen Moltmann, *God in Creation* (Minneapolis: Fortress, 1985).

Tillich.[41] Tillich portrays the arts and sciences as raising questions that theology answers on the basis of its own normative resources. He is particularly interested in entering into a dialogue with those arts and sciences that articulate the deepest questions with which the contemporary world is struggling. This leads him to enter into dialogue with surrealism in art, psychoanalysis in psychology, and existentialism in philosophy. These perspectives, he believes, have come to terms with modernity's overly optimistic belief in human progress and reason. They portray human consciousness as caught in a web of forces beyond rational control, forces that can be threatening and destructive. This darker picture of the modern condition raises the question theology must answer. One of the ways Tillich responded in his theology was by portraying God's grace as offering people the courage to be in the face of the threats of nonbeing.[42]

Tillich's method of correlation has been criticized as one-sided. The arts and sciences raise the question; theology provides the answer. This led David Tracy and Don Browning to develop a *revised correlational* model of theology's dialogue with other fields.[43] The conversation here is more mutual. The arts and sciences offer both questions and *answers* in this dialogue. The insights of contemporary feminism or evolutionary thinking, for example, do far more than raise questions that the Christian tradition can then answer. They have the potential of eliciting major revisions of the Christian tradition on the basis of new knowledge emerging outside the Christian community. Moreover, theology also raises critical questions to its dialogue partners. Don Browning, for example, has raised devastating questions about the optimistic assessment of human beings found in much humanistic psychology.[44] Is it really adequate to portray human beings solely in terms of their self-actualizing potentials? In the revised correlational model, theology's dialogue with other fields takes the form of a mutually critical conversation in which the parties are equals. Questions and answers are offered by all participants in this dialogue.

41. Paul Tillich, *Systematic Theology*, vol. 1 (Chicago: University of Chicago Press, 1951); cf. Tillich, *Theology and Culture* (New York: Oxford University Press, 1959).

42. Paul Tillich, *The Courage to Be* (New Haven: Yale University Press, 1952).

43. David Tracy, *Blessed Rage for Order: The New Pluralism in Theology* (New York: Seabury Press, 1979); Browning, *A Fundamental Practical Theology*.

44. Don Browning, *Generative Man: Psychoanalytic Perspectives* (Philadelphia: Westminster, 1973); Browning, *Religious Thought and the Modern Psychologies: A Critical Conversation in the Theology of Culture* (Philadelphia: Fortress, 1987).

Both of these models of correlation have been criticized as being preoccupied with questions of cognitive meaning and as privileging dialogue within the academic community. Such critics contend that the real crisis confronting theology is not one of meaning but one of human suffering, and the goal of theology's dialogue with other fields is to contribute to social transformation that alleviates this suffering. This led Matthew Lamb and Rebecca Chopp to develop the *revised praxis method of correlation*, which situates the dialogue between theology and other fields in a broader conversation than rational exchange between academic disciplines.[45] What is brought into a mutually influential relationship is the praxis of new social movements committed to human liberation and the praxis of the Christian community. Praxis is the struggle against some concrete form of oppression and includes theoretical reflection that guides this struggle. Critical social theories, for example, play an important role in critiquing ideologies that legitimate dominant social patterns and in helping social movements become clear about their goals. In the revised praxis correlational model, thus, the first and most important dialogue is between movements and communities sharing common emancipatory goals. The dialogue between theology and other fields is a second step, arising out of transforming praxis and helping to guide this praxis. A nice example of this model is found in Elaine Graham's work, described above.

Transformational Models of Cross-Disciplinary Dialogue

Transformational models portray the dialogue between theology and other fields as a conversation between people who speak different languages. When this conversation is between people from cultures with very different worldviews, mutual understanding is difficult. Some aboriginal tribes, for example, do not have a Western, linear view of time but live in cyclical time rooted in the rhythms of nature. Some also have a concept of "dream time" when the gods established the world, a time that can be reentered in rituals, festivals, dreams, spiritual journeys, and visions. For Westerners to grasp this view of time, they must enter the very different linguistic world in

45. Matthew Lamb, *Solidarity with Victims: Toward a Theology of Social Transformation* (New York: Crossroad, 1982), chapter 3; Rebecca Chopp, "Practical Theology and Liberation," in *Formation and Reflection: The Promise of Practical Theology*, ed. Lewis Mudge and James Poling (Philadelphia: Fortress, 1987), pp. 120-38. Cf. Chopp's *The Power to Speak: Feminism, Language, God* (New York: Crossroad, 1989).

which aboriginals live, either literally or imaginatively. At a later point, when they try to explain to others what they have learned, it will not be as simple as translating aboriginal ideas into equivalent terms in their native language. Such terms do not really exist in their own language. They face the more difficult challenge of moving from one language world to another.

The transformational model of theology's dialogue with other fields is similar to a conversation between people who speak different languages. Different fields are viewed as engaged in different language games with their own grammars and vocabularies (positive analogy), even when they are conducted in the same natural language (negative analogy). Disciplines have their own distinctive subject matter, oriented to a particular level of reality. They construct and comprehend the social and natural "objects" of their field with the language and practices used to investigate them. Moving from one field to another, thus, is not a matter of simple translation, taking the terms of one field and finding equivalent terms in another (positive analogy). Rather, it is a matter of transforming what is learned from another field by placing it in a different disciplinary context. Two versions of the transformational model have emerged in recent theology: the Chalcedonian approach and the ad hoc "correlational" approach.

The *Chalcedonian model* is developed somewhat differently in the work of James Loder and Deborah van Deusen Hunsinger; here I describe Loder's perspective.[46] Loder portrays the dialogue between theology and other fields as guided by the theological grammar of the christological formulations of the Council of Chalcedon.[47] This grammar consists of three rules that characterize the relationship between the human and divine in Jesus Christ: indissoluble differentiation, inseparable unity, and indestructible order.

46. Deborah van Deusen Hunsinger, *Theology and Pastoral Counseling: A New Interdisciplinary Approach* (Grand Rapids: Eerdmans, 1995). The two best recent discussions of Hunsinger's and Loder's theological methods are Theresa F. Latini, "From Community to *Communio*: A Practical Theology of Small Group Ministry" (Ph.D. diss., Princeton Theological Seminary, 2006), pp. 316-18; Dana R. Wright, "Ecclesial Theatrics: Toward a Reconstruction of Evangelical Christian Theory as Critical Dogmatic Practical Theology: The Relevance of a Second 'Barthian Reckoning' for Reconceiving the Evangelical Protestant Educational Imagination at the Metatheoretical Level" (Ph.D. diss., Princeton Theological Seminary, 1999).

47. James Loder and Jim Neidhardt, *The Knight's Move* (Colorado Springs: Helmers and Howard, 1992); James Loder, *The Logic of the Spirit: Human Development in Theological Perspective* (San Francisco: Jossey-Bass, 1998).

First, in Christ the human and divine are differentiated, coexisting without the reduction of one to the other. Jesus is not merely a very good human being with certain godlike qualities; nor is he a god who only appears to be human. He is both human and divine, coexisting in a *differentiated* whole. Second, the divine and human coinhere in an inseparable *unity*. As the mediator of the relationship between God and humanity, Christ necessarily is both human and divine. He brings salvation to the world as the true human being before God and as the true God with human beings. Third, the relationship of the human and divine follows an *asymmetrical order*, with the divine having logical and ontological priority over the human. Christ does not become God's Son by virtue of his life of faith and obedience; he is God's Son who enters fully into finite existence.

Loder argues that the three rules of this theological grammar can guide theology's dialogue with other fields. First, the knowledge given to faith is unique and not to be confused with other forms of human knowledge. Theology, thus, must be differentiated from the arts and sciences. Second, theology cannot carry out its work without entering into a dialogue with other forms of human knowledge; they are inseparably joined in a bipolar unity. Third, the relationship between theology and other fields follows an asymmetrical order, with theology retaining "marginal control" over the knowledge of other fields when they are brought into its own forms of discourse. In short, theology listens to and learns from other fields. But it transforms their insights according to the rules of its own theological grammar.

Hans Frei offers an *ad hoc correlational* model of cross-disciplinary dialogue.[48] His use of the term "correlational" does not imply a relationship of mutual influence between equals, as described above. When theology enters into a dialogue with other fields, it transforms their insights as they are placed in the altogether different language game of theology. This is because theology is grounded in the unique cultural-linguistic matrix of the Christian community in which first-order statements of Christian belief and practice are made. Theology is second-order discourse that describes the grammar or internal logic of first-order language and assesses such language critically. This cultural-linguistic matrix of Christian theology sets it apart from other forms of scholarship.

When theology enters into a dialogue with other fields, thus, it appro-

---

48. Hans Frei, *Types of Christian Theology*, ed. George Hunsinger and William Placher (New Haven: Yale University Press, 1992).

priates their insights in an ad hoc manner. This means two things. First, the knowledge and methods of other fields are not appropriated as a system but in bits and pieces, just as we might take over words from another language without taking over the entire linguistic system (e.g., carousel, *différance*). Second, the knowledge of other fields is placed in the service of the distinctive task of theology: Christian self-description and evaluation. In several of his writings, for example, Frei draws on contemporary literary and hermeneutical theories.[49] But he does not allow such theories to provide theology with a systematic set of procedures or ordering concepts. These must be derived theologically. Where literary and hermeneutical theories are helpful to theology, they are used; where they are not, they are discarded. In other words, they are appropriated in an ad hoc way, not as a system.

A Transversal Model of Cross-Disciplinary Dialogue

This is the most recent model of theology's dialogue with other fields and is closely identified with the work of the philosophical theologian Wentzel van Huyssteen, who is influenced by Calvin Schrag's understanding of transversality.[50] The concept of transversality appeared simultaneously in a number of fields.[51] In mathematics it refers to a line's intersection of two or more lines or surfaces without achieving coincidence. Think of the way sticks touch and diverge in a game of pick-up-sticks. In physiology it is used to describe the networking of bands of fibers. In these disciplines and others, transversality means "lying across, extending over, intersecting, meeting and converging without achieving coincidence."[52]

---

49. Hans Frei, *The Eclipse of Biblical Narrative: A Study in Eighteenth and Nineteenth Century Hermeneutics* (New Haven: Yale University Press, 1974); Frei, *Theology and Narrative: Selected Essays,* ed. George Hunsinger and William Placher (New York: Oxford University Press, 1993); Frei, *The Identity of Jesus Christ: The Hermeneutical Basis of Dogmatic Theology* (Philadelphia: Fortress, 1975).

50. J. Wentzel van Huyssteen, *The Shaping of Rationality: Toward Interdisciplinarity in Theology and Science* (Grand Rapids: Eerdmans, 1999); van Huyssteen, *Alone in the World? Human Uniqueness in Science and Theology* (Grand Rapids: Eerdmans, 2006); Calvin Schrag, *The Resources of Rationality: A Response to the Postmodern Challenge* (Bloomington: Indiana University Press, 1992), chapter 6; Schrag, "Transversal Rationality," in *The Question of Hermeneutics,* ed. T. J. Stapleton (Dordrecht: Kluwer Academic, 1994).

51. Schrag, *The Resources of Rationality,* p. 148.

52. Schrag, *The Resources of Rationality,* p. 149.

Felix Guattari extends the root metaphor of transversality to dialogue in his description of the interaction of groups in psychiatric hospitals.[53] In such settings, power, decision making, and communication are situated in a network of groups: the treatment team, the patient's family, hospital administrators, physical or art therapists, and patients on the ward. All may contribute to the program and process of healing, but this depends on the degree of transversality in the communication of these groups. It is a matter of dialogue across this social network in various directions: between the treatment team and patient, the family and hospital administrators, patients and orderlies, etc. Communication flows downward, upward, and across the transversal networking of these groups. As Guattari puts it: "Transversality is a dimension that tries to overcome both the impasse of pure verticality and that of mere horizontality; it tends to be achieved when there is a maximum communication among the different levels and, above all, in different meanings."[54]

The transversal model of cross-disciplinary dialogue extends this picture of transversality to the conversation between members of different fields. This model pictures the relationship of the disciplines as an interacting network of different fields and contends that the human quest for intelligibility is strengthened by rational communication across this network (positive analogy). In a specific dialogue between the members of different fields, the values and perspectives of the conversation partners may overlap at points. A biblical scholar may share a common commitment to feminism with a dialogue partner in sociology. Yet, they may diverge sharply in their evaluations of religion and the ways they conduct research. Cross-disciplinary dialogue, thus, explores points of intersection and divergence at various levels (positive analogy). This sort of rational communication is possible because the members of different fields share common resources of rationality, in spite of their differences.[55] They use interpretive strategies, justify their claims through argumentation, and disclose truths that are fallible or subject to future reconsideration. These features are common to *all* forms of rationality. They make it possible for the members of different fields to engage in rational communication across disciplinary lines.

---

53. Schrag, *The Resources of Rationality,* pp. 153-54.

54. Quoted in Schrag, *The Resources of Rationality,* pp. 152-53.

55. The concept of the common resources is taken from Schrag and van Huyssteen, cited above.

Models of Cross-Disciplinary Dialogue

- *Correlational:* Mutual influence
  - method of correlation
  - revised method of correlation
  - revised praxis method of correlation

- *Transformational:* Distinct language worlds require transformation, not simple translation
  - Chalcedon
  - Ad hoc correlation

- *Transversal:* Intersection and divergence of disciplines that share resources of rationality

---

We gain further insight into this model by comparing it to those examined above. Unlike the transformational approach, the transversal model presupposes a more fluid and dynamic understanding of the relationship between the disciplines. Disciplines are not pictured as distinct language games but as networks that transverse one another and share the common resources of rationality. While this model has much in common with the correlational approach, it gives greater attention to the pluralism found in virtually every field today.[56] In light of this pluralism, cross-disciplinary dialogue must become more concrete than is typically the case in correlational models. It is not, for example, a matter of the field of theology entering into a conversation with the field of psychology. Rather, it is a matter of this particular theologian working in these specific ways entering into a conversation with that particular psychologist working in equally specific ways. Transversality, thus, is person- and perspective-specific. It explores areas of overlap and divergence in a concrete dialogue between particular people or perspectives.

56. In addition to the writings of Schrag and van Huyssteen, see also Wolfgang Welsch, *Vernunft: Die zeitgenössische Vernunftkritik und das Konzept der transversalen Vernunft* (Frankfurt: Suhrkamp, 1995). Some of Welsch's articles are now available in English at http://www2.uni-jena.de/welsch/start.html.

Toward the Pragmatic Task

In this chapter we have examined the normative task of practical theological interpretation and various models of cross-disciplinary dialogue. The conversation between theology and other fields is a part of *all* the tasks of practical theological interpretation. It was treated in the present chapter because the normative task poses the question of practical theology's relationship to other disciplines most clearly. Normative theological perspectives provide interpretive guides with help in determining what they ought to do. But they do not tell them how to move particular episodes, situations, and contexts toward desired ends. This is the pragmatic task of practical theological interpretation, to which we now turn.

CHAPTER 4

The Pragmatic Task:
Servant Leadership

———◦❀◦———

Between 1990 and 2000 the total membership of the Presbyterian
Church (USA) shrank by 411,769 people, a decline of 11.6 percent.[1]
This follows decades of declining membership since the 1960s, a trend also
found in other mainline Protestant denominations. During the same decade, the membership of the Episcopal Church declined by 5.3 percent, the
United Methodist Church by 6.7 percent, the Evangelical Lutheran Church
in America by 2.2 percent, and the United Church of Christ by 14.8 percent. While these statistics reflect relatively low birthrates and the natural
attrition of the death of older members, they also raise difficult questions.
Do they reflect a lack of congregational vitality in these denominations or
social trends far beyond the congregational level? Are they a sign of low-
commitment Christianity in dying denominations or of these denominations' willingness to tackle controversial social issues in an era when America has become increasingly conservative? Do the congregations of these
denominations remain nostalgic for the days of cultural power and influence, or have they begun to embrace their role in American culture as "mi-
nority" churches?

This chapter focuses on the pragmatic task of practical theological in-

1. The statistics cited here are drawn from a presentation by John Marcum, "Trends and
Changes in Mainline Denominations," at the annual meeting of the Religious Research Association, Salt Lake City, Utah, November 2002.

terpretation: the task of forming and enacting strategies of action that influence events in ways that are desirable. Practical theology often provides help by offering models of practice and rules of art. Models of practice offer leaders a general picture of the field in which they are acting and ways they might shape this field toward desired goals. Rules of art are more specific guidelines about how to carry out particular actions or practices. In light of the trends noted above, this chapter focuses on the pragmatic task of *leading change*. The leaders of mainline congregations face not only the external challenge of a changing social context, but also the internal challenge of helping their congregations rework their identity and mission beyond the era when they were at the center of cultural influence and power. We begin by exploring a model of leadership that is illustrated with a case study. We then place this model in a theology of servant leadership. We conclude by examining an open systems model of organization change and a case study that puts flesh and bones on the process of leading change in one concrete congregation.

Three Forms of Leadership

Let us begin by examining three forms of leadership commonly distinguished in leadership theories.[2] One is *task competence*. This is the ability to excel in performing the tasks of a leadership role in an organization. In most congregations, for example, leaders carry out tasks like teaching, preaching, running committees, leading worship, and visiting the sick. Carrying out these tasks with competence is an important part of leadership.

Transactional leadership is the ability to influence others through a process of trade-offs. It takes the form of reciprocity and mutual exchange: I will do this for you, and in return you will do that for me. In the leadership of organizations, this takes place in two basic ways: (1) meeting the needs of those involved in an organization in return for their contribution

---

2. The distinction between transactional and transforming leadership goes back to James M. Burns, *Leadership* (New York: Harper and Row, 1978). It has been widely developed by others. See Michael Hackman and Craig Johnson, *Leadership: A Communication Perspective* (Prospect Heights, Ill.: Waveland Press, 1996); W. Warner Burke, *Organization Change: Theory and Practice* (Thousand Oaks, Calif.: Sage, 2002), chapters 4, 9; Robert Quinn, *Deep Change: Discovering the Leader Within* (San Francisco: Jossey-Bass, 1996); Quinn, *Building the Bridge as You Walk on It* (San Francisco: Jossey-Bass, 2004).

to the organization, and (2) making political trade-offs to deal with competing agendas of different coalitions in an organization so it can best accomplish its purpose. In the business world this takes the form of a contract: meeting employees' financial needs in exchange for their work. In voluntary organizations, legal contracts may not be involved but reciprocal, contractlike exchanges are still made. Leaders gain support for the organization by responding to needs that will lead people to participate: the chance to give back to society, to make friends, or to become a part of a community where they are known and accepted. In congregations, leaders make these kinds of trade-offs in a variety of ways. They respond to the desire of parents to raise good children by offering quality educational programs and youth ministries. They meet the needs of people who are looking for a meaningful, face-to-face community by offering small-group ministries. In return, leaders hope members will support the congregation by giving money and volunteering their time.

Transactional leadership also involves political trade-offs. Leaders must deal with the competing agendas of different coalitions in their organization. In congregations these coalitions often become apparent when the budget is formed. Those people committed to the music program may ask for funding to hire musicians for special music at Easter or Christmas, while parents of youth may lobby for money to hire a full-time youth minister. Leaders must negotiate these competing agendas through compromise, persuasion, and trade-offs. The political dimension of transactional leadership, however, goes far beyond forming a budget. Different coalitions often have very different agendas for their congregation, including the activities and values it should support. Transactional leaders enter the fray and use their influence to help the congregation best accomplish its mission.

Transforming leadership involves "deep change," to borrow Robert Quinn's apt phrase.[3] It is leading an organization through a process in which its identity, mission, culture, and operating procedures are fundamentally altered. In a congregation this may involve changes in its worship, fellowship, outreach, and openness to new members who are different. It involves projecting a vision of what the congregation might become and mobilizing followers who are committed to this vision.

Leading deep change is costly and risky. Leaders must carry out the

---

3. Quinn, *Deep Change.*

Three Forms of Leadership

- *Task Competence:* Performing well the leadership tasks of a role in an organization.

- *Transactional Leadership:* Influencing others through a process of trade-offs.

- *Transforming Leadership:* Leading an organization through a process of "deep change" in its identity, mission, culture, and operating procedures.

"internal work" of discerning their own core values, as well as the "inner voice" of the organization they are leading.[4] They must confront their own hypocrisy in failing to embody the values they espouse and must alter their behavior to model with integrity the sorts of changes they would like to see in their organization. Such leadership also is costly and risky because it almost inevitably encounters resistance. The dominant coalition of an organization is especially likely to resist deep change, for it stands to lose power and control. Moreover, deep change is messy. It usually is not a linear process unfolding along the lines of a rational plan. As the organization moves through a period in which old patterns no longer work and new ones have not yet emerged, it often feels chaotic. Such times often are filled with conflict, failures, and dissatisfaction, as well as new vitality and experimentation. During such periods, transformational leaders must remain committed to their internal vision, even as they empower others to reshape their vision.

All three forms of leadership are needed in congregations. Pastors, teachers, committee chairs, and caregivers must be competent in carrying out their respective tasks. Congregations also need transactional leaders who are responsive to the needs that bring people to congregations and are willing to enter the political fray of competing agendas to enable different groups to work together. But today, especially in mainline congregations, it is transforming leadership that is most needed, leadership that can guide a congregation through a process of deep change.

4. Quinn, *Deep Change*, p. 201.

Bobo's Burial

A number of years ago I taught a course for students who had just completed yearlong internships in congregations between their second and third years of seminary. A particularly memorable case study written for this course illustrates the importance of the three forms of leadership described above.

Nancy Wilson grew up and attended college and seminary in the Southeast. She was pleased when she learned her internship was in the Midwest, in a blue-collar Presbyterian congregation of around 150 members in a small town about one hundred miles east of St. Louis. Indeed, she was so eager to explore another part of the country that when the pastor of her placement left the church less than three weeks before she was to begin, she decided to go anyway. As she put it: "I got to live in the manse for the entire year and experienced what it's like to preach every Sunday. I wouldn't trade my experience for anything, even after 'the incident.'"

"The incident" was the focus of her case study. It took place three months after she arrived. During her first months as pastor, she carried out a systematic plan of home visitation to get to know every family in the church. One family she became particularly fond of was a brother and sister, Harvey and Blanche. They were both in their late sixties and lived in the family house that they inherited after their mother died five years earlier. In a private conversation, Blanche shared with Nancy that Harvey had been hit by a car during childhood and had suffered brain damage, leaving him "slow," in Blanche's words. "It pretty much fell to me to take care of him, and mother too after her stroke," Blanche reported. Blanche was an elementary school teacher until her retirement several years earlier. She had never married.

The year before Nancy came to the church, Blanche had been diagnosed with breast cancer. She had a double mastectomy and extensive chemotherapy. During this period the church worked closely with a social worker to provide Harvey the support he needed to live at home while Blanche was hospitalized. By the time Nancy arrived on the scene, Blanche said she was "back to normal." She was in worship every Sunday and served as a Sunday school teacher and the leader of the women's circle. Blanche told Nancy about her health difficulties during her first visit and mentioned in passing that the hospitalization had left them $7,000 in debt, making it hard for them to get by on their fixed income.

During the weeks following this visit, Nancy quietly began spreading the word of Blanche and Harvey's situation among the leaders of the church. Drawing on the pastor's discretionary fund and money quietly raised by word of mouth, Nancy presented Blanche with a check for $2,500 a month later. "You should have seen the smile on her face," Nancy reported. "It was pure joy. After all she had done for others, people were actually doing something special for her."

Several weeks later, Nancy received a phone call from Blanche. She was in tears. "Bobo was just hit by a car. Will you come over tomorrow so we can bury him?" Bobo was the family dog and, in Nancy's view, was treated by Harvey and Blanche as "one of the family, as a kind of child." When she called the next day to set up a time to come over for Bobo's funeral, Blanche told her to meet them at two in the afternoon at Longview, the local cemetery, where they owned a family plot and their mother was buried. When Nancy arrived, a small group of friends were gathered around a freshly dug cemetery plot with a small, child's coffin ready to be lowered into the ground. Having never conducted a funeral of *any* sort, Nancy had decided to pretty much follow the funeral liturgy of the Presbyterian book of worship and offer a few comments about God's love for all of creation, including family pets. The funeral went smoothly as far as she could tell, and she returned with Blanche and Harvey to their home where they talked for a while.

When Nancy returned to the church manse late that afternoon, there were *ten* voice messages on the answering machine. Apparently, Blanche had thanked one of the church members attending the service for making it possible to give Bobo such a nice funeral. Nancy was later to learn that Blanche had spent a large portion of the money given to her by the church to prepare the burial site and purchase the casket. As word got around, Nancy was inundated with phone calls from angry church members. Nancy reported, "Pretty much the gist of all these calls was that the church had been 'used' and they never would have given money to help Harvey and Blanche if they had known it would be put to such a wasteful purpose." The church leaders who helped raise the money were receiving phone calls as well.

Pretty soon "Bobo's Burial," as it came to be known, was the talk of the town. "At first, I had this really deep sense of shame," Nancy reported. "I felt like I had let the church down. But when I started hearing the little jokes about us being 'the dog-burying church' and me being the 'pet-preacher,' I got mad. Did we really do such a bad thing in providing Harvey and Blanche financial support?"

What sort of leadership might Nancy offer in response to this episode? Certainly, *task competence* is important. In her description of this episode, Nancy called herself "green as a baby tree" when it took place. She had not even graduated from seminary and was flying solo in a church and region that were unfamiliar. She was inexperienced and just starting to develop competence in the tasks of ministry. Her classmates raised two issues of competence.

A number challenged the way Nancy had provided financial assistance to Harvey and Blanche. They wondered how wise it was to give money without the guidance of a church policy. As one person put it: "Of course, we want to be gracious in our love of people in need, but we ought to provide assistance that is genuinely helpful. What if they're using the money to buy drugs or alcohol?" Another student shared that the pastor of his intern church had a policy of never giving money directly to people who came to the church office or parsonage. He sent them to a local gas station or restaurant where the church had an account for this purpose. As the discussion unfolded, Nancy began to reconsider her actions. "Maybe I should have gotten the treasurer to write a check directly to the hospital," she conceded.

Nancy's classmates were quite supportive of her insight about the psychological importance of Bobo to Blanche. They also worried that Blanche might become marginalized and ridiculed in her own congregation and were eager to hear the steps Nancy took to make sure this did not happen. They framed this in terms of Nancy's ability to offer competent pastoral care to Harvey and Blanche and to help the church respond in a caring way.

Leadership in the form of task competence is important. It is necessary to solve problems like the one Nancy faced, as well as to perform well the ongoing tasks of ministry. But what if Nancy comes to believe that leading this congregation involves more? What if Bobo's Burial leads her to recognize fundamental problems in the culture, operating procedures, and mission of this congregation? What if she decided that it is not enough to solve the immediate crisis and restore the status quo? Likely, both transactional and transforming leadership will be needed if she initiates a process of change.

Admittedly, there are real constraints on Nancy's leadership. Yet, it is often only through the testing of limits that we are able to discern how constraining they really are. Nancy will be at the church for only a short time. Yet leaders often plant seeds of change that do not germinate until they are gone. What about Nancy's youth and inexperience? Without question, these are real obstacles to gaining the congregation's trust, especially in a small, family-like congregation in which pastors and newcomers often are perceived as outsiders. But it might be possible to turn this constraint to Nancy's advantage and use it to leverage more leadership from the people, not the pastor. What about the constraints of the size and resources of the church? How much change could Nancy really expect from a 150-member congregation with limited financial resources? Yet churches this size are the norm in most mainline Protestant denominations. Seventy percent of all Presbyterian churches have 200 or fewer members, for example, and the median size is 109 members. If change cannot take place in a congregation like the one Nancy is leading, then there can be no doubt that mainline denominations are on the road to slow death.

What strategies might Nancy have used to initiate a process of change? The first thing she would need is a better understanding of the crisis facing the congregation, which would clarify the primary target of change. As it turns out, Nancy had already begun to grasp this crisis. "In one of my first visits to an older member," she recalled, "she told me, 'They're going to have to close the doors of this church in about twenty years if something doesn't happen. I'm glad I won't be around to see it.' You know, the next time I stood in the pulpit and looked out at all the gray heads, I remembered that woman's words. They *would* be dead in twenty years if there wasn't some sort of renewal."

Bobo's Burial shocked Nancy enough to lead her to take a hard look at the congregation. She began to recognize deep-seated patterns in its culture. The former pastor had led the congregation for fifteen years and was a trusted member of this family-like congregation. Its members were very comfortable with a "wagon-wheel" pattern of leadership in which the pastor is at the center of all decision making, which radiates outward to others like the spokes of a wheel. It is little wonder that church leaders trusted the judgment of their inexperienced intern pastor when she asked them to raise money for Blanche and Harvey. They were used to deferring to the pastor in decision making.

If this congregation is to undergo a process of deep change, then this wagon-wheel style of leadership will need to be altered. If I had been Nancy's supervising pastor during her internship, I would have encouraged her to consider questions related to transactional and transforming leadership:

- How might she foster a sense of urgency about the need for change? Probably, the older woman quoted above is not the only person in the congregation worried about its long-term prospects.
- What sort of vision of a desired future might she help the congregation form? This vision must be both compelling and realizable.
- How might she turn her inexperience and embarrassment over Bobo's Burial to her advantage? She could probably use this episode as a way of encouraging others to take a more active role in leading the church and to trust their own judgment. She might use this tactic to initiate a process of empowering others.
- Where are the potential sources of new members and what does the church have to offer these members? What will it take for the congregation to transition from a family-like church to a welcoming church?
- What strategies might Nancy use to influence the congregation's vision of the pastor it will hire? If she is successful in helping its members begin to imagine an alternate future, then how might she guide them in imagining the sort of pastor who will travel with them toward this future?

A Spirituality of Servant Leadership

The distinction between task competence, transactional leadership, and transforming leadership provides us with a first language to think about leading change. Yet, it tells us very little about the *goal* of change: Change to what end and for what purpose? This is determined by reflection on the purpose of an organization and its ability to achieve this purpose in a particular setting. In the church, this involves theological reflection on several key questions: What is the mission of the congregation? How is this mission best carried out in a congregation's present context? What role do leaders play in guiding the congregation toward the fulfillment of its mission, and what changes might need to take place for this to occur?

Here I answer these questions by reflecting on Jesus as the embodiment of God's royal rule in the form of a servant. While Christ as the "suffering servant" of God is used in the New Testament to portray his priestly office, it is clear that this theme also is used to describe the nature of God's royal rule. Christ redefines the nature of power and authority by taking the form of a servant. He teaches his followers that servanthood is fundamental to the mission of the community of disciples and leadership within this community. When two of Jesus' disciples ask him to seat them at his right and left hands when he comes into his glory, Jesus replies: "You know that among the Gentiles those whom they recognize as their rulers lord it over them, and their great ones are tyrants over them. But it is not so among you; but whoever wishes to become great among you must be your servant, and whoever wishes to be first among you must be slave of all. For the Son of Man came not to be served but to serve, and to give his life a ransom for many" (Mark 10:42-45).

Kings in Israel

From the beginning there were dissenting voices in Israel when the people asked God to give them a king like the other nations (1 Sam. 8:4-7), and it is clear that kingship proved to be a mixed blessing in Israel. While the monarchies of David and Solomon ushered in an unprecedented period of prosperity, security, and "high" culture, it is equally clear that the centralization of power in court and temple gave rise to serious abuses from the start. We see a sign of things to come when David sends Uriah to his death because he desires his wife, Bathsheba, leading to a confrontation with the prophet Nathan (2 Sam. 12). Things quickly grow much worse under Solomon, the very epitome of the "wise" king and son of David and Bathsheba. To finance his program of expansion and building, Solomon reorganized the old tribal boundaries into twelve districts for the purpose of taxation and to consolidate his power. He initiated a program of slave labor, using the people Israel conquered. He even conscripted 30,000 Israelites to work on his projects, sending them to the labor camps one month out of every three (1 Kings 5:13-18). When Solomon died and the people demanded relief, his son Rehoboam told them their yoke would become even heavier under him (1 Kings 12). Eventually this led to civil war and the division of Israel into two kingdoms.

The people asked for a king like the other nations, and this is what they got. Yet amid the royal ideology used to legitimate the centralized power of court and temple, we can discern a theology of the ideal king, appointed by

God to ensure covenant fidelity in Israel and to see that justice is done. Psalm 72:1-2, 12-14 provides a nice example:

> Give the king your justice, O God,
>   and your righteousness to a king's son.
> May he judge your people with righteousness,
>   and your poor with justice. . . .
> For he delivers the needy when they call,
>   the poor and those who have no helper.
> He has pity on the weak and the needy,
>   and saves the lives of the needy.
> From oppression and violence he redeems their life;
>   and precious is their blood in his sight.

This sort of portrait of the ideal king later became a part of Isaiah's eschatological hope, God's promise of a time when a messianic king would rise to establish God's justice and righteousness among the people, seen here in Isaiah 9:6-7:

> For a child has been born for us,
>   a son given to us;
> authority rests upon his shoulders;
>   and he is named
> Wonderful Counselor, Mighty God,
>   Everlasting Father, Prince of Peace.
> His authority shall grow continually,
>   and there shall be endless peace
> for the throne of David and his kingdom.
>   He will establish and uphold it
> with justice and with righteousness
>   from this time onward and forevermore.

Jesus the Messiah: God's Royal Rule in the Form of a Servant

One of the most important innovations of New Testament Christology was the use of the suffering servant passages of Deutero-Isaiah (Isa. 40–55) to portray Jesus as the Messiah. These are found in Isaiah 42:1-4, 49:1-6, 50:4-9, and 52:13–53:12. As Donald Juel notes, pre-Christian Jewish traditions did not customarily view these passages as referring to the Messiah.[5] Likely, Christians were drawn to the Servant Songs to rethink traditional concepts of messiahship in light of Jesus' death and resurrection, portraying the Messiah as one who is humiliated and vindicated and who suffered vicariously on behalf of the people. Of special interest for our purposes is the way the imagery of the suffering servant is associated with God's royal rule as manifested in Jesus' messianic life and death. The cross is portrayed as a paradigm of Christ's faithfulness to God in carrying out his messianic vocation.[6] As the long-awaited Messiah who establishes God's reign in healing the sick, welcoming social outcasts, and calling for justice, Jesus encounters conflict and resistance from those in power. Yet he trusts and obeys God in representing God's royal rule, even to the point of death on the cross. This is not suffering for suffering's sake, but suffering as self-giving love in carrying out his messianic vocation. Jesus' disciples are told to take up their cross and follow him (Mark 8:34) and to join in the *koinonia*, or fellowship, of his suffering (Phil. 3:10). Power and authority within the community of disciples are to take the form of a servant like that of their Lord.

These themes are found throughout the New Testament; here we examine only the way they are treated in Mark and Paul. In Mark's narrative of Jesus, the "messianic secret" of Christ's true identity is only gradually disclosed. During the first part of Mark's Gospel, Jesus is portrayed as a miracle-worker, virtually indistinguishable from other such figures in his world. But as the story unfolds, the miracles are less prominent, the conflict intensifies, and Jesus tells his disciples three times that he must suffer and die. Each time he tells them of his impending suffering, they do not really comprehend what this means. Only with his death and resurrection do they finally begin to understand the meaning of his suffering and death as a ransom "for many" and as sealing a new covenant with God (14:22-24). This transforms their understanding of discipleship. Reflecting on Mark, Richard Hays writes: "The *norm* for discipleship is defined by the cross. Jesus' own obedience, interpreted as servanthood (10:45), is the singular pattern for faithfulness."[7]

5. Donald Juel, *Messianic Exegesis: Christological Interpretation of the Old Testament in Early Christianity* (Philadelphia: Fortress, 1988), chapter 5.

6. Richard Hays, *The Moral Vision of the New Testament: A Contemporary Introduction to New Testament Ethics* (San Francisco: HarperSanFrancisco, 1996), p. 197.

7. Hays, *Moral Vision*, p. 84.

Paul's theology of the cross offers one of the most profound interpretations in the New Testament of Christ's suffering and death and its meaning for the community of Christ's followers. One of the most important passages in which this theology comes to expression is Philippians 2:6-11, where Paul draws on the Servant Songs of Deutero-Isaiah to portray the nature of God's royal rule.[8] Richard Bauckham argues that this passage presupposes the broader context of Isaiah 40–55, which offers Isaiah's vision of a new, eschatological exodus in which God will act to redeem Israel in the sight of the nations and for the sake of the nations.[9] Paul, in effect, portrays Christ as the fulfillment of this eschatological salvation in the form of the suffering servant and as creating a new community of Jews and Gentiles, which signals the beginning of the gathering of the nations. Bauckham points to some of the connections between Philippians 2:6-11 and Deutero-Isaiah as follows:[10]

Philippians 2:6-11	**Isaiah 52–53; 45**
[Christ Jesus], though he was in the form of God, did not regard equality with God as something to be used for his advantage but	
poured himself out,	53:12: because he poured himself out
taking the *form* of a slave,	
being born in human *likeness*	(52:14; 53:2: form . . . appearance)
and being found in human *form,*	
he *humiliated* himself	(53:7: he was brought low)

---

8. I follow here the interpretation of this passage by Richard Bauckham, *God Crucified: Monotheism and Christology in the New Testament* (London: Paternoster Press, 1998), chapter 3, as well as that of Richard Hays, *Moral Vision*, pp. 28-31, and Gordon Fee, *Philippians*, IVP New Testament Commentary Series (Downers Grove, Ill.: InterVarsity, 1999), pp. 83-112. Interpretation of this passage is much debated. N. T. Wright and James Dunn, for example, interpret it as expressing an Adam Christology, not a servant Christology. See N. T. Wright, *The Climax of the Covenant: Christ and the Law in Pauline Theology* (Minneapolis: Fortress, 1991), chapter 4; James Dunn, *The Theology of Paul the Apostle* (Grand Rapids: Eerdmans, 1998), pp. 281-88.

9. Bauckham argues persuasively that this material was widely used in the Christian community to bring Hebrew Scripture and the history of Jesus into a relationship of mutual interpretation. In addition to the Philippians passage, he also examines the use of this material in Revelation and John. See *God Crucified*, chapter 3.

10. Bauckham, *God Crucified*, p. 59.

becoming obedient to *the point of accepting death* — even death on a cross.	53:12: . . . to death
Therefore also God *exalted him to the highest place* and conferred on him the Name that is above every name,	53:12: Therefore . . . 52:13: he shall be exalted and lifted up and shall be very high.
so that at the name of Jesus *every knee should bend,* in heaven and on earth and under the earth, *and every tongue should acknowledge* that Jesus Christ is Lord, to the glory of God the Father.	45:22-23: Turn to me and be saved, all the ends of the earth! For I am God, and there is no other. By myself I have sworn, from my mouth has gone forth in righteousness a word that shall not return: "To me every knee shall bow, every tongue shall swear."

We might interpret this passage along the following lines.[11] The preexistent Christ did not understand his equality with God as something to be used for his own advantage. Rather he entered fully into the human condition and gave expression to God's self-giving love in the form of service, obedience, and self-humiliation for others, even to the point of a particularly shameful death. Therefore, he is exalted and lifted up by God, sharing in God's sovereignty over all things and receiving the divine Name and the worship of creation. Divine sovereignty and servanthood are closely related in this passage. As Bauckham puts it: "Paul is reading Deutero-Isaiah to mean that the career of the Servant of the Lord, his suffering, humiliation, death and exaltation, is the way in which the sovereignty of the one true God comes to be acknowledged by all the nations."[12] This entails two things. The Lord is a servant. God rules in the form of self-giving love. The Servant is Lord. The one who came in the form of a servant now shares in God's sovereignty. Indeed, he is now described in ways that are *exclusive* to God in Deutero-Isaiah (i.e., as possessing the divine Name and as worthy of worship by creation).

11. See, particularly, Bauckham, *God Crucified*, pp. 57-58; Fee, *Philippians*, pp. 89-102; Hays, *Moral Vision*, pp. 28-31.

12. Bauckham, *God Crucified*, p. 59.

Throughout Philippians Paul appeals to this portrait of God's royal rule in the form of a servant to describe the life of the community of Christ's followers. Two times he points to his own participation in Christ's suffering as an example for the Philippians to imitate, just as he imitates Christ. Through the hardship of his imprisonment the gospel has advanced (1:7, 12); though he had the standing of a pious Jew, he gave up this status to serve the gospel of Christ (2:2-11). Imitating this pattern, the Philippians are to stand firm in the face of their own persecution for the sake of the gospel (1:27-30; 2:17) and are to set aside their petty bickering and seek, not their own advantage, but unity and mutual love in their relationships with one another (2:14; 2:2-4). In this way they participate in the One who rules in the form of a servant.

Paul's use of the Servant Songs of Isaiah to portray Christ's royal rule represents nothing less than a reversal of the way power is conventionally understood. Power is not a matter of resources, might, or status. Nor is it a matter of wielding influence for one's own advantage. Rather, power preeminently is self-giving love in which the needs of others and the community take precedence. It is a matter of love that is willing to suffer with and for others. This reversal of conventional notions of power is found throughout Paul's letters. Paul portrays the members of congregations as *incorporated* into Christ's death in their baptisms and as called to *imitate* Christ's self-giving love in their relationships with one another and their neighbors. Here I call attention to three ways Paul uses the reversal of power in servanthood as a norm for his congregations.

First, congregations are to be characterized by relationships of mutual care and service, which build up the body. We might call this "one-anothering," for Paul commonly describes the mutuality of this sort of community in terms of the way people care for, serve, comfort, build up, and are at peace with *one another*. Those with power and social status are to voluntarily subordinate their "rights" to the needs of "the weak," just as Paul does in renouncing his "right" to financial support by his congregations (Rom. 15:1-3; 1 Cor. 8:1–11:1). Paul uses the norm of mutual love to criticize spiritual pride, which "puffs up" those who view themselves as spiritually advanced, and factionalism in which groups seek their own advantage in the church.

Second, the Christian community is not to reduplicate the hierarchies of power and social status found in the surrounding culture because its oneness comes from Christ. This is perhaps best expressed in a baptismal formula used in Paul's churches: "There is no longer Jew or Greek, there is no longer slave or free, there is no longer male and female; for all of you are one in Christ Jesus" (Gal. 3:28; cf. 1 Cor. 12:13; Col. 3:9-11).[13] One of the more remarkable aspects of many of Paul's churches was the way they transgressed the social boundaries of Greco-Roman culture by bringing together people from these groups and knitting them together in a new "family" in which they related to each other with mutuality and equality on a regular basis. In these communities, leadership and ministries were not apportioned along the lines of conventional social roles but by the one Spirit to build up the one body. Paul draws on the norm of the oneness of the community in Christ to criticize congregations that allow status and power hierarchies of the surrounding culture to creep into the church.[14] For example, he criticizes the Corinthian community because it is giving the best seats at the fellowship meal preceding the Lord's Supper to those with the greatest social status (1 Cor. 11:17-28). He also criticizes this community because believers are taking fellow believers to court, taking advantage of a judicial system biased in favor of those with wealth and social status (6:1-11).

Third, Paul teaches his congregations that they are to reject power in the form of violence and retribution and, rather, are to practice nonviolent love. In Romans 12:14-21 he echoes Jesus' teaching about nonviolent love in the Sermon on the Mount. Paul primarily has in mind Christians' relationships with their neighbors. They are to resist the reciprocity of power found in the surrounding culture: if your neighbor does you harm, then you are to reciprocate in kind, doing your neighbor harm in return. The cycles of violence and revenge this sort of reciprocity of power sets in motion were ever present in Paul's world, as they are in our own. In contrast, Christians are to leave vengeance to God (v. 19). They are to bless (v. 14), empathize with (v. 15), and meet the needs (v. 20) of those who do them harm. Such actions will heap "burning coals" on the heads of their enemies and may even transform a relationship of antagonism into one of

13. For discussion of this verse as a baptismal formula, see J. Louis Martyn, *Galatians*, Anchor Bible (New York: Doubleday, 1997), pp. 373-83; Donald Juel, "Multicultural Worship: A Pauline Perspective," in *Making Room at the Table: An Invitation to Multicultural Worship*, ed. Brian Blount and Leonora Tubbs Tisdale (Louisville: Westminster John Knox, 2000), pp. 42-59.

14. For interpretation of the relevant passages, see Richard Hays, *First Corinthians*, Interpretation (Louisville: Westminster John Knox, 1997).

mutual respect. In this way the Christian community gives visible expression to the self-giving love of Christ, who exercised God's royal rule in the form of a servant.

Many other parts of the New Testament portray Christ's power and authority with the imagery of the suffering servant.[15] But enough has been said to make my basic point. God's sovereign, royal rule takes the form of self-giving love in Christ. The Lord is a servant, and the Servant is the Lord. Power and authority are redefined. A reversal takes place. Power as domination, or power over, becomes power as mutual care and self-giving. Power as seeking one's own advantage becomes power as seeking the good of others and the common good of the community.

Theologians have offered two helpful concepts to describe congregations that embody this reversal of power and authority: the church as a contrast society and as a catalyst of social transformation.[16] As a *contrast society*, congregations embody in their internal relationships and their relations with their neighbors an alternative to power and authority as conventionally practiced in the world. Domination, violence, and advantage seeking are not true power. God's power takes the form of a servant who embodies self-giving, suffering love. A congregation that takes the form of a servant represents an alternative to the ways of the world. It opens up a new set of possibilities that may have a *catalytic* effect, evoking social transformation. Conflicts do not have to be resolved with violence. Well-being is not gained by pressing one's own advantage. Security is not achieved through domination. There is no certainty that congregations will be able to influence their local and national communities in the direction of these alternatives. But it is certain that these alternative possibilities are unlikely to even arise unless congregations first give them visible expression in their own lives and their relations with their neighbors. As a contrast society, they serve as a sign and

15. One thinks of John's description of Jesus washing the feet of his disciples and the way he links the "lifting up" of Christ on the cross to the disclosure of God's glory. One also thinks of Revelation's description of Christ in the throne room of God as the slaughtered Lamb.

16. The concept of the church as a contrast society is found in Gerhard Lohfink, *Jesus and Community: The Social Dimension of Christian Faith* (Philadelphia: Fortress, 1984). Jürgen Moltmann draws on Lohfink's work and adds the concept of the church as a catalyst of social transformation in *The Church in the Power of the Spirit: A Contribution to Messianic Ecclesiology* (New York: Harper and Row, 1977), chapters 3, 4.

witness to God's royal rule in the form of a servant. As a catalyst of social transformation, they serve as a sign and witness to the possibilities of new creation, which anticipates provisionally the consummation of God's royal rule.

Servant Leadership

In this portrait of a congregation as a contrast society and catalyst of social transformation, we find the answer to questions raised earlier: If the leaders of mainline congregations face the challenge of leading change, what is the goal of that change, to what end and purpose is the change? What is the mission of the church? Mainline congregations can be on the road to slow death, or they can form a new understanding of their mission. Paradoxically, losing their power and influence represents a chance to gain a more biblical and authentic understanding of true power and influence. They are not to yearn nostalgically for the time when they were at the center of power and authority but to change in ways that more fully embody the reversal of power and authority found in their servant Lord. Their ability to influence the direction of their local community and nation will come not from their social status and resources but from their ability to hold up an alternative set of possibilities, which may have the effect of catalyzing social transformation.

It is best, thus, to think of servant leadership in the following way: *Servant leadership is leadership that influences the congregation to change in ways that more fully embody the servanthood of Christ.* It is not primarily a matter of personality traits, like being self-effacing, mild-mannered, or overly responsible. To the contrary, leading a congregation to change in ways that more nearly approximate its mission as a contrast society and social catalyst will take courage, resolve, and the ability to empower others. While servant leadership may involve suffering, this is *not* suffering for suffering's sake. It is suffering in the pursuit of one's calling, or vocation, suffering in the face of conflict and resistance. To gain practical guidance in imagining what servant leadership actually involves, let us return to the three forms of leadership described in the first part of this chapter. What do task competence, transactional leadership, and transforming leadership look like when they are forms of servant leadership? These may be conceptualized along the lines of a continuum:

A Spirituality of Servant Leadership

Task competence
informed by
humility

——————————————————

Transforming
leadership as leading
deep change

Transactional leadership
as meeting "deepest needs"
and boundary crossing

Task Competence and Humility

Acquiring task competence takes commitment, hard work, and experience. There is no other way to develop expertise in the tasks of ministry. Yet task competence in the service of leading change requires more than these things. It requires humility. Humility is not to be mistaken for false modesty or being meek and mild. Rather, it is the virtue of a contrast society in which power and authority are viewed along the lines of Christ's self-giving love. As Gordon Fee points out: "*Humility* is a uniquely Christian virtue, which, like the message of a crucified Messiah, stands in utter contradiction to the values of the Greco-Roman world, which generally considered humility not a virtue but a shortcoming."[17]

The roots of true humility are found in Hebrew Scripture's understanding of "creatureliness." As Fee puts it, "It has to do with a proper estimation of oneself, the stance of the creature before the Creator, utterly dependent and trusting. Here one is well aware both of one's weaknesses and of one's glory (we are in God's image, after all) but makes neither too much nor too little of either."[18] Considered from the perspective of Christ's servanthood, humility goes even further. It involves treating the needs of others and the common good of the community as having a claim on one's conduct.[19]

Task competence pursued with humility entails two things. First, it involves allowing the concrete needs of those in the community and the

17. Fee, *Philippians*, p. 88.
18. Fee, *Philippians*, p. 88.
19. While many passages in the New Testament portray humility as leading Christians to consider the needs of others as *greater* than their own, this is qualified by the themes of mutual subordination and "one-anothering" in which mutuality receives greater emphasis. Humility, thus, is not seeking one's own advantage or prerogatives to the exclusion of the needs of others or the well-being of the community.

well-being of the community as a whole to influence the competencies leaders develop. Often the process of leading change involves learning new skill sets that stretch leaders beyond their comfort zones. In humility, leaders consider what the community needs, not just what they do well already or might like to do. Second, it involves acknowledging their creatureliness, as described by Fee. All leaders have limitations. They can do important things in leading change, but they cannot do everything. In humility they will need to rely on others. In part, this is because they have particular strengths and weaknesses as leaders. They need to form a realistic understanding of their competencies as well as their limitations.

Transactional Leadership: Persuasion and Boundary Crossing

Transactional leadership, we can recall, has to do with making trade-offs of two sorts: (1) leaders strive to make the congregation a place where the needs of people are met in return for their support and participation, and (2) leaders enter the political fray of competing agendas of different coalitions in order to help the congregation accomplish its mission. How are these two dimensions of transactional leadership handled by servant leaders committed to the vision of the congregation as a contrast society and catalyst of social transformation? On the surface it would seem that the contract-like logic of trade-offs would have no place in this kind of congregation. This is too simple. What is needed is a shift from the model of contract-as-fair-exchange to the model of covenant-as-service-of-God.

How does this alter the transactional task of meeting needs in return for support and participation? Servant leaders strive to make their congregations responsive to the needs of others. But they distinguish between people's felt needs and their "deepest" needs. Felt needs are shaped by the society in which people live. Many people today, for example, experience the bureaucratic institutions of their work, health care, insurance, schools, and government as impersonal and alienating. They long for a community in which people know each other by name and relate in personal ways. This sort of felt need is real, and servant leaders will do well to help their congregations respond to such needs. But they go further. Felt needs are not necessarily people's "deepest" needs. Time and time again Jesus reframed the needs and questions people brought to him in order to point them to the deeper needs of their life in relation to God: Master, what must I do to inherit eternal life? Shouldn't we stone this adulterous woman to protect the moral sanctity of the people? In the same way, servant leaders are responsive to the felt needs that bring people to their congregations. But they also help such people recognize their "deeper" needs as participants in a covenant community whose mission is to give witness to God's self-giving love. They do so in two especially important ways.

First, they offer members a path of discipleship in which the needs of others gradually become as important as their own. The logic goes something like this: Just as we are a community that is responsive to your needs, you, as a member of this community, are now to respond to the needs of others. Self-concern is not your deepest need. Rather, you will find yourself as you lose yourself in caring for others.

Second, servant leaders guide their congregations toward caring for the needs of people who are different from themselves. Jesus was constantly crossing social boundaries to bring God's love to those who were not among the "good people" of Israel: the sick, the marginalized, the poor, and even the corrupt like Zacchaeus. Early Christian communities gave witness to this sort of boundary crossing by bringing together people with radically different social standing in the Greco-Roman world: slave and free, men and women, Greeks and Jews, and rich and poor. It is precisely at this point that the congregation as a contrast society breaks with the logic of contractual exchange and becomes a covenant community based on its oneness in Christ Jesus. When transactional leadership takes the form of contractual exchange, then members think of the purpose of the church as meeting the needs of people "like us." As long as the church meets *our* needs, we will give it our support. Little regard is given to the needs of others in very different social circumstances. A covenant community, in contrast, crosses over to the needs of others. With joy and thanksgiving they receive the gift of God's self-giving love. And in return, they offer this love to others by welcoming and serving those who are different from themselves.

What about the political dimensions of transactional leadership? How do servant leaders handle this? Surely they will not allow themselves to get caught up in political maneuvering and trade-offs. Paul provides us with guidance in answering these questions. Most of the time he used the "political clout" of his apostolic authority in the form of *persuasion*.[20] One of

20. There are times when Paul exercises his authority more directly, as with the member of the Corinthian community living in a sexual relationship with his stepmother (1 Cor. 5:1-13). Paul tells the Corinthians directly what they are to do. They are to expel this individ-

the best examples is the way he handled the meat-eating controversy in 1 Corinthians 8–10. The issue of eating meat sacrificed to idols was highly controversial in the early Christian community, comparable to the divisiveness of many contemporary churches over gay and lesbian issues. Paul handles this issue by articulating the perspectives of all parties in the dispute, the "weak" and the "strong." He attempts to persuade the congregation to adopt a position in which individuals are free to follow the dictates of their consciences, as long as they take account of the needs of other parties in the debate. In other words, Paul does not remain aloof from the political fray. He enters into it and attempts to persuade all sides to resolve this issue along the lines of mutual love, not seeking their own advantage.

Transforming Leadership and the Fellowship of Christ's Suffering

Transforming leadership, we can recall, is leading a congregation through a process of deep change. Fundamental alterations of its identity, culture, operating procedures, and mission occur. Transforming leadership is the sort of leadership most needed in mainline congregations today. Such leadership is costly and risky. It will encounter resistance and conflict, failures and disappointments. But leaders who give themselves to this sort of leadership come closest to the sort of servant leadership found in Jesus. Like Christ, they will suffer the hardships of leading their congregations to become the sorts of communities God wants them to be. They will enter into the fellowship of Christ's suffering. Here I draw attention to three paradoxes of their suffering with and for Christ.

You Will Find Your Way Only by Getting Lost   At various points in this book I have used the analogy of maps to describe the tasks of practical

---

ual from the church in the hope that he will change his conduct and, thereby, be saved (v. 5). This sort of direct assertion of authority is rare in Paul's letters and should be even rarer among contemporary leaders. Yet, there may be times when conflict and resistance to change are so egregious that leaders must directly intervene to bring them to an end. Suppose the church has begun to welcome into the community people of other races, cultures, sexual orientations, or classes, and certain members refer to them with slurs like "white trash," "wetbacks," and worse. Such conduct must be confronted directly and the authority of leaders asserted. When this occurs, such people often leave the congregation, and leaders can only hope, like Paul, that this will lead to a change of heart.

theological interpretation. Particularly in chapter 2, I described the importance of relying on theoretical maps to interpret particular episodes, situations, and contexts. Lacking such maps, congregational leaders are likely to become "Lost, No Map, Inadequate Clothing," as the headline from chapter 2 summarized it. Without taking back this affirmation of thoughtful, informed leadership, I now want to underscore the inadequacy of such maps in the actual process of leading deep change. Pragmatically, the challenge leaders face is journeying into unknown territory. Indeed, unless they are willing to get lost, they will never find their way. Why is this the case?

Most basically, it is because deep change is discontinuous with the past. Old maps that may have worked well in other churches, prior eras, or earlier stages of life cannot provide guidance through unknown territory. Finding your way involves traveling down one path only to find it blocked and then doubling back to move in a different direction. It is a matter of not really knowing the way ahead, taking risks, and getting lost — yet continuing to venture into the unknown. For many leaders the experience of "not knowing" and loss of control will be threatening. It is a genuine experience of powerlessness. It calls for the sort of faithfulness to God found in Christ. Trusting God in the midst of "not knowing" is a key part of the spirituality of servant leaders.

You Will Gain Power by Empowering Others   Deep change usually begins on the margins of a congregation and only gradually becomes an accepted goal as people see the need for change and are empowered to shape the sorts of changes that will occur. Transforming leaders, thus, must be willing to suffer the risks of marginalization. Often this occurs because a dominant coalition in the congregation holds great power in defining its "organizational reality" and resists the possibility that things might be done differently. Chris Argyris describes such coalitions as maintaining assumptions that are "undiscussable."[21] These assumptions are woven so deeply into the current life of an organization that to bring them up is to risk a negative reaction by others or to appear crazy and stupid. Deep change involves confronting the undiscussable and risking the marginalization this may entail. It often originates in a position of relative powerlessness.

21. Chris Argyris, *Increasing Leadership Effectiveness* (New York: Wiley, 1976), p. 16.

Change initiatives are likely to remain on the margins of a congregation unless leaders convince others of the need for change and empower them to shape this process. Servant leaders do not make themselves the center of change. Rather, they give power away. Jesus worked intensively with a small group of disciples who later were pivotal in spreading the gospel and offering leadership in the early Christian community. So too, Paul stayed with new congregations for a short time to train local leaders and then left. This is the way power works in servant leadership. Leaders gain power by empowering others. This too is a key dimension of the spirituality of servant leaders.

The Less You Are Attached to the Congregation, the Deeper Your Relationships   What do I mean by "attached" here? This is key. I am using attachment in ways that resemble Gerald May's discussion of this concept.[22] I have in mind leaders' dependence on the congregation for personal affirmation, security, and self-worth, as well as for professional achievement and power. Such attachment can have an addictive quality, creating forms of dependence that disable leaders' ability to think for themselves or risk conflict. Congregational leaders who are attached to their congregations in this way are displacing their longing for God, who alone is the ultimate source of their affirmation, security, and worth, on to a community that, in the end, will not be able to fully meet these needs.

Transforming leaders cannot be attached to their congregations in this way. Why? One reason is that deep change almost inevitably provokes conflict and resistance. Leaders who depend on their congregations for personal affirmation and professional status cannot endure the trials and tribulations of deep change. Their decisions and actions are often driven by fear, personal needs, or the desire for professional success. They are not

---

22. See Gerald May's description of attachment in *Addiction and Grace: Love and Spirituality in the Healing of Addictions* (San Francisco: Harper and Row, 1988). While human beings are created for love, May contends, they "displace" their "longing for God on to objects of attachment" (p. 92). Such attachment has an addictive quality. As May puts it: "Addiction exists wherever persons are internally compelled to give energy to things that are not their true desires. . . . *Attachment,* then, is the process that enslaves desire and creates the state of addiction" (p. 14). He illustrates this claim with security addictions, in which human beings search compulsively for security in possessions, power, human relationships, and, today we might add, military and surveillance systems (pp. 31-36). Attachment to such things is every bit as powerful as addiction to alcohol.

based on what needs to take place for the congregation to fulfill its mission as God's people. In the face of conflict and resistance, servant leaders hold fast to the vision and values that motivated them to initiate the process of change, even when receiving negative feedback from others. This does *not* mean that transforming leaders are stubborn, close-minded, and cut off from others. Paradoxically, the opposite is often the case. As they empower others to join them in the process of change, new energies are released and relationships formed. People are free to challenge one another as well as support one another. Mutual commitment and care often emerge. At their best, relationships among those leading change model for the congregation the sort of community it might become. Attachment gives way to "one-anothering." This too is a dimension of the spirituality of servant leaders.

Organization Change: An Open Systems Model

To this point, we have focused primarily on the role of leadership in initiating change. What about the congregation as a whole? How does change take place in a community? Moreover, our focus has primarily been on the internal life of the congregation, building it up as a contrast society that is faithful to its mission as God's people. What about the church's role as a catalyst of social transformation? We find help in answering these questions in the literature of organization change, which is engaged here as an interdisciplinary dialogue partner. I give special attention to theories that portray organizations as open systems.

Open Systems Theory: An Overview

Open systems theory is part of a family of theories in the "new synthesis" of the life sciences based on the concept of the web of life. It portrays living organisms as open systems that interact with their external environments in order to survive. "Open," thus, indicates the way all forms of life are dependent on and in continual interaction with the environment in which they reside. They draw energy and resources from the environment, transform them to maintain themselves, and turn them into output. "System" indicates the interconnection of the various parts, or subsystems, within the boundaries of the life-form. While the parts of the human body, for example, are highly differentiated and specialized, they work together in an integrated fashion and are connected by feedback loops. This internal system, in turn, is connected to feedback loops between the organism and its environment, which are guided by a mechanism of knowing that allows the organism to respond selectively to the environment. When internal and external feedback are aligned, the organism maintains a state of homeostasis, or equilibrium, in its interactions with its context. Equilibrium can be disrupted in one of two ways. Internal subsystems can fall out of alignment with one another. When cancer invades a vital organ in the body and it can no longer carry out its function, the entire system enters a state of disequilibrium. This also can occur when the organism's relationship with its context becomes misaligned. Because of a drought, it can no longer procure food resources; a new species has migrated to its context, which preys on its young. Thus far we have used individual life-forms as an example of open systems. But individual life-forms are nestled within other systems. Most mammals, for example, form systems for reproduction, protection, and food gathering. These systems, in turn, are nestled in other natural and social systems, which make up the web of life.

When open systems theory is applied to organizations, attention is given to the internal system of the organization, composed of interrelated subsystems, and the organization's interaction with its context, composed of other systems with which it exchanges resources. Here, too, change may be provoked by internal or external factors. Internal subsystems may grow out of alignment with one another, creating the need for change. A new preacher, for example, may have altered the worship service, making it more informal and using contemporary music. Many younger families with children have been attracted to the church as a result. But the educational subsystem is out of alignment with these changes in the worship service. Its allocation of space and recruitment of teachers cannot handle the influx of children in the church school. Internal change in one part of the congregational system, thus, has created a crisis for another subsystem. This misalignment has temporarily thrown the system into a state of disequilibrium. It must develop new structures and feedback loops before a new state of equilibrium is achieved.

Change in the organization also may be due to external factors, provoked by changes taking place in the systems with which it exchanges resources. For example, a congregation may be located in a small town in which all the manufacturing plants have closed down over the past decade, their work shipped abroad. This has left few good jobs for workers, and consequently many of the young people in the community have moved away to find work. As the financial and human resources of the community have declined, the congregation has declined as well. As a system nestled within other systems, it must discern how it will cope with these changes in the economic systems of its local context, nestled within changes in the global economic system.

Open systems theory supplements our focus on leadership in the first part of this chapter. It situates leadership within the congregation as an organizational system, composed of subsystems and interacting with other systems in its environment. It offers a model of change that takes account of factors internal and external to the organization, as well as their interaction. An open systems perspective on congregations provides insight into a number of issues. Here I focus on only three, posed in the form of questions facing leaders of congregational change.

What vision of congregational change best captures the mission of the congregation in its particular context?

Open systems theory encourages congregational leaders to think contextually.[23] If congregations are organizational systems interacting with other systems, then the congregation's mission will take concrete shape in relation to its context. A key part of leading change is forming a vision of what the congregation might become, what it would look like if it carried out its mission in contextually relevant ways. Throughout this book, context has been used flexibly, referring to local, regional, national, and international systems with which the congregation interacts. Congregations, thus, may form a vision of what they would like to become, oriented to micro- or macrocontexts. They may be deeply concerned about the impact of the global economic system on Africa and develop partnerships with congregations in that part of the world to provide resources for education and health care and to alleviate poverty. Or they may direct their attention to their local context, responding to similar issues. Congregations with strong missional orientations often respond to micro- and macrocontexts simultaneously.

Leading a congregation toward this sort of mission requires forming

---

23. For a helpful overview of different approaches to contextual theological thinking, see Stephen Bevans, *Models of Contextual Theology* (Maryknoll, N.Y.: Orbis, 1992).

and communicating a vision of what the community might become, a vision that is both compelling and realizable. This requires *both* contextual thinking *and* systemic thinking. Leaders often focus more on the former than on the latter. This will be apparent in the case study that follows. It describes leadership that helped a congregation change from an inward-looking, Sunday-morning congregation to one committed to serving the needs of its urban context. It is a profound and inspiring example of congregational change. Underdeveloped in this case, however, are systemic forms of thinking. By this I mean reflection on the systemic causes of particular problems. It is important for congregations to provide financial assistance to those in need, but it also is important for them to reflect on the economic, educational, and social systems that are contributing to poverty. Offering a helping hand and advocating justice should go hand in hand. As you read the case study that follows, consider some of the ways the leaders might have attended to systemic thinking in the change process.

What sort of process of change is needed in my congregation: revolutionary or evolutionary change?

Organization change theory commonly distinguishes two patterns of change: revolutionary and evolutionary.[24] Both can result in deep change in the congregational system. Connie Gersick describes *revolutionary* change in organizations with the concept of punctuated equilibrium. This includes three basic ideas.[25] First, all organizations possess a *"deep structure,"* the interconnected subsystems of the organization and the way it relates to the environment. Second, this deep structure is maintained during *equilibrium periods.* Third, *revolutionary periods* occur when this equilibrium is punctuated and the deep structure of an organization is altered. This is experienced as a major jolt to the system and involves significant and rapid change. Old structures collapse; new groups and leaders come into power; the identity and operating procedures change in visible ways. Revolutionary change, thus, typically involves a major crisis in an organization and is marked by a clear transition from "before" to "after."

In contrast, *evolutionary change* is incremental. It usually begins with alterations in a subsystem of an organization, creating small changes that

24. Burke, *Organization Change,* chapter 4.

25. Connie Gersick, "Revolutionary Change Theories: A Multilevel Exploration of the Punctuated Equilibrium Paradigm," *Academy of Management Review* 16, no. 1 (1991): 10-36. This is summarized in Burke, *Organization Change,* pp. 64-67.

are continuous with the past, which build on, improve, and modify the current system. Evolutionary change often does not result in deep change. Yet a number of organization theorists argue that it has the potential to do so. Karl Weick and Robert Quinn summarize this perspective as "the idea that small continuous adjustments created simultaneously across units, can cumulate and create substantial change. That scenario presumes tightly coupled interdependencies."[26]

"Tightly coupled interdependencies" refers to a high degree of inter-action and influence across the subsystems of an organization. Changes in one part of the system necessarily reverberate throughout the whole. This often is *not* the case in congregational systems. The youth group, likely, is not "tightly coupled" with the church council. Changes in one do not necessarily influence the other. Incremental changes in congregations, thus, often remain confined to the subsystem in which they occur. But this is not always the case. Leaders may work to diffuse innovation in one subsystem to other subsystems, eventually impacting the congregational system as a whole. The leaders of a congregation with which I am familiar decided to change its formal and distant culture to one of greater sharing and intimacy. They started by making all new members classes a small-group experience. They then started a small-group ministry in the congregation and hired a staff person to lead this. When people rotated off committees, they did their best to have them replaced by people participating in a small group. They trained and empowered leaders to alter the operating procedures of committees to include times of sharing and prayer. Over time, innovation in one subsystem was diffused to the whole.

Deep change, thus, can follow the paths of revolution or evolution. One of the questions leaders face, thus, is which of these paths will work best in their particular congregation. Does the system need a major jolt? Or can small, incremental changes in one subsystem impact the entire congregation over time? As you read the case study that follows, ask yourself which of these patterns best captures the way change took place in this particular congregation.

How might I support change at different levels of the congregation?
Warner Burke identifies three levels of an organization that are affected

---

26. Karl Weick and Robert Quinn, "Organization Change and Development," *Annual Review of Psychology* 50 (1999): 375, quoted in Burke, *Organization Change*, p. 68.

by a comprehensive process of change: individual, group, and total sys-tem.[27] Resistance and support are found at all three levels. It is important, thus, for leaders to think of change not only in terms of the congregational system as a whole, but also in terms of particular individuals and groups, which may be engaging the process of change in very different ways.

The Individual Level. Individuals respond to the process of organiza-tion change in a wide variety of ways. This has to do with their personali-ties, life histories, investment in the organization, and values and beliefs. It is very important for leaders to pay attention to this level of organization change. We have examined one of the most important ways they might do so: by empowering individuals to shape the process of change. As a rule of thumb, involvement and participation by individuals lead to greater com-mitment to the process of change. Often this is supported by leadership education or by "coaching," informal support and reflection in personal conversations. Since attention has already been given to the importance of empowering individuals, I focus here on a common source of resistance to change at the individual level: the experience of loss.

Many individuals experience congregational change as a kind of loss. Often the people who are most strongly identified with the congregation respond in this way. They feel that they are losing something of value. They are losing familiar routines like singing favorite hymns or knowing every-one on a first-name basis. They may feel they are losing a position of influ-ence that has provided them with a great deal of personal meaning. Or they may feel they have lost the ability to choose, that change is being forced down their throats when they are happy with the way things are.

It is important for leaders to acknowledge these feelings of loss by indi-viduals and the resistance they often engender. Such feelings are a natural response to change. A helpful perspective comes from the field of grief work. When grieving over the loss of a loved one, individuals often must express their pain and anger before they can bring closure to their grief. In-deed, people who repress such feelings or bring closure too quickly may continue to experience unresolved grief many years after their loss. This is a helpful way of thinking about what may be going on when individuals appear to be resisting change. They may be experiencing it as a loss and need leaders who are not afraid of their need to express pain and anger be-fore they can move on.

27. Burke, *Organization Change,* chapter 5.

This, of course, does not explain all forms of resistance by individuals. Some may have a vested interest in keeping things the way they are or may just be contrary. Such individuals may adopt a completely negative stance toward change, subverting it, or whining about it, or withdrawing. There is no magical way of dealing with such people. Sometimes the passing of time or seeing the fruits of change will bring them around, but not always. While leaders must do their best to care for such individuals, they cannot let them sabotage the process of change. They must remain internally committed to their vision.

In the case study that follows, pay attention to the individual level of change. You will catch glimpses of some of the reasons that certain individuals come to be deeply invested in the change process.

The Group Level. All organizations contain groups: specialized subsystems that accomplish some aspect of the organization's purpose. Burke argues that groups are the most important subsystem in an organization for three reasons: (1) they are the primary interface between the individual and the organization; (2) they are the focal point of social relationships and support of the individual; (3) they determine the individual's primary sense of organizational reality.[28]

While groups play these roles in many congregations, this is not true of all. Sunday morning worship often accomplishes the first and the third. In family churches, moreover, how things are done (i.e., a sense of the organizational reality) is tacitly held and widely diffused, not rooted in groups. Yet in many congregations, groups do play these roles. Church school classes or small-group Bible studies often are the primary source of support of individuals (#2). Likewise, the primary point of connection with the congregation for many children and youth is often their Sunday school class or the youth group, not Sunday morning worship (#1). Moreover, adults can find committee work deadly dull or highly challenging, communicating something quite important about the congregation's organizational reality (#3).

The group level of the congregation as an organization, thus, is very important to keep in mind in leading change. If groups sometimes play the sorts of roles Burke describes, then they can form a formidable line of resistance to deep change. Conversely, they can serve as a key source of change. In the case that follows, pay attention to the way the pastor relies

---

28. Burke, *Organization Change,* p. 97.

on groups to leverage change. Some of these groups were brought into being during the change process, while others already were in existence.

The Total System Level. It also is helpful for leaders to think of the process of change in terms of the entire congregational system, the phases it passes through and the steps leaders must take to guide them through this process. As you read the case study, see if you can spot these phases and steps.

Robert Quinn offers a four-stage model of organization change, which he calls the transformational cycle.[29] (1) *Initiation* — a leader, group, or leadership team develops a strong sense of the need for change and begins to form a vision of the desired future; it starts acting on this vision and taking risks. (2) *Uncertainty* — those leading change begin to engage in more serious forms of experimentation and innovation; likely, at least some of these new initiatives fail, leading to doubt and uncertainty on the change agents' parts and strengthening resistance; leaders feel lost, but if they (and the organization) can tolerate this period of uncertainty, it deepens their vision and opens up new lines of action. (3) *Transformation* — innovation gradually spreads to the organization as a whole, leading to deep change in its identity, mission, culture, and operating procedures; new energy is released and relationships formed. (4) *Routinization* — the organization moves into a new state of equilibrium; new roles and structures have been developed and mastered; specific problems can be handled by the new organizational system.

John Kotter studied more than one hundred organizations that intentionally initiated a process of deep change and reached the conclusion that transformation efforts often fail.[30] He drew two lessons from his research. First, deep change passes through a series of phases that require considerable time and energy. Skipping steps to speed up the process usually does not pay off in the long run. Second, critical errors in any of the steps can have a devastating impact on the entire process. Here are the eight steps he identified, along with potential errors along the way:

1. Establishing a sense of urgency (error: failing to persuade others that change is needed or the organization faces a crisis situation).

29. Quinn, *Deep Change*, pp. 167-69.
30. John Kotter, "Leading Change: Why Transformation Efforts Fail," in *Harvard Business Review on Change* (Boston: Harvard Business School Publishing, 1991), pp. 1-20; Kotter, *Leading Change* (Boston: Harvard Business School Press, 1996).

2. Forming a powerful guiding coalition (error: failing to assemble a group to lead the change effort and to allow them to use their gifts and creativity to shape this process).

3. Creating a vision (error: failing to develop a compelling and realizable picture of the desired future that is relatively easy to communicate).

4. Communicating the vision (error: failing to use every means possible to communicate the vision; failing to embody this vision in the actions, not just words, of the guiding leaders).

5. Empowering others to act on the vision (error: failing to support active participation in the change process by equipping people with the knowledge and skills they need, by rewarding them in appropriate ways, and by removing obstacles to change they may face).

6. Planning for and creating short-term wins (error: trying to change everything all at once or starting with a particularly sticky problem instead of small changes that generate confidence in the process).

7. Consolidating improvements and producing still more change (error: declaring victory too soon; changing the culture of an organization takes time, and declaring victory prematurely kills a sense of urgency and momentum).

8. Institutionalizing new approaches (error: failing to develop leadership beyond those people involved initially in the process of change, new leaders who understand and embody the paradigm shift that has occurred).

In this section we have reflected on the process of congregational change by entering into a dialogue with theories of open systems and organization change. This literature is quite rich, and we have considered only three of the ways it might help leaders think about congregational change. But these three are important, as will be evident in the following case study. This case draws on a project originally written for a doctor of ministry program.

A Case Study of Congregational Change

Old Union Congregational Church is located near the financial district of a large city in the Northeast. At the time this case study was written, it had 527 members, with an average attendance of around 225 adults at the 11:00

A.M. Sunday worship service (the only service offered). Children and youth combined numbered 115 in the 9:30 A.M. Sunday school, and 45 youth participated in the middle school and high school youth groups, which met on Wednesday evenings. Old Union has a long and distinguished history. Prior to the Civil War, it was a rallying point of the abolitionist movement in the city, a fact proudly noted on a plaque on the front of the church building and in the narrative history of the church commissioned for its 150th anniversary. Most of its older members and families do not live near the church but commute from the suburbs.

The church also has a relatively large number of young adults. This is the result of a singles ministry started in the 1980s, created to attract the young adults moving into the gentrified neighborhoods to the east of the church. Approximately 125 young adults participate weekly in its various programs, which include weekday volleyball and basketball leagues in the church gym, a Friday evening roller-skating party in the gym followed by a social hour at the local pub, and a Sunday school class with an average attendance of 50 young adults. A number of gays and lesbians participate as welcomed members. This singles ministry is supported by a full-time staff person, Betsy Everding, who graduated with a master's degree in recreational ministries from a well-known school of Christian education. Every year Betsy organizes a "fellowship trip" for the group, which typically involves around 50 people. Two years earlier the group hiked a portion of the Pacific Crest Trail in northern California and finished their trip in wine-country inns of Sonoma County. The previous year the group biked around the lakes of northern Italy.

Several blocks to the west of the church is a neighborhood with a high rate of unemployment, poverty, and single-parent families, an area commonly known as Parker Hill. Traditionally an African American neighborhood, Parker Hill's population has changed over the past decade with the arrival of a large number of Latino families and young adults. Many of these Latinos work for construction companies, bakeries, restaurants, and as domestics. Despite their cultural and economic differences, the African American and Latino communities have coexisted with relatively few problems until recently, when the neighborhood experienced an upsurge of violence between the Crips (African American) and Latin Kings (Latino), who are fighting for control of the drug traffic in the area.

When Paul Davis came to Old Union as senior pastor three years earlier, he knew he faced certain challenges. As he put it in a doctor of ministry paper, "Old Union was rich in resources and tradition but poor in leadership and mission." Paul followed a pastor, Dr. Barry O'Grady, who served the church for fifteen years, before his retirement. In Paul's view, preaching was Dr. O'Grady's primary ministerial focus. "He was a wonderful storyteller and used humor a lot in his sermons. I have the impression that his preaching bordered on religious entertainment. Easy-listening preaching — fun, easy to follow, and totally focused on the ways God helps you solve the problems of everyday life and enhances your personal happiness and relationships." During summers Dr. O'Grady had two standing golf dates with some of the most powerful members of the church council, who lived in the suburbs.

The focus on Sunday morning worship was augmented by a high-powered music program, funded by a $5 million endowment left to the church by a former member who specified in her bequest that it be used exclusively for the music program. The church had a full-time choir director, Evert Moorly, a part-time organist, and a thirty-member choir, which included seven people paid small stipends in order to attract gifted vocalists from the community. None of the paid soloists were members of the church. As Paul put it, "They came; they sang; they left." The church typically underspent the earnings of this endowment and managed it wisely, so that it had grown to slightly less than $6 million.

Reflecting on his first year at Old Union, Paul wrote, "I was struck by how much energy went into Sunday morning. Other than the young adult and youth programs, most organized activities took place on Sundays and focused on worship, preaching, music, and Christian education." Three times in the fall and the spring the congregation had "Committee Days." It offered a catered meal immediately after worship, which was followed by committee meetings that focused on specific areas like music, education, mission, and the building. The chairs of these committees stayed on for the church council that met at 2:30 P.M. "For a commuting church," Paul noted, "this was an effective way of taking care of church business. But it reinforced the idea that church was a Sunday-only activity. What happened the rest of the week was between scattered individuals and God — far away from the church and its urban setting. Most members don't know much about the African Americans and Latinos living only a few blocks from the church. They might have read about the gang violence in the newspaper but didn't really see it as their problem."

There were notable exceptions to this indifference to Old Union's urban context. Several members who lived in the suburbs but worked in the financial district were deeply concerned about the upsurge of gang violence. One of these people, Serene Hastings, was on the mayor's task force to deal with the gang problem. Betsy Everding (the staff person for young adults) let Paul know that the current leader of the singles ministry, Peter Hardwick, had approached her recently about getting the young adults to do more than "fun and fellowship," in his words. A gay man, Peter had experienced taunting and teasing because of his sexual orientation during high school and was the victim of a violent episode of gay bashing after leaving a bar several years earlier, putting him in the hospital. He told Betsy, "I know personally if people stand by and let discrimination and violence happen, real victims experience real pain. I don't want us to be a bunch of bystanders."

The mission committee also had long advocated greater involvement by the church in the city. "It is frustrating," said its current leader, Tony Marco. "There is a handful of people who volunteer a lot in the Catholic church's night shelter and soup kitchen and in the crisis center located in Bethel Baptist. But it's just a few of us. And we run into a brick wall every time we try to get our church to do something *as a church*. The church council always says something like, 'Hey, that's a great idea. Go ahead and do it.' But seven people by themselves can't start a program, especially when they're already volunteering in other programs."

Over a four-year period Paul Davis led Old Union through a process of deep change, initiated during his third year as senior pastor. He helped transform the church from a Sunday morning, inward-looking church to a church that is mission-oriented and uses its building, finances, and leadership resources to address the problems of its urban context. A detailed description of Paul's leadership in this process would take a chapter in its own right. Here, space permits me to provide only a year-by-year summary of some of the strategies and initiatives that brought this change about. The subtitles are mine.

Year 1: Vision Casting and Creating a Sense of Urgency

1. *Building a guiding coalition.* Paul built strong personal relationships with people who were committed to getting the church more involved in the city, including those described above. He met with them individually and

solicited their ideas. Finally, he gathered them at his house for a Saturday dinner. During dessert he asked them if they'd like to join a "revolution" that would get the church more involved in the problems of the downtown area. His guests were enthusiastic and decided to have a dinner meeting twice a month to get the ball rolling. This "guiding group" provided the key players in forging a vision of change for Old Union and in initiating the change process. Its members became very close personally.

2. *Social networking and forming an initial vision.* Paul intentionally began to visit every community leader, pastor, program, and organizer he could find working near the church. At some point he asked them two questions: (1) What is the most important problem facing this area right now? (2) What would it take to start dealing with that problem? Again and again the same answers came back to him: the gang violence, and keeping the young people out of these gangs. As Paul began to feed back what he was hearing to the guiding group, it gradually began to develop the sense that the church should focus on the youth of Parker Hill. At this point they referred to this simply as the "Good Neighbor Project."

3. *Planting seeds of change in worship and Christian education.* Paul stopped using the lectionary in his preaching and began to choose biblical texts that put the issues of mission, loving others, and care for the vulnerable before the church. He also introduced a new item in worship. Once a month someone offered a five-minute Minute for Mission in which he or she talked about a personal experience of church mission from the present or past. During the spring Paul asked all classes in the church school to study four passages from Jeremiah during the same month, which he preached on as well. The family camping weekend in the spring focused on Jeremiah 31:31-34 and 2 Corinthians 3:1-6, using intergenerational activities. Paul drew together the most creative educators in the church to write a curriculum for these educational activities and introduced them to the vision beginning to emerge in the guiding group.

4. *Gaining control of the nominating committee.* This committee nominates the chair and members of all church committees and the at-large members of the council. When two people rotated off this committee, Paul encouraged it to replace them with individuals he knew were sympathetic to the vision of change that was beginning to emerge.

Year Two: Taking Risks, Experimenting, and Innovating

1. *Initiating the "blue-ribbon panel."* Paul asked Tony Marco, the chair of the mission committee, to go one more time to the council and to tell them that his committee wanted to do something for the youth of the Parker Hill area, explaining some of what Paul had learned about the way children and youth were being recruited by the gangs. If the council agreed with this idea, Tony was to ask for a formal vote of support, which would be recorded in the minutes. As expected, with little discussion or investment, the council voted to let the mission committee proceed with the project. Several weeks later when Tony announced in a Minute for Mission the formation of a "blue-ribbon panel" to begin work on this project and listed the names of the outstanding people on the panel, several of the members of the council were surprised. Only half of the panel were people from the guiding group; it included a broad spectrum of church members, including a youth representative.

2. *Forming an initial plan.* This panel took its work seriously and came up with an ambitious three-point plan. First, use the church gym and fellowship hall for after-school activities that include tutoring, recreation, and a substantial snack. Second, tap into the music endowment to fund a recording studio open to Parker Hill youth and start an integrated children's choir composed of church and neighborhood kids. To encourage participation, this choir would take an annual trip that was part vacation and part performance, funded by the church. Third, work cooperatively with the mayor's task force, with Serene Hastings as liaison. Make the church available for community meetings and offer free office space for any local initiatives that might emerge from the task force. The panel called this plan the Jeremiah Project, picking up on themes raised in Paul's preaching on Jeremiah. The motto of the project came from Jeremiah 9:23-24: "Boast not in wisdom or wealth but the love and justice of the Lord."[31]

3. *Reworking position descriptions of church staff and hiring a new staff person.* The church staff, blue-ribbon panel, and representatives of the personnel committee came together as an ad hoc planning committee to ex-

---

31. Jer. 9:23-24 reads in full: "Thus says the LORD: Do not let the wise boast in their wisdom, do not let the mighty boast in their might, do not let the wealthy boast in their wealth; but let those who boast boast in this, that they understand and know me, that I am the LORD; I act with steadfast love, justice, and righteousness in the earth, for in these things I delight, says the LORD."

plore how the present staff might reallocate their time to support the Jeremiah Project. Betsy was excited about providing leadership for the after-school program. The choir director was a close friend of Peter Hardwick, who approached him before the meeting and sold him on the project. He agreed to direct the new children's choir if someone else would recruit the children. The group also recommended that the church hire a new staff person who would spend one-third of his or her time working with church youth and two-thirds as a community youth worker. This person would oversee the recording studio. The personnel committee voted to enact these recommendations at its next meeting, raising the salaries of Betsy Everding and Evert Moorly by $5,000 and recommending the creation of the new staff position. This position and Evert Moorly's raise were funded by the music endowment. These recommendations were approved at a special called meeting of the congregation in January. The church advertised the new position during the spring and hired an African American seminary student graduating in May, Lowell Jones.

4. *Linking spirituality and outreach.* While Paul was heartened by these initiatives, he was afraid the members of the congregation would fall into the trap of hiring church staff to do ministry *for* them, instead of becoming engaged directly in ministry themselves. This particularly worried him because of the strong Sunday morning emphasis of the church. He was familiar with the Roman Catholic JustFaith program, which combines spirituality and social service, and came to believe that it might provide a helpful model for Old Union. He decided to make this concern his primary leadership focus over the next few years, even though he had no background in spiritual direction or mission groups. He asked Jan Starling, a stay-at-home mom with two children in elementary school, to help him with this project, and together they attended the introductory JustFaith workshop. Jan turned out to be a brilliant leader. Over the next three years she started ten mission groups among the suburban members of the congregation. Some were composed entirely of women and some were couples groups. Jan and Paul developed a format that included prayer, Bible study, and sharing. All participants had to agree to volunteer in some form of service at least once a month, and the group's sharing focused largely on this experience. Jan was quite persuasive at encouraging them to participate in one of the congregation's new mission programs, securing a steady supply of volunteers for the after-school program and recording studio. Paul started two lunch-hour, downtown groups for members working in the financial district.

5. *Starting the after-school program.* Betsy started this program in February; it ran two days a week. Paul used the social network he had developed to get the word out. That spring thirty elementary and middle-school children participated.

6. *Changing leadership in the church council.* In January the nominating committee nominated Serene Hastings and Peter Hardwick to serve as at-large members of the council when two people rotated off.

Year Three: Lost, No Map, Inadequate Clothing

1. *Expanding the after-school program.* During the fall the after-school program expanded to five days. The program was *too* successful. Of the 150 children who signed up, 75 were accepted, with the hope that all children might soon be able to participate. Betsy quickly tabled any idea of expanding the program as she was overwhelmed by what she already was handling. As she put it, "I went from a low-maintenance, fun job that I knew how to handle to one that I basically didn't know how to do. If I hadn't been so committed to what we were trying to accomplish and hadn't gotten so much support from Paul, I don't think I would have stayed with it." One of the biggest problems she faced was securing enough volunteers. She also faced discipline problems. Betsy was not used to having young people tell her, "Shut your face, girl" (and much worse), and laughing at her when she corrected their behavior. Some middle-school girls were caught smoking marijuana in the church restroom, and Betsy suspected that more of this was going on than she knew about. One day several gang members showed up, sauntered around the gym until they stopped in front of Betsy and told her: "Hey, bitch. We heard you don't like us. Don't get in our business." They then strutted out, while a hush fell over the gym. Gang graffiti began to appear on the side of the church. As soon as it was removed, it would re-appear. The December meeting of the council was extremely tense, with a number of concerns raised by the "old guard." As Paul describes this meeting, "They basically were saying out loud what I was feeling, that we had bitten off more than we could chew. All of us were dealing with problems we didn't know how to handle. Once the blue-ribbon panel came up with a change-plan, it went out of business and we didn't have any infrastructure to deal with the programs as a whole. It felt like we were lurching from crisis to crisis, which was pretty much what the council said."

2. *Program successes.* Not all was bad news, however. Under Jan Starling's leadership, the mission groups continued to expand, providing a steady stream of volunteers to the new programs. The community children's choir was into its second year of practicing weekly, performing monthly, and traveling on a mission/recreation trip every summer. The recording studio had not really taken off, however. Lowell Jones was an instant hit with the church's youth but was finding it harder to connect with Parker Hill's youth.

3. *Resistance to change.* For the first time, Paul was beginning to get secondhand reports of grumbling about his leadership. The gist of the complaints was that he was spending so much time on his "pet projects" that he was not taking care of church business. He had tried to start a "care team" that would help him handle hospital visitation. The hospitals used by members were scattered around the city and suburbs, and it often took Paul half a day just to visit one person. When he brought up the idea of a care team to share the hospital visitation with him, he encountered strong resistance. Even Serene Hastings and Peter Hardwick, now on the council, said the timing was not right for this program. One council member stated bluntly what at least some church members were feeling: "Look, Paul. It's all right to try and save the world, but you've got to take care of business here too. Otherwise, the folks paying the bills will stop supporting you."

4. *Paul and Betsy seek help.* Feeling overworked and stressed out, Paul and Betsy both got into therapy. Paul also located a spiritual director, with whom he met monthly. Betsy used her professional development money to attend a conference for inner-city teachers working with at-risk children.

Year Four: A Sea Change

1. *The church council owns the process of leading change.* A number of people rotated off the church council and were replaced by people deeply committed to and involved in the process of change, including two participants in Jan Starling's mission groups. During the fall the council for the first time began to serve as the organizing center of the change initiative. They voted to change the operating procedure of the council for a two-year period. They would continue to meet on Committee Days to deal with committee reports and standard church business. The council and appropriate staff would also meet monthly on a Wednesday evening (when

the youth groups met) to deal with business related to the Jeremiah Project. The council gradually became a highly creative problem solver. For example, it recommended that Betsy hire four single mothers from the Parker Hill area to help her in the after-school program.

2. *Welcoming the Pentecostals.* Paul was approached by a Latino Pentecostal pastor who asked if the church would let his congregation use the sanctuary for its Sunday evening worship. It currently was meeting in a member's home. The pastor told Paul he had heard that Old Union was trying to relate to the community. Paul agreed to take his request to the next council meeting, and it decided to make the sanctuary available on a trial basis (for a year). By the end of the year, this congregation had grown to 125 people, 5 of whom were volunteering in the after-school program on a regular basis.

3. *Jan Starling's continued leadership.* Jan's mission groups continued to thrive. She entered a local Quaker program in spiritual formation and was given funding by the congregation to attend a workshop on spiritual direction in small groups. Paul asked her to consider becoming a part-time staff member, expanding her responsibilities to include individual spiritual direction and retreats, as well as the mission group. Jan decided to think it over.

4. *Rap 'n' roll.* Lowell Jones finally figured out a way to publicize the recording studio and use it to get Parker Hill youth involved. With the disc jockeys from an African American radio station and a Latino one, he got the church to sponsor a rap 'n' roll contest for local musicians between the ages of thirteen and eighteen, offering prize money totaling $10,000 (supplied by the music endowment) and a chance to cut a compact disk in the studio, which would be played on the two radio stations. The contest attracted thirty-five groups from around the city, each of which performed in a festival-like atmosphere in a park in the Parker Hill area. After this event, the recording studio was in great demand. Lowell recruited several musicians to offer classes in the studio on writing music, performing live, etc. He also started a Friday afternoon program called "Back Talk" in which the participants had to create a song that "talked back" to a line of graffiti that Lowell had spotted around the neighborhood that week. The songs were judged by the group, and the winners got to take their family out to dinner the next evening at the church's expense (again, with money from the music endowment).

5. *Celebrating change.* Serene Hastings approached Paul about planning

a special Sunday evening community service to celebrate the new begin-
nings taking place over the past four years. She invited the mayor to bring a
word of thanks from the city and the local media to cover the event. One
newspaper featured the church in its Sunday morning religion section. All
choirs sang, and Paul preached on the church's abolitionist heritage. The
Pentecostal congregation, which was still meeting in the sanctuary, was invited to participate. The service proved to be a spectacular success.

Year Five: How Far Can We Go?

The fifth year was just beginning when Paul wrote up this case for his doctor of ministry project. The total membership of Old Union had grown
slightly during the four-year process of change. Five families had left the
church because they were unhappy with the changes taking place; but the
church had taken in seventeen new families, mainly a by-product of Jan
Sterling's mission groups. Old Union remained almost entirely white, and
Paul was beginning to wonder how to deal with this.

Concluding Reflections

This case study puts flesh and bones on the models of leadership and organization change outlined in earlier parts of this chapter. Paul Davis and
Betsy Everding experienced all the paradoxes of transforming leadership.
They knew firsthand what it was like to get lost before finding their way,
the power that comes from empowering others, and the importance of not
deriving their personal and professional worth from how things were going at Old Union at any given time. The guiding group, blue-ribbon panel,
and ad hoc planning committee played pivotal roles in forming a vision
and initiating the process of change. This began at the margins of Old
Union and gradually moved to the center, redefining the ways it invested
its resources, its identity and mission, and even the operating procedures
of the church council. Under Paul and Betsy's leadership, a contextually
relevant vision of the church's mission was articulated and gradually
owned by the congregation.

I view Paul as pulling off a quiet revolution at Old Union. He initiated
a process resulting in deep change at Old Union in a relatively short period

of time and with only a modest amount of resistance and conflict. The congregation moved from an inward-looking, Sunday-only church to one that was committed to serving the needs of its urban setting throughout the week. In my brief summary, we only catch glimpses of Paul's attention to the individual, group, and total system levels of organization change. But we do gain some insight into the important role specific individuals played, the way Paul leveraged change at the group level, and the phases of change in the congregational system.

My description of this case is far more linear than the actual process of change itself. It fails to capture what change feels like from the inside. Betsy Everding better expresses this in part of a poem written immediately after she was confronted by gang members in the church gym during the third year of the change process. Her poem captures the pain that servant leaders often experience in the midst of leading change.

Eyes of malice,
Burning white-hot with hate.
Staring back, I shudder;
My vision slowly dims and darkness surrounds me.
Lead me, O Lord, along paths I no longer can see
Unless you light my way,
I will surely stumble and fall.

Teaching Practical Theology
in Schools of Theology

In this epilogue I focus on theological education and, primarily, address professors of practical theology currently teaching in theological education. What are the implications of the preceding chapters for the teaching of practical theology in schools of theology? To answer this question, two issues are addressed. First, we explore some of the ways courses in practical theology can help students develop the knowledge, attitudes, and skills of practical theological interpretation. Second, we examine the changing role of practical theology in contemporary theological education. Here I ask the question: What is the unique contribution of practical theology to the theological enterprise as a whole at the end of the theological encyclopedia?

Pedagogies of Practical Theology

Our first question is how courses in practical theology might help students develop the knowledge, attitudes, and skills of practical theological interpretation. What sorts of pedagogical strategies will help them learn how to carry out the descriptive-empirical, interpretive, normative, and pragmatic tasks in response to particular episodes, situations, and contexts? Before describing specific strategies that contemporary practical theologians often use, it will be helpful to consider three larger educational issues. Here I draw on the educational theory of Howard Gardner and his colleagues.

General Educational Issues

Clarity about the Endstates Promoted by the Curriculum of Practical Theology

Gardner uses the term "endstates" to describe knowledge, attitudes, and skills that are valued by a particular community and are necessary for its adult members to carry out certain roles or to create certain products.[1] Endstates guide the selectivity inherent to education. They determine the knowledge, attitudes, and skills worth teaching and learning. A central argument of this book is the importance of conceptualizing the endstates of courses in practical theology in terms of the four interrelated tasks of practical theological interpretation: descriptive-empirical, interpretive, normative, and pragmatic. Each task is complicated in its own right and includes qualities of the person, like attentiveness and thoughtfulness, as well as capacities based on the acquisition of knowledge and skills. Often, particular courses focus primarily on only one or two of these tasks. A course in congregational studies, for example, may focus on the descriptive-empirical and interpretive tasks while an advanced course on small-group Bible study may concentrate on the pragmatic task. In course planning, it is important to be clear about the tasks of practical theological interpretation that are primary.

In light of the selective focus of particular courses, education toward the endstates of practical theological interpretation is accomplished by the curriculum of practical theology as a whole. This requires intentional planning by the entire department. Below we will examine the concept of educational pathways that enable students to develop greater competence in practical theological interpretation over time. Working together as a department requires professors to move beyond the "silo mentality" of the

1. Howard Gardner, *Frames of Mind: The Theory of Multiple Intelligences* (New York: Basic Books, 1983); Gardner, *The Unschooled Mind: How Children Think and How Schools Should Teach* (New York: Basic Books, 1991); Gardner, *Multiple Intelligences: The Theory in Practice — a Reader* (New York: Basic Books, 1993); Gardner, *The Disciplined Mind: What All Students Should Understand* (New York: Simon and Schuster, 1999).

theological encyclopedia in which they think of their courses exclusively in terms of specialized task competence, with no regard to their contribution to the broader outcomes of student learning. In the final part of this epilogue, we examine the emergence of this mentality in the encyclopedic paradigm of theology. Planning particular courses in light of endstates promoted by the entire department of practical theology has four implications.

1. *Conceptualizing task competence in terms of the broader endstates of practical theological interpretation.* At a number of points in this book I have indicated some of the reasons why focusing exclusively on task competence in courses in the subdisciplines of practical theology is too narrow a practice. It fails to help students grasp the interconnectedness of ministry within the congregational system as a whole and within the web of life. It also fails to attend to leadership issues that go beyond task competence. Thinking solely in terms of task competence binds leaders to roles in the congregation as it *presently* is organized. It does not address the sorts of issues involved in transactional and transforming leadership.

This does not mean that courses should not focus on helping students learn the specialized knowledge and skills of a particular subfield. Preaching, teaching, and pastoral care are complex in their own right, and courses in these areas must help students acquire the language and skills involved in these ministries. Yet it also is important that competence in these areas is taught in terms of an understanding practical theological interpretation that is shared across departmental offerings. In this way students acquire a common language and habits of reflection, even as they learn the specialized concepts and skills of a particular form of ministry. This will equip them to spot the deep connections between various forms of ministry. It also will ensure that task competence is not taught in a decontextualized manner. Is it really possible to teach or preach in ways that are timely and relevant without attention to what is going on in particular contexts, critical reflection on why this is going on, and how the Christian community ought to respond? Is it possible to offer care to individuals or families without consideration of contextual factors that are contributing to their suffering? Specialization remains, but it now is part of an interconnected web of practical theological interpretation woven across the course offerings of the entire department.

2. *The importance of integrating the four tasks of practical theological interpretation.* This takes place at two levels. Within courses that focus pri-

marily on task competence and on one or two of the tasks of practical theological interpretation in relation to this task, it is important that at least some attention be paid to the other tasks. For example, if a course emphasizes preaching informed by congregational studies (emphasizing the descriptive-empirical and pragmatic tasks), this sort of integration can be handled by pointing students toward knowledge and skills learned in other courses. Suppose they have discovered in their research on a particular congregation a loosely bound, highly individualistic ethos. They might be asked: In light of what you've learned about the church in theology and Bible, how adequate do you find this pattern? In other courses, what have you learned about the social roots of individualism in contemporary America?

Integration also takes place at a second level. The curriculum of practical theology ought to offer upper-level courses that make this sort of integration central. Such courses would consistently feature the interaction of the four tasks, as well as the ways they help leaders grasp the interconnections of various forms of ministry within the congregational system and within the web of life.

3. *The importance of educating the capacity for cross-disciplinary thinking.* A consistent theme of this book is the importance of the dialogue between theology and other fields, both other theological disciplines and the arts and sciences. Each task of practical theology confronts a unique set of interdisciplinary issues. Moreover, congregational leaders commonly face multidimensional problems, which require the vantage points of several fields (as we saw in the discussion of alcoholism). Furthermore, the congregation as an open system, nestled within other systems, requires leaders who are adept at exploring systems beyond the church, drawing on disciplines appropriate to these systems. It is difficult for me to imagine a course in practical theology in which cross-disciplinary issues are not involved. While cross-disciplinary thinking may receive sustained attention in only some courses, it should receive at least some attention in every course.

4. *Attending to the person of students.* Practical theological interpretation is not simply a matter of learning techniques, despite what students sometimes think. Rather, it involves good judgment in quite particular circumstances. It takes key attitudes like the willingness to attend to others with openness and thoughtfulness and to "suffer" the risks of raising difficult normative questions and of leading change. Attending to the *person* of students — helping students grow, change, acquire new self-understandings,

and form a realistic picture of their strengths and limitations — is an important part of education in practical theology. It requires a quality of teaching, coaching, and mentoring that is highly personal. How to accomplish this in a classroom setting, especially in large classes, is one of the greatest challenges facing professors of practical theology. At a minimum, it requires feedback mechanisms of two sorts: (1) evaluation of student performances by the professor and peers, and (2) self-reflection by students that enables them to form a more realistic image of their strengths, limitations, and growing edges.

Teaching for Understanding as the Goal of Courses in Practical Theology

Gardner and his associates portray understanding as the ability to draw on knowledge, attitudes, and skills learned in one context to address relatively novel problems in different contexts.[2] To put it briefly, "understanding is the ability to think and act flexibly with what one knows."[3] It requires more than rote learning: providing standard answers to set questions on tests or in papers. Understanding means that students can extend what they have learned beyond the original setting in which knowledge and skills were initially acquired. For obvious reasons, teaching for understanding is a critical goal in courses on practical theology. Such courses are preparing students to interpret and respond to episodes, situations, and contexts that are messy and unique.

The great enemy of understanding in education is the drive for coverage. This is the attempt to cover all aspects of a subject matter in depth through required reading and lectures. It puts students in the position of constantly racing to learn the next new thing. They never have the chance to integrate what they have learned or to circle back to material or activities already covered to deepen their initial learning. The great friend of understanding is student performances, which are evaluated with publicly stated criteria and are repeated in a spiral-like fashion.[4] This allows stu-

2. Martha Stone Wiske, ed., *Teaching for Understanding: Linking Research with Practice* (San Francisco: Jossey-Bass, 1998); cf. Tina Blythe and Associates, *The Teaching for Understanding Guide* (San Francisco: Jossey-Bass, 1998).

3. This brief definition is offered by David Perkins in Wiske, *Teaching for Understanding*, p. 40.

4. Wiske, *Teaching for Understanding*, pp. 41-44, 51-54, 72-76.

dents to correct deficiencies in earlier learning and to extend their learning to new contexts.

Student performances can take many forms: a written test, a paper, participation in class discussion, writing up a critical incident or case study, or an embodied activity like preaching, teaching, or role playing a pastoral conversation. What separates a performance from conventional learning is the requirement that students go beyond the information given. This means they must demonstrate knowledge and perform skills they have already begun to learn in the face of relatively novel circumstances, which require thoughtfulness and creativity on their part. Feedback, moreover, is formative, not merely summative, giving students the chance to correct mistakes and improve their performances on the basis of feedback.

Developing Educational Pathways

According to Gardner, *educational pathways* are trajectories in the curriculum that allow students to deepen their knowledge, attitudes, and skills over time.[5] Everything cannot be learned all at once in a curriculum, because complex knowledge and skills are gradually built up in a cumulative fashion. To project such pathways, the entire department of practical theology must work together. This enables them to sequence course offerings on two levels simultaneously: increased competence in particular tasks like preaching, teaching, or pastoral care and greater proficiency in practical theological interpretation. To accomplish both things, introductory courses must focus on more than task competence. They must introduce students to the basic structure of practical theological interpretation in relation to this task. Upper-level courses ought to be able to assume that this structure has already been learned.

Departments working together in designing educational pathways make it possible for courses to build on and deepen what has already been learned in other courses. An upper-level course in preaching or pastoral care, for example, may build on empirical research skills acquired in an introductory course on congregation studies. An advanced course in Christian education may build on a communication model learned in a required preaching course. This sort of cross-fertilization of courses is rare

5. Technically, Howard Gardner uses the term "pathways of understanding" in *The Disciplined Mind*, pp. 215-17.

in departments of practical theology (and theological education generally) and reflects the "silo" mentality of the theological encyclopedia.

In structuring educational pathways, it may be helpful for departments to draw on models, which chart developmental trajectories in the acquisition of critical thinking, reflective judgment, creativity, and skills.[6] Hubert and Stuart Dreyfus, for example, describe five levels in the acquisition of skills: novice, advanced beginner, competent performer, proficient performer, and expert.[7] Novices rely heavily on rules offered by experienced "authorities" to guide their actions and tend to evaluate their performances in terms of how well they follow such rules. At the level of competent performer, following rules in this fashion plays little role in skillful performance; they have been internalized and form a part of taken-for-granted, background knowledge. Rather, people now focus on developing competence in recognizing and sorting out different kinds of situations, based on a system of classification and their past experience. They learn to spot interrelated signs of depression or alcoholism in particular people, for example, and to draw on ways of responding to such people that have proven effective in the past. At the highest levels of skillful performance, people begin to rely on judgments that are highly intuitive and holistic. Classificatory systems and past experience give way to assessments and actions that fit this particular situation involving these particular people. On-the-spot evaluations and adjustments can be made as action is unfolding: e.g., a sermon is altered in midstream because the preacher senses it is falling flat or a pastoral counselor recognizes a moment of insight has emerged in the counselee and spends time helping him or her consolidate it.

The Dreyfus model of skillful performance may be helpful in planning an educational pathway in a department of practical theology. It allows the

6. See the following, for example: William Perry, *Forms of Intellectual and Ethical Development in the College Years: A Scheme* (Troy, Mo.: Holt, Rinehart and Winston, 1970); Hubert Dreyfus and Stuart Dreyfus, *Mind over Machine: The Power of Human Intuition and Expertise in the Era of the Computer* (New York: Free Press, 1986); J. Mezior and Associates, *Fostering Critical Reflection in Adulthood: A Guide to Transformative and Emancipatory Learning* (San Francisco: Jossey-Bass, 1990); Patricia King and Karen Strohm Kichener, *Developing Reflective Judgment: Understanding and Promoting Intellectual Growth and Critical Thinking in Adolescents and Adults* (San Francisco: Jossey-Bass, 1994); Darcia Narváez et al., eds., *Post-conventional Moral Thinking: A Neo-Kohlbergian Approach* (Mahwah, N.J.: L. Erlbaum Associates, 1999).

7. Dreyfus and Dreyfus, *Mind over Machine,* chapter 1.

department to consider the level of skillful performance characterizing the majority of their students as they enter a curriculum and how particular courses might help them move toward more complex levels. Similar models chart developmental trajectories in critical thinking, creativity, and reflective judgment. These might prove helpful in planning educational pathways as well.

Pedagogical Strategies of Practical Theology

Beyond these general educational goals of a curriculum of practical theology, a number of pedagogical strategies might be used to teach students certain aspects of practical theological interpretation in particular courses. Here I point to teaching strategies commonly used by contemporary practical theologians.[8]

1. *The interaction of modeling and student performances to teach the pragmatic task.* This strategy involves the presentation of a model of good practice, which is followed by student performances that seek to embody certain features of this model. Sometimes the model is an actual performance by the professor: role playing a pastoral conversation or teaching a class with a method students are learning. Or the model may be performances that have been audiotaped or videotaped or written up in the form of a verbatim conversation or case study. After they have encountered this model performance and analyzed it, individual students or teams then offer performances that embody certain features of this model (which often is related to assigned reading as well). Sometimes student performances take place in a class practicum or live setting (i.e., a congregation, hospital, day-care center, etc.). These may be audiotaped or videotaped or written up. Or they take the form of an action plan, which projects an intervention strategy, lesson plan, written sermon, and so forth.

Models of good practice are a powerful way of helping students to do more than *think* about practice; in them they actually experience it. They also help students learn that imitation alone will not take them very far.

8. The Spring 2006 Biennial Meeting of the American Association of Practical Theology, held at Vanderbilt University Divinity School, focused on pedagogies of practical theology. A number of the strategies offered here emerged from the outstanding presentations of this gathering.

Try imitating a sermon of Martin Luther King, Jr., just listened to in class, or the interaction patterns of an experienced pastoral counselor, observed on a videotape. While students gain a great deal from such models, they quickly learn that their own performances must be responsive to the particularities of the situation in which they take place and are profoundly influenced by their personality, gender, cultural background, and unique strengths/limitations. It is helpful, thus, to supplement models of good practice with rules of art: open-ended guidelines that provide direction in carrying out an activity but require the creativity, skills, and good judgment of the performer in a particular context. Such rules play their most important role relatively early in the learning process.

2. *Using case studies and critical incident reports to practice practical theological interpretation in relation to particular episodes, situations, and contexts.* This is a well-established pedagogical strategy in professional education, including clinical pastoral education. It is an extraordinarily helpful way of teaching the sort of contextual thinking used in practical theology. It gives students the opportunity to learn the unique contribution of each task of practical theological interpretation, as well as to explore the mutual influence of these tasks. At the most elementary level, students reflect on the case or critical incident by moving around the hermeneutical circle of practical theological interpretation one task at a time. At a more advanced level, their reflection becomes more like a spiral, circling back to tasks repeatedly as new insights emerge at other points on the circle.

Often, it is helpful to use case studies or critical incident reports written by someone who is not a member of the class. This may help students learn how to write good cases or reports. It also may free them to give honest feedback and to focus on the tasks of practical theological interpretation without worrying about how a fellow student will respond. At the same time, having students write cases and reports in which they are directly involved has many advantages. Not only do students learn to distance themselves (i.e., to stand back) from events in which they participate, but they also have the opportunity to learn a disciplined way of approaching such events as they are still unfolding. Just as students learn the habits and skills of biblical interpretation by exegeting particular texts, here too they learn the habits and skills of practical theological interpretation by exegeting particular cases and episodes in which they are actors.

3. *Repetitive question-asking to integrate task competence and practical theological interpretation.* Katherine Turpin spoke eloquently of the role of

repetitive question-asking at a recent meeting of the American Association of Practical Theology, and her comments fit nicely with a central tenet of teaching for understanding.[9] Gardner and his colleagues argue that teaching for understanding should make use of publicly articulated evaluation criteria.[10] Students know in advance the standards by which their performances will be evaluated. Not only is this fair, but it also signals to students the key elements of good performance (i.e., "This is what we are going to be looking for in your teaching, preaching, or caregiving"). It allows students to shape their performances to these standards *prospectively* and enhances the ability to provide feedback that is *formative*. On the basis of such criteria, evaluators can offer students specific assessments of strengths, weaknesses, and ways of improving their performances (which they typically are allowed to carry out in light of this feedback).

In effect, Turpin broadens the idea of public evaluation criteria beyond situations in which student performances are being assessed. Standards of reflective practice are turned into questions, which are used repeatedly to explore a wide range of performances in the course, including models of good practice, case studies, student performances, and so forth. By way of illustration, let us take some of the criteria of good preaching, which might be extracted from Fred Craddock's *Preaching* and *As One without Authority*.[11]

In these books Craddock portrays good preaching as biblical, inductive, and fitting; as creating an appropriate form; and as offering hearers something to think about, feel, or do. These are turned into questions: Is the sermon grounded in solid exegesis of the text? Does it allow listeners to experience the journey the preacher has traveled in arriving at the central theme of the sermon? Is the sermon related to its time and place in a fitting way? What form does the sermon take, and how does this form shape the expectations of the listeners? What does the sermon ask listeners to think about, feel, or do during the actual preaching event? Again and again, students are asked to put these questions to the sermons they hear, write, and

9. Katherine Turpin, "On Teaching and Religious Education" (paper presented at the Biennial Meeting of the American Association of Practical Theology, Vanderbilt University Divinity School, Spring 2006).

10. Wiske, *Teaching for Understanding*, pp. 71, 76-81.

11. Fred Craddock, *Preaching* (Nashville: Abingdon, 1985); Craddock, *As One without Authority: Revised and with New Sermons* (St. Louis: Chalice, 2001).

deliver. Over time they become second nature and provide categories that students may use in the future to prepare their sermons.

Repetitive question-asking is useful in teaching, caregiving, and any other form of skillful performance that may be the focus of courses in practical theology. It is important, however, for such questions to involve more than task competence. They also should teach students how to approach tasks like preaching in ways informed by practical theological interpretation. The questions gleaned from Craddock's writings, for example, move far in this direction. Questions about the text and working inductively are inherently normative. Asking if a sermon is fitting involves descriptive-empirical and interpretive judgments. The form and action of the sermon are pragmatic in nature. If task-specific questions are portrayed as specialized forms of a more basic structure of practical theological interpretation, then students will be in a much better position to discern the underlying unity of their various courses in practical theology and to integrate what they are learning from course to course. They also will learn how to spot the interconnections of various forms of ministry, an important step toward thinking systemically and not solely in terms of task competence.

4. *Theories of interpretation link closely with case studies/critical incidents or practice.* Courses in practical theology commonly study theories of the arts and sciences. Courses in Christian education, for example, often assign readings on human development, multiple intelligence theory, and gender theory, and in preaching, books on communication theory, hermeneutics, and congregational studies. Courses on pastoral care often use texts on depth psychology, family systems, social analysis, gender theory, and cultural anthropology (e.g., culture-specific forms of healing). These sorts of texts play an important role in the interpretive and pragmatic tasks. They deepen students' understanding of the context of ministry and offer models of practice. It is helpful if the role a book is playing in the course is explicitly framed in terms of its contribution to one of the tasks of practical theology. For example, a professor might tell students: "While Diana Eck's book on religious pluralism, *A New Religious America,* might not provide you with much help in how to teach a particular class (the pragmatic task), it offers a great deal of help in your interpretation of the context of contemporary ministry in the United States. This is why we are reading it in this course."

Two of the most helpful ways of helping students learn how to draw on theories in practical theological interpretation are bringing them to bear on particular cases/incidents and planning and assessing performances. For example, in reflecting on a rural congregation that has "circled the wagons" in the face of many changes in the local community, Eck's book might provide a helpful way of interpreting the adaptive challenge the congregation faces. Theory is used to understand and explain why certain patterns are occurring in this case. Other books may be more helpful in the pragmatic task, providing a model of practice that can be used to design and assess student performances. For example, Murray Bowen has written a number of books on family systems and the importance of self-differentiation within such systems. One of his texts might serve as the starting point for an action plan in which students think through how they might work with a family in their congregation with a teenage son who is acting out. Theory informs practice, and its relevance is immediately apparent.

5. *Portfolios of performance and self-reflection.* While less common, student portfolios are used by some practical theologians in their courses. We commonly think of a portfolio as a collection of paintings or photographs by an artist that were created over time. In a similar manner, student portfolios in education gather together a student's work over the course of the semester.[12] A portfolio of sermons or lesson plans, for example, allows students to recognize what they have learned in the course, as well as providing the basis for summative evaluation by the professor.

Such portfolios also can serve as a powerful way of attending to the *person* of students in the course. One professor I know, for example, requires students to write a personal reflection paper on every theory of Christian education studied in her course. After reading about faith enculturation theory, they reflect on their own enculturation. When studying critical pedagogies, they reflect on settings and persons who helped them learn to think critically about their values, relationships, and social context. At the end of the course, students look back at their portfolios of personal reflection papers. They integrate what they have learned about themselves and evaluate the theories studied in terms of their own experience.

12. For an introduction see Steve Seidel et al., *Portfolio Practices: Thinking through the Assessment of Children's Work,* NEA School Restructuring Series (Washington, D.C.: National Education Association, 1997).

Practical Theology at the End
of the Theological Encyclopedia

Most Protestant seminaries and divinity schools today continue to educate their students along the lines of the encyclopedic paradigm of theology. By this I mean a pattern of theology forged during the modern period that focuses on specialized academic disciplines organized around the fourfold theological encyclopedia: biblical studies, church history, dogmatic theology/Christian ethics, and practical theology.[13] Theological schools are organized into departments based on each of these fields, and students are required to take courses in each department. This fourfold pattern is the product of a specific history shaped by a particular set of problems confronting theology in the modern research university.

The Legacy of the Theological Encyclopedia

The encyclopedic paradigm emerged in response to two broad-reaching intellectual and institutional shifts of the modern period: (1) the rise of modern science as the driving force of research and technological innovation, and (2) the secularization of institutions giving shape to everyday life. While these two trends influenced every aspect of modern life, they came together in the modern university. For most of Western history theology had an important, even privileged, place in academic institutions. In the medieval university, for example, it was viewed as the "queen" of the arts and sciences. In the humanistic education emerging from the Reformation of the sixteenth century, it had an unquestioned role in all levels of education. Catechisms, for example, were studied in primary education, and theology had a special place in university curriculums.

All of this was to change with the rise of the modern university. First, modern science now set the terms of research and academic teaching in this setting. Universities were no longer charged with the task of handing on the cultural and religious inheritance of the past. Rather, they now had the task of carrying out scholarly research that yielded new knowledge in the present. Natural science, especially, served as the paradigm case of this

---

13. For the history of the theological encyclopedia, see Edward Farley, *Theologia: The Fragmentation and Unity of Theological Education* (Philadelphia: Fortress, 1983).

research. It was seen as unlocking the secrets of the natural world, which issued in new forms of technology with very tangible applications in industrializing societies. Second, the modern university now was one of many social institutions that were secularizing. Theology no longer held a privileged position in the university as a community of "scientific" scholars. Indeed, the question theology faced was whether it had any place at all in the modern research university. The encyclopedic paradigm of theology was a way of responding to this question.

The term "encyclopedic paradigm" is taken from a particular genre of literature that emerged during this period, the theological encyclopedia. Most of us are familiar with encyclopedias that bring together knowledge from many different fields. In their early days, such encyclopedias did more than provide access to a broad array of information. They provided a picture of the "tree of knowledge," describing various fields of science and their relationship to one another. Theological encyclopedias were a subspecies of this genre. They too provided an overview of the various branches of theology, describing the specialized focus of each branch and the branches' relation to one another. They often were used to introduce first-year students of theology to the curriculum as a whole. I am less interested in the genre of theological encyclopedia, however, than I am in the pattern of theology it reflects.

Friedrich Schleiermacher offered one of the earliest and most influential theological encyclopedias in his *Brief Outline on the Study of Theology*.[14] He wrote this book to defend theology's place in the modern university, prompted by his leadership and teaching in the University of Berlin, founded in 1819. Schleiermacher's defense consisted of two basic arguments.

In his first line of argument, Schleiermacher portrayed theology as a "positive" science comparable to the sort of scholarship supporting law and medicine. A positive science draws on the research of other, fully scientific fields to support a profession that contributes to the well-being of society. While doctors do not carry out research themselves, their medical practice is informed by such research. Medicine, as such, is a positive science, as are law and theology. This allowed Schleiermacher to argue that just as society needs doctors and lawyers, it also needs clergy, for religion

14. Friedrich Schleiermacher, *Brief Outline on the Study of Theology*, trans. Terrence Tice (Richmond: John Knox, 1966).

makes an important contribution to the lives of individuals and to the common good.

Schleiermacher's second line of argument had to do with the way theology should be organized as a scholarly enterprise in a research university. While the subject matter of theology remained the Christian religion, it now was to be divided into three specialized fields: philosophical theology, historical theology, and practical theology. Each branch of theology was to use forms of scholarship found in cognate disciplines (disciplines that were "closely related" or "similar"). Philosophical theology was to determine the "essence" of Christianity using methods appropriate to philosophy. Biblical studies and church history, as branches of historical theology, were to use the scholarly methods of historical research. Since Schleiermacher wrote before the advent of the social sciences, he had greater difficulty describing the scholarly methods of practical theology. At times he described it as offering a "theory of practice," providing models for the practice of ministry grounded in research and theory. At other times he described practical theology as developing "rules of art," open-ended guidelines that help clergy carry out specific tasks like preaching and teaching but require their own creativity and good judgment. As we shall see, Schleiermacher's uncertainty about the scholarly task of practical theology reflects a particular understanding of the relationship between pure and applied science or, more generally, between theory and practice. For our purposes, it is enough to underscore a basic point. We see here the beginning of specialization and the loss of theology's own distinctive rational operations, as it is enjoined to take over those of cognate fields.

Schleiermacher's specific proposal about the organization of theology into three branches was not widely accepted and was quickly supplanted by the fourfold pattern with which we are familiar today. Yet his argument about the sort of specialized scholarship that ought to characterize theology in a modern research university was virtually a charter for the encyclopedic paradigm of theology as it unfolded in Europe and North America. This pattern has four key features.

1. Theology is divided into specialized, relatively autonomous fields.
2. Each field pursues its distinctive tasks along the lines of a modern research discipline, with a specialized language, methods of inquiry, and subject matter. The standards and research methods of theology, thus,

are the same as those of other research disciplines in the university at a given point in time.

3. The goal of theological scholarship is the production of new knowledge. Theology that is "scientific" is not concerned directly with application but is concerned with the pursuit of original scholarship.

4. The specific task of practical theology is to relate the scholarship of the other theological disciplines to the work of clergy and congregations.

The third point clearly was not a part of Schleiermacher's original proposal. The whole purpose of his description of theology as a "positive" science was to argue that theological scholarship ought to serve clergy education because clergy, as leaders of the Christian religion, make an important contribution to the well-being of society. But this argument was persuasive only as long as Western nations remained at least nominally Christian. Across the modern period, secularization was to erode its plausibility, and the present reality of religious pluralism makes it doubly difficult to defend. Increasingly, the specialized theological disciplines viewed the production of new knowledge as an end in itself, more oriented to academic guilds and scholarly publication than to the church.

To summarize, within the encyclopedic paradigm, each theological discipline is specialized and relatively autonomous, uses the methods of cognate fields, focuses on the production of new knowledge, and relates to ecclesial practice indirectly, leaving this to practical theology. Over time this paradigm gave rise to a "silo mentality" in schools of theology. Just as farmers store grain and corn in independent silos, so too each field and department maintained the harvest of its specialized research in its own disciplinary silo. The interconnection of the fields of theology and of subdisciplines within these fields became more and more tenuous. While this pattern was an important way of coping with the challenges of the modern research university, it is questionable whether it is adequate to the challenges of our postmodern context.

Indeed, theological schools that are organized along these lines may be characterized as "shell institutions" in the sense of sociologist Anthony Giddens.[15] From the outside, "shell institutions" look the same as they have in the past. But internally they are no longer capable of carrying out the work

15. Anthony Giddens, *Runaway World: How Globalization Is Reshaping Our Lives* (New York: Routledge, 1999), pp. 18-19.

they need to perform. National governments today, for example, are having great difficulty ensuring the economic well-being of their citizens in the face of global economic systems. So too, families are having difficulty carrying out the tasks of primary socialization in the face of the shaping power of education, media, and peer groups. The "shell" remains, but the internal organization is not up to the challenges of a new context. Such is the case of theological schools organized along the lines of the encyclopedic paradigm of theology.

Beyond the Encyclopedic Paradigm

If two of the driving social forces giving rise to the modern research university were modern science and secularization, both forces are evaluated quite differently in our postmodern context. Across the modern period, modern science fostered a mood of great optimism based on the hope that its achievements might usher in a new era in which the problems of economic scarcity and disease might finally be overcome. Today, science is viewed with much more caution — and even fear. Sociologist Ulrich Beck describes this new mood as the awareness that we live in a "risk society."[16] Scientific achievements have unleashed forces potentially more devastating than anything faced by human beings in the past.

If the gradual secularization of social institutions during the modern period seemed to imply the gradual disappearance of religion in the future (or a radically diminished role), this also is called into question today. Religion has continued to play an important role in social change, as seen in the civil rights movement in the United States, the struggle against apartheid in South Africa, and the "velvet revolutions" ending communism in Eastern Europe. Moreover, the recovery and reinvention of local religious traditions around the world is a widespread response to the intrusion of economic and cultural globalization. This flies directly in the face of the secularization thesis, which appears to better describe western Europe than the entire world. Likewise, the rise of conservative Christian, Islamic, and Hindu movements and their impact on public and political institutions call secularization into question. Even the relatively moderate version of the secularization thesis — that religion would be confined to the private sphere — appears far-fetched today, as religious communities vie

---

16. Ulrich Beck, *Risk Society: Towards a New Modernity* (Thousand Oaks, Calif.: Sage, 1992).

for theocratic control of various societies, on the one hand, or for a legitimate public presence in pluralistic societies, on the other.

Reconsideration of the role of science and religion in society calls into question the problematic to which the encyclopedic paradigm of theology was a response. Indeed, we are now living in a new postmodern intellectual context quite different from modernity. This can be characterized in terms of four key shifts.

1. *From science as the exemplar of scholarship in all fields, including theology, to affirmation of the variety of ways scholarly research is conducted, including theology.* The key to this shift is that modern science — especially natural science — is no longer viewed as the paradigm case of rationality and scholarly research. In the past, much of science's intellectual authority was based on its claim to objectivity and universality. In our current postmodern intellectual context, such claims have given way to a much clearer understanding that science is an interpretive activity, drawing on the models and methods of particular research traditions that change over time. Different fields like the arts, humanities, and human sciences no longer look to natural science for their own scholarly orientations. This raises serious questions about the way the encyclopedic paradigm portrays theology as taking over the standards and research methods of cognate fields. Rather, theology today has both the freedom and obligation to articulate its own subject matter and forms of scholarship.

2. *From disciplinary specialization in relatively isolated fields to cross-disciplinary thinking as the center of scholarly research.* The tendency toward greater and greater specialization by relatively autonomous disciplines has given way to an affirmation of the importance of cross-disciplinary forms of research and thinking, the task of bringing several disciplines to bear on a research project or issue. It is true that some fields are highly specialized today. But the broader intellectual context of such specialization has taken a marked turn toward cross-disciplinary work, which includes interdisciplinary and multidisciplinary approaches.

For example, the Human Genome Project, which identified the approximately 20,000 or 25,000 genes in human DNA and the sequences of the 3 billion chemical base pairs that make up human DNA, obviously was a research project in genetics. But it was genetics informed by a dialogue with the disciplines of microbiology, chemistry, computer science, and ethics, to name but a few. Today, research problems and social systems are viewed as too complex to be fully comprehended by a single discipline.

This raises serious questions about the encyclopedic paradigm's tendency toward disciplinary specialization and isolation. If theological disciplines are reclaiming their own voice and perspective today, they are doing so as part of a cross-disciplinary conversation with other fields of theology and with various nontheological dialogue partners.

3. *From the ideal of universality, consensus, and progress to pluralism and rational dissensus.* The scientific ideal of the modern research university was based on a strong commitment to the values of universality, consensus, and progress. Here again, natural science was viewed as exemplary. Its experimental methods supposedly yielded "facts" based on "observations" that served as the foundation of explanations of the "laws" of the natural world. Such methods and findings were publicly available to other scholars and, if replicated and confirmed by other scientists, yielded knowledge with the claim of universality, that is, as true beyond the context of discovery. Such knowledge was viewed as the basis of consensus within the scientific community and of cumulative progress over time.

Today this scientific ideal is largely abandoned in many fields and has been reconceptualized within natural science itself. One reason is the interpretive "turn" examined in the introduction: the recognition that science carries out its work in particular research traditions that change over time. Yet, as we also have seen, this is not merely a matter of change over time — e.g., the shift from Newtonian to quantum physics — which might be interpreted as a form of progress. Rather, diverse and competing paradigms *within* the same field at the same time are quite common today.

Moreover, pluralism and rational dissensus — well-reasoned disagreement across different perspectives — are viewed as signs of strength and vitality in a field, not universality and consensus. Nor is scholarship viewed as progressing in a linear, cumulative fashion but through imaginative leaps and paradigm shifts. Indeed, the very notion of progress in a strong sense plays little role in many fields. Rather, fields like literature, ethics, and anthropology view themselves as dealing with subjects and problems that are not amenable to cumulative advances or resolution. They deal with issues that are context-specific, on the one hand, and perennial, on the other.

4. *From a sharp distinction between disinterested, pure scholarship and applied science to the recognition that scholarship is grounded in and oriented toward practice, reflecting constellations of value, interest, and power.* The distinction between pure and applied science had a great impact on the way practical theology was conceptualized in the theological encyclopedia.

Within the fourfold pattern, biblical studies, church history, and dogmatic theology/ethics were viewed as engaging in pure research and practical theology in application. This might be pictured along the lines of a relay race. In the theological encyclopedia, each theological discipline runs its own leg of the race and, as such, has its own distinctive contribution to make. Practical theology is located in the final position, running the anchor leg. It has the task of bringing the baton across the finish line to the church. It mediates the scholarly findings of other fields to church leaders in terms of practical application. This relay race model is challenged along three lines today.

First, the recovery of theology's distinctive subject matter and forms of scholarship has freed many Christian theologians to reconsider the relationship of their work to Christian practice. Indeed, many have come to view their scholarship as grounded in and oriented toward contemporary Christian practice in both the church and public life.[17] It is no longer helpful, thus, to view practice as the province of practical theology alone. This has important implications for the sort of scholarship that Christian scholars produce. While they rightly continue to write technical books and articles oriented to their academic guilds, they also provide resources for congregations and Christian communities engaged in social transformation.

For example, Bible scholars write commentaries used by preachers and teachers and draw on insights emerging out of base and womanist communities and the "academy of the poor."[18] Church historians offer congrega-

17. The following is a brief sampling of biblical scholars who link their work explicitly with contemporary Christian practice, and it would be easy to identify scholars in other theological disciplines working in the same way: Brian Blount, *Cultural Interpretation: Reorienting New Testament Criticism* (Minneapolis: Fortress, 1995) and *Can I Get a Witness: Reading Revelation through African American Culture* (Louisville: Westminster John Knox, 2005); Richard Hays, *The Moral Vision of the New Testament* (San Francisco: HarperSanFrancisco, 1996); Stephen E. Fowl, *Engaging Scripture: A Model for Theological Interpretation* (Oxford: Blackwell, 1998); Luke Timothy Johnson, *Scripture and Discernment: Decision Making in the Church* (Nashville: Abingdon, 1983) and *Living Jesus: Learning the Heart of the Gospel* (San Francisco: HarperSanFrancisco, 1999); Beverly Roberts Gaventa, *Mary: Glimpses of the Mother of Jesus* (Columbia: University of South Carolina Press, 1995); Fernando Segovia and Mary Ann Tolbert, eds., *Reading from This Place,* vol. 1, *Social Location and Biblical Interpretation in the United States* (Minneapolis: Fortress, 1995); Elisabeth Schüssler Fiorenza, *In Memory of Her: A Feminist Theological Reconstruction of Christian Origins* (New York: Crossroad, 1983); Gerald West, *Biblical Hermeneutics of Liberation: Modes of Reading the Bible in the South African Context* (Maryknoll, N.Y.: Orbis, 1995).

18. See Gerald O. West, *The Academy of the Poor: Towards a Dialogical Reading of the Bible* (Sheffield, U.K.: Sheffield Academic Press, 1999).

tions short introductions to church tradition, as well as new narratives that recover the contributions of neglected figures and groups, like women. Dogmatic theologians write catechisms, commentaries on catechisms, and short introductions to Christian doctrine for leaders of congregations. They also portray doctrine as shaping the Christian life and as guiding social transformation.[19] Christian ethicists provide churches with models and guidelines with which to think about ethical issues in everyday life and controversial social issues. Philosophical theologians address contemporary issues like evolution, genetics, and human consciousness, helping ordinary Christians think about the relationship between their faith and contemporary science. It no longer is helpful, thus, to picture the relationship between theological scholarship and Christian practice along the lines of a relay race in which practical theology hands the baton of application to church leaders.

Second, it is widely recognized today that scholarship itself is a form of practice. Scholars carry out certain activities in their research. They examine texts, artifacts, and contemporary communities. They use linguistic practices that frame what they find and how they communicate with other scholars and publics. It is unhelpful and even misleading to think of scholarship as "pure," as removed from practice. It *is* a particular constellation of material and linguistic practices.

Third, and closely related to the preceding point, it is widely recognized that practices of scholarship are embedded in constellations of value, interest, and power, which structure their field, the institution in which they work, and the social systems that impact the life chances of human beings and other species in the contemporary world. For the sake of illustration, let us focus on the institutions in which scholars work.

Much research today in higher education is funded by corporate, governmental, or grant-making institutions and reflects their interests. Moreover, every academic community is characterized by certain power relations in the form of reward systems (tenure, promotion, salary), departmental status (as perceived by students, faculty, and administrators), and decision-making structures (e.g., administrative hierarchies, departmental chairs, and informal leaders). It is naive to believe that scholarship is not affected by this con-

---

19. See the quite different perspectives of Ellen Charry, *By the Renewing of Your Minds: The Pastoral Function of Church Doctrine* (New York: Oxford University Press, 1997), and Jon Sobrino, *Christology at the Crossroads: A Latin American Approach,* trans. John Drury (Maryknoll, N.Y.: Orbis, 1978).

stellation of power relations, which privileges certain values over others. If academic research, not resources for congregations, is alone rewarded with tenure, then scholars feel the pressure to carry out this sort of research. The converse is true as well. Scholarly practices, thus, are embedded in constellations of value, interest, and power. Whose interests do they serve, whose voices do they privilege, and what values do they promote?

This deals a devastating blow to the relay race model of the encyclopedic paradigm, which confined practice to the application of practical theology. In our postmodern context, scholars face the challenge of "double reflexivity": (1) reflecting on their own field (and their own perspective within this field) as a form of scholarly practice, and (2) reflecting on the contribution of their field (and their own research) to the web of life, the interlocking natural and social systems in which life is lived.

Practical Theology at the End of the Theological Encyclopedia

This leaves us with one final question. If all forms of scholarship, including those of theology, are implicated in various forms of practice, what remains of the so-called practical fields? What model of practical theology is viable at the end of the encyclopedic paradigm? Over the course of this book I have articulated the answer given by many contemporary practical theologians in the course of their work.

Practical theology as an academic field has its own distinctive research program. It makes its own constructive contribution to the theological enterprise as a whole and to the ongoing conversation of humankind in its quest for intelligibility. It carries out four mutually related intellectual operations: the descriptive-empirical, interpretive, normative, and pragmatic. This distinguishes practical theology from other forms of theology and from the social sciences, even as it overlaps these fields in certain ways.

At the same time, practical theology, like other fields today, engages in a robust conversation with other disciplines, including other theological disciplines and the arts and sciences. It is not self-enclosed. Cross-disciplinary thinking is an inherent part of each of its four tasks. In its empirical work, it necessarily engages social science and makes choices about the research methods and approaches that are best suited for its own research. In its interpretive work, it engages the social sciences, natural sciences, and philosophy to place particular episodes, situations, and contexts in a broader explanatory framework. In constructing a normative perspective, it enters into a dialogue with dogmatic theology, Christian ethics, philosophical ethics, and normative social theory. In its pragmatic task, it engages action sciences like education, therapy, organization change theory, and communication theory. At every point, thus, practical theology engages in cross-disciplinary thinking. But at no point does it merely take over the methods and frameworks of cognate fields. It engages them critically, as part of a cross-disciplinary conversation in which the distinctive theological perspective of practical theology retains its own voice.

As I have noted many times in this book, practical theology is a highly pluralistic field today. Practical theologians carry out the four tasks in remarkably different ways. They give more attention to some of these tasks than to others. They view them as related to one another in different ways. They engage quite different conversation partners from various fields. This pluralism is a sign of vitality. But it is helpful in our pluralistic, postmodern intellectual context to periodically articulate what the philosophical theologian Wentzel van Huyssteen and others call a wide reflective equilibrium.[20] Across the great variety of perspectives in a particular field, what do its current members share? Where are the points of convergence in their work, even as they diverge sharply in other ways?

This is what I have attempted to articulate in the four interrelated, intellectual operations of practical theology, the tasks that contemporary practical theologians actually carry out in their work. Equilibriums are made to be punctuated, as we have seen, and reflective equilibriums are no different. They are fragile and tenuous. But they do provide a helpful way for the members of a field to talk to each other instead of past each other. If this book has strengthened the possibility of this sort of conversation within practical theology as an academic field, as well as the conversation between practical theology and the church, then it has served its purpose.

---

20. J. Wentzel van Huyssteen, *Alone in the World? Human Uniqueness in Science and Theology* (Grand Rapids: Eerdmans, 2006), pp. 31-34. See also Kai Nielsen, "Searching for an Emancipatory Perspective: Wide Reflective Equilibrium and the Hermeneutical Circle," in *Anti-foundationalism and Practical Reasoning*, ed. Evan Simpson (Edmonton: Academic Press, 1987); Calvin Schrag, *The Resources of Rationality: A Response to the Postmodern Challenge* (Bloomington: Indiana University Press, 1992); Francis Schüssler Fiorenza, *Foundational Theology: Jesus and the Church* (New York: Crossroad, 1984).

Name Index

Name Index

Hunter, Rodney, viii

John of Salisbury, viii
Johnson, Craig, 26
Jorgenson, Danny, 60
Juel, Donald, 185

Keck, Leander, 35
Kotter, John, 206
Krestan, Jo-Ann, 110

Lamb, Matthew, 167
Loder, James, 168-69
Long, Thomas, 25, 36

McKenzie, Alyce, 88
Melchert, Charles, 87
Mikoski, Gordon, ix
Miller-McLemore, Bonnie, 15-16, 46
Murphy, Roland, 93

Nelson, James, 110, 120
Niebuhr, H. Richard, 139-47, 162

Patton, Michael, 60
Pieper, Josef, 82

Plummer, Ken, 64
Poling, James, 107, 167

Quinn, Robert, 203, 206

Ratzsch, Del, 124
Ricoeur, Paul, 21, 149, 162
Roof, Wade Clark, 42

Schleiermacher, Friedrich, 232-33
Schrag, Calvin, 171
Schweitzer, Friedrich, viii
Seow, C. L., 95, 96
Smith, Christian, 41-42
Stewart, John, viii

Tillich, Paul, 166
Tisdale, Leonora Tubbs, 36-37, 38
Tracy, David, 166
Turpin, Katherine, 227-28

Van Huyssteen, Wentzel, viii, 170, 241
Ven, Johannes van der, viii, x, 149
Von Rad, Gerhard, 91

Wuthnow, Robert, 42

Subject Index